Over the past few years, Jan Marsh has established herself as the major authority on the women of the Pre-Raphaelite circle through the ground-breaking study *Pre-Raphaelite Sisterhood* and the equally innovative *Legend of Elizabeth Siddal*. Her hallmarks are readability and meticulous research, which have opened up a whole new field of feminist inquiry. In 1991 she curated the inaugural exhibition of Siddal's paintings and drawings at the Ruskin Gallery, Sheffield and presented a BBC radio programme on the Legend of Elizabeth Siddal. Jan Marsh is currently preparing a major biography of Christina Rossetti and continuing research into artists of the Victorian period.

Also by Jan Marsh

Edward Thomas: A Poet for his Country

Back to the Land: The Pastoral Impulse in
Victorian England 1880–1914

Pre-Raphaelite Sisterhood

Women Artists and the
Pre-Raphaelite Movement
  (with Pamela Gerrish Nunn)

The Woman's Domain: Women and the
English Country House

The Legend of
Elizabeth Siddal

JAN MARSH

Q
Quartet Books

First published in Great Britain by Quartet Books Ltd in 1989
A member of the Namara Group
27/29 Goodge Street
London W1P 1FD

Reprinted in paperback in 1992 by Quartet Books Ltd

A catalogue record for this title is available from the British
Library

ISBN 0 7043 0170 9

Printed and bound by
The Cromwell Press, Broughton Gifford, Melksham

Pre-Raphaelite, they say: I sit for hours
and peer at painted women in a book,
peer as into mirrors,
lest my face forsake

me, and the fable of my hair.

Gillian Allnutt, *Lizzie Siddall: Her Journal 1862*

Contents

Acknowledgements

The author would like to thank the following for their contributions to the making of this book: Gillian Allnutt, Sharon Buckley, Peter Cormack, Marion Edwards, Lady Iddesleigh, Jennifer Kavanagh, Mark Samuels Lasner, Dr E. Mackerness, the late Lady Mander, Susan Lowndes Marques, Hilary Morgan, Pamela Gerrish Nunn, J. M. Olive and Sheffield Local Studies Library, Mrs E. Oliver, Nell Penny, Kate Perry and the Mistress and Fellows of Girton College, Lorraine Price, Lyndal Roper and History Workshop, Ray Watkinson, Zina Sabbagh and Chris Parker, Quartet Books.

Preface

Strictly speaking, this book is not a biography, although it deals almost exclusively with biographical material. It is, specifically, the study of a biographical history or, as designated here, a biographical legend, which has been told and retold during the past hundred years with varying elements and emphases.

It is, however, also a quest for what may, with qualifications, be described as the real Elizabeth Siddal, and concludes with an appraisal of the information now available about this elusive historical figure, and my own contribution to the process of discovery and mythmaking.

The known facts about Elizabeth Siddal's life are few; knowledge of her personality, opinions and emotions is even scantier. Of her 'true self' only her paintings, drawings and poetry survive, and these do not admit of simple biographical analysis.

Readers seeking new information and a new interpretation of Elizabeth Siddal's life and work will find a good deal published and discussed here for the first time. Those hoping for a definitive account, however, may be disappointed, for the main message of this book is that such biographical accounts cannot exist and should not be sought; every historical narrative and analysis of past events is as shaped by its own circumstances as by those it attempts to describe.

I hope that many more chapters, from other perspectives, will in the future be added to the ever-changing legend of Elizabeth Siddal.

[The chronological bibliography given at the end has been extended for the paperback edition, indicating once more the perennial appeal of Lizzie's story.]

1

The Overgrown Grave

When I first went there, several years ago, the place was overgrown and derelict. It was closed to the public, and the Friends of the Cemetery had only just begun the work of reclamation. I went in with a volunteer group which spent weekend afternoons with billhooks and bow saws, felling high sycamores, lopping branches and brambles and vainly attempting to plant new shrubs in narrow chinks between close-packed tombstones.

It was a true wilderness, with few landmarks, for woodland had all but obliterated the burial ground. The small team of volunteers acted like explorers, retracing their steps to make sure they were covering new territory, and repeatedly checking the new planting, staked out with coloured labels, lest the small bushes and stems suffocate under the luxuriant brambles. It was a confusing, unmapped place, the paths all but impassable. Trees and saplings grew between and from every grave, thrusting up through blocks and beds, tilting headstones askew. Creeper and ivy curled and billowed over the monuments, brambles curtained the kneeling angels, rampant cow parsley grew shoulder-high, masking large family tombs, which leant sideways, their iron-grilled doors open to wind and birds.

A Friend of the Cemetery led me on a mystery tour, indicating a loyal carved dog lying on the tomb of the last of the barefisted prize fighters, a large ragged lion above a menagerist, and the last resting places of a few famous figures. (This is the wrong side of the cemetery for household names: Karl Marx and George Eliot lie across the road.) But my guide's destination, when revealed, was the Rossetti grave – 'You know, where his wife was buried' – what's her name, now? It's just slipped' –

'Oh – you mean Lizzie Siddal?' I said, dredging from my memory a name I did not know it possessed.

'That's it! Poor Lizzie! She's here somewhere, on the edge of the meadow.'

I could see no such pastoral place in the midst of the jungle. My guide gestured in a circular manner. 'It's like a meadow here in summer – or will be when we've cut down the trees,' she said. I foresaw buttercups and cats' tails and scabious. 'She's just to the west of here somewhere: let's see if we can find her.'

But the undergrowth and overgrowth were such that we could find no named grave, though we stripped and scraped ivy and moss from a dozen headstones. As there were thousands to choose from, crammed into curving rows with barely an inch between, it was a fruitless search. Briars and branches festooned everything, as thick and rambling as those concealing the Sleeping Beauty.

To push aside the leaves, to negotiate the nettles and to step and jump across the uneven marble slabs, slippery and green and growing toadstools, was a macabre experience. Uncountable long-decayed corpses lie buried below the dead foliage and rotting logs, from which a whole new world of wildlife has risen.

Today, the reclamation of Highgate Cemetery has so progressed that there are teams of conservationists working full-time on the site, clearing the paths, restoring the tombs, rehabilitating the funeral chapels and beavering away to create a well-managed urban nature reserve. It's less spooky, but more accessible. Daily now, there are conducted tours: tombs of interest, the Egyptian Avenue, the sunken circle of lock-up vaults, the ghastly Catacombs with little glass windows to peer in on shelves of crumbling coffins, and all the more or less famous residents: Rowland Hill of the Penny Post, Charles Cruft of the Dog Show, Carl Rosa of the Opera, Jacob Bronowski of *The Ascent of Man* – and Elizabeth Siddal.

The last time I went on the conducted tour was a fresh early-summer afternoon, with the leaf buds still unfolding. Twenty assorted tourists were escorted by a young woman wearing a trailing patchwork skirt, silk scarf and long loose hair, herself a latter-day Pre-Raphaelite. We followed her up and round and down again, pausing at each tomb of significance for scraps of historical information. The cemetery, we were told, had been established because the churchyards of London were full to bursting, with noxious fumes rising from half-buried coffins, the result of cholera, smallpox and plague.

Ivy still wrapped itself round most of the monuments, but here and there were newly naturalized cowslips and forget-me-nots, together with wild garlic and ground elder. We listened to our guide's gruesome and amusing facts: 150,000 bodies, two acres left unconsecrated for suicides and sectarians, an ancient cedar tree retained as the focal point, under which, we were assured, William Shakespeare himself had directed an open-air masque.

We paused to peer into Julius Beer's magnificent mausoleum, decorated by Islamic craftsmen. Nearby, Charles Dickens had selected a grass plot for his infant daughter, who loved sunlight and fresh air. For six years, the mistress of F. W. Woolworth visited his embalmed corpse in its glass-covered coffin weekly, to change his shirt, until the body was taken back to America.

The last and longest stop in the itinerary was the Rossetti grave, where the inmates were described in loving detail. The inventory concluded with the person I had come for:

Elizabeth Eleanor, better known under the name Lizzie Siddal, the Pre-Raphaelite model who can be seen in all the famous paintings. The most famous of these is the picture of Ophelia, by John Everett Millais, where Ophelia is drowning in the river, and she posed for this lying in a bath of water. She was consumptive, always weak and ailing. She suffered dreadfully, during the painting of the lovely picture, for the sake of art, and her father sued Millais for fifty pounds.

Lizzie was Dante Gabriel Rossetti's lover and model for ten years and eventually they got married. She was very beautiful, very pale and had long red hair. But less than two years after they were married, she died of an overdose of laudanum, which she was taking for her consumption. It was either that or suicide. Rossetti was overcome by grief, or guilt, and while the coffin lay in his room for six days before the funeral he kept asking the doctor to say that she was not dead after all, but in a trance from the laudanum. But the doctors assured him that she was dead, and while the coffin was open he put into it his manuscript poems, Lizzie's favourite poems, in a notebook she had asked him to have bound, saying that since she was gone he had no more use for them.

Then, six years later, he wanted to publish his poems to make some money, and he agreed to the exhumation. In an exhumation a canopy is set up over the grave and a bonfire lit to provide light, and then

3

the grave is opened and the coffin lifted. Rossetti didn't attend himself, but five of his friends were there, standing around, and one who was himself a poet later explained how when the coffin was opened, Lizzie's face was still as beautiful as ever, and her red hair shone in the firelight. Rossetti never really recovered from the experience, although when his poems were published in 1870 he earned eight hundred pounds from them in the first year, so it was worth it.

Duly impressed, whether by the romantic or financial aspects of the tale, we followed our guide back to the main path and thence to the funeral chapels at the gate, where she gave a pretty speech on the cost of conserving the cemetery – for legal reasons the tours are free – and ended by inviting us to contribute. As we did so, I reflected that Elizabeth Siddal still has a distinct value to the custodians of her tomb.

The summary of Elizabeth Siddal's story provided by the cemetery guide is no more or less fanciful than others which have been related over the years since her burial at Highgate in 1862. It contains the key 'facts' by which Elizabeth Siddal is known – to a wider public than one might expect, for her fame extends far beyond those who visit her grave. Even when her name is forgotten, she is remembered as the red-haired model who sat to the Pre-Raphaelite Brotherhood for some of their most famous paintings, and who died tragically. Pathos and romance attach themselves to her image.

This book began as a straightforward biographical inquiry, looking as it were behind the image. Having first investigated the life of Elizabeth Siddal for inclusion in *Pre-Raphaelite Sisterhood*, my earlier study of the painters' models, mistresses and wives, I was keen to extend the research. Subsequent discoveries and suggestions – no book is written without new material coming to light *after* publication – indicated new lines of inquiry and the possibility of filling further gaps. In addition, the reception of *Pre-Raphaelite Sisterhood* made me aware of the large symbolic role played by Elizabeth Siddal both in the histories of Pre-Raphaelitism and in individual responses to the world of Pre-Raphaelite painting.

In the month when I began working on this book, for example, the colour supplement of a Sunday newspaper published a feature on up-and-coming stars, dressed as figures from the past – a game of self-definition by affinity. Bryony Brind, principal dancer with the Royal Ballet, chose to appear as Ophelia – as in the paintings rather than the play. Dressed in a blue, bosom-exposing silk gown with gold embroidery and clutching a handful of herbs and flowers, which with ivy leaves were also twined in her loose spreading hair, she posed with an anxious expression to simulate madness before a blue background strewn with artificial leaves and ferns, her bare foot extended as if stepping gingerly into the stream that was to be her watery grave. Bryony explained:

> My fantasy role – as a Pre-Raphaelite heroine – is an extension of my own life. To me, these paintings mean romance, and beautiful, luminous colour. They are full of mystery: nothing in them is what it seems. You can see from the expression in the subject's eyes that often she is searching for something outside the canvas. The effect is bewitching, mesmerizing – like my own world in the theatre.[1]

Such carefully staged acting-out of legend is rare, but points to a still vital tradition. The story of Elizabeth Siddal lives on, and sometimes takes strange twists. 'Tell me,' a man said to me recently, 'is that story about the bath true? How that woman – I forget the name – posed for a painter lying in a bath, and was drowned? Did that really happen? Did she really drown?'

'Can you confirm that story about the picture of Beatrice?' asked someone else on another occasion. 'I was told authoritatively that it was painted after Lizzie's death – from life, as it were, with the corpse propped up on the bed, so that Rossetti could paint from it directly. Is that true?'

I had to confess that this was one story I hadn't heard, although I can see where its origins lie: in the posthumous nature of the *Beata Beatrix* canvas, in the gruesome tale of the exhumation, and in the notion of Rossetti as an artist tormented by female beauty. In the manner of an urban legend, this particular tale shaped itself in the telling to reflect the current image of Lizzie as a model so exploited for her beauty that even in death she was made to pose for a painting.

As these accretions of myth indicate, Elizabeth Siddal is one of those ancillary figures in the history of art whose story is of

limited intrinsic interest but who possesses extraordinary symbolic significance for a large number of people. So my research,
starting as a chronological reading of the source material with the
purpose of assessing the dates and provenance of each fact and
anecdote and, as I thought, of stripping away the brambles of
mythology from the overgrown grave, soon became fascinated
by the changing ways in which the persona of Elizabeth Siddal
has been represented over the years, like a soft clay pot constantly
shaped and reshaped and filled with new meanings. This plasticity
is indeed her chief feature, for the ways her legend has been
related during the past century tell us only a limited amount about
the historical person, but a great deal about succeeding views of
femininity, prevailing sexual politics and, within the ideologies
of gender, about the sense of mystery (or mystification, as some
would have it) surrounding the artist and the work of art. It is
thus an index of changing attitudes, and an account of how history
and biography are continually rewritten, according to the preoccupations of the age, while always claiming to be true.

I

Recollections

1

Recollections

2

Dimmed in Death

Elizabeth Siddal's story really began, not with her birth, the date and place of which long remained unknown, but with her death in 1862. It was not a romantic beginning. Under the heading 'Death of a Lady from an Overdose of Laudanum', on 14 February the *Daily News* reported:

Yesterday Mr Payne held an inquest at Bridewell Hospital, on the body of Eliza [*sic*] Eleanor Rosetti, aged 29, wife of Dante Gabriel Rosetti [*sic*], artist, of no. 14 Chatham Place, Blackfriars, who came by her death under very melancholy circumstances. Mr Rosetti stated that on Monday afternoon, between 6 and 7 o'clock, he and his wife went out in the carriage for the purpose of dining with a friend, at the Sablonniere Hotel, Leicester Square. When they had got about halfway there his wife appeared very drowsy and he wished her to return. She objected to their doing so and they proceeded to the hotel and dined there. They returned home at 8 o'clock when she appeared somewhat excited. He left home again at 9 o'clock, his wife being then about to go to bed. On his return at half past 11 o'clock he found his wife in bed, snoring loudly and utterly unconscious. She was in the habit of taking laudanum and he had known her take as much as 100 drops at a time and he thought she had been taking it before they went out. He found a phial on a table at the bedside which had contained laudanum, but it was then empty. A doctor was sent for and promptly attended. She had expressed no wish to die, but quite the reverse. Indeed, she contemplated going out of town in a day or two and had ordered a new mantle which she intended to wear on the occasion. He believed she took the laudanum to quiet her nerves. She could not sleep or take food unless she used it. Mr Hutchinson of Bridge street, Blackfriars, said he had attended the deceased in her confinement in April with a still-born child. He saw her on Monday night at half past 11 o'clock and found her in a comatose state. He tried to rouse her but could not, and then tried the stomach pump without avail. He injected several quarts of water in the stomach and washed it out, when the smell of laudanum was very distinct. He and three other medical gentlemen stayed with her all night and she died at 20 minutes past 7 o'clock on Tuesday morning. The jury returned a verdict of 'Accidental Death'.[1]

Laudanum is the tincture of opium (from which heroin is also derived) and was freely available and regularly used in the mid-nineteenth century as both a painkiller and tranquillizer.

Elizabeth's body joined that of her father-in-law in the Rossetti family grave plot in the new cemetery at Highgate, and in the years that followed, as her husband's fame as painter and poet grew, she was remembered only by a small circle of family and friends.

Gabriel vacated the apartment at Blackfriars, moving to a large house facing the river on Cheyne Walk in Chelsea, a few miles upstream. Here his wife's pictures were hung round the dining room, and his portraits of her filled a portfolio, so that her presence was ghostlike, shadowy and silent. Out of deference to the widower's grief, visitors spoke of her rarely, in hushed tones.

Rumours circulated, however. On Gabriel's own death, the daughter of his physician (one of the four medical men to attend on the night of Elizabeth's death) noted in her diary that 'for two years he *saw* her ghost every night!'[2] Whether or not this was true, her spirit was certainly invoked (as was revealed many years later) by her husband when, at the height of contemporary enthusiasm for spiritualist seances in the mid–1860s, Gabriel endeavoured to communicate by means of a spirit medium, inquiring whether she was happy 'on the other side'.[3] The small group of friends who participated in this endeavour, including Gabriel's sceptical brother William Michael, professed themselves struck by the uncanny accuracy of some answers to his questions but, as the fashion waned, the seances were soon abandoned.

They were also kept secret, for Gabriel's pious mother Frances Lavinia Rossetti and sisters Maria and Christina held firm Christian beliefs that would not have countenanced spiritualist parlour games. Yet Christina, at least, seems to have shared a sense of her sister-in-law's unquiet shade, and many readers must surely have interpreted the title poem in her second volume of verse, *The Prince's Progress*, published in 1866, as an indirect comment

on her brother's marriage. This long ballad tragedy laments the
death of a woman kept waiting by her prince and lover:

> Too late for love, too late for joy,
>   Too late, too late!
> You loitered on the road too long,
>   You trifled at the gate:
> The enchanted dove upon her branch
>   Died without a mate;
> The enchanted princess in her tower
>   Slept, died, behind the grate;
> Her heart was starving all this while
>   You made it wait.

> Ten years ago, five years ago,
>   One year ago,
> Even then you had arrived in time,
>   Though somewhat slow;
> Then you had known her living face
>   Which now you cannot know:
> The frozen fountain would have leaped,
>   The buds gone on to blow,
> The warm south wind would have awaked
>   To melt the snow.

> . . .

> You should have wept her yesterday,
>   Wasting upon her bed:
> But wherefore should you weep today
>   That she is dead?
> Lo, we who love weep not today,
>   But crown her royal head.
> Let these be poppies that we strew,
>   Your roses are too red:
> Let these be poppies, not for you
>   Cut down and spread.

In the poem's allegory of a man repeatedly diverted on his journey
towards his beloved, those who knew the Rossettis would have
found it hard not to read oblique references to the long-postponed
marriage and untimely death of the author's sister-in-law. Gabriel

11

was indeed involved in the composition, suggesting to Christina that she 'turn the dirge into a narrative poem'[4] and also in the design, producing in December 1865 two illustrations for frontispiece and title page, showing the Princess watching in vain for her lover, and the Prince arriving to find her laid on the funeral bier. In neither image does the Princess bear Elizabeth's features, but this does not preclude a partly biographical meaning to the tale.

Some months earlier, Gabriel had begun a pictorial commemoration of his wife in a painting of Dante's beloved Beatrice. This was a figure with special meaning on account of his own baptismal names (Gabriel Charles Dante Rossetti, later rearranged as Dante Gabriel Rossetti), his father's lifelong study of Dante Alighieri, his own translation of the *Vita Nuova* and his namesake's reputation as one of the great mystical poets and lovers of the Western world. Earlier in his career, Rossetti had painted Elizabeth as Beatrice Denying Dante's Salutation at a Marriage Feast. The posthumous image depicted Beatrice at the moment of her death, 'suddenly rapt from earth to heaven' as if in a trance. Later titled *Beata Beatrix*, it was based on a 'life-size head of my wife, begun many years ago', as Rossetti told a prospective client in 1863;[5] it was completed slowly, between 1864 and 1870.

The images of poem and painting resonate. Both *Beata Beatrix* and *The Prince's Progress* contain an enchanted dove, the flame of love and life, the opium poppy of sleep and death, the slow hours of the sundial, and the bride between sleep and waking, life and death:

> . . . red and white poppies grow at her feet . . .
> But the white buds swell, one day they will burst,
> Will open their death-cups drowsy and sweet –
> . . . .
> Does she live? – does she die? she languisheth
> As a lily drooping to death,
> As a drought-worn bird with failing breath –
> . . . .
> Is she fair now as she lies?
>   Once she was fair;
> Meet queen for any kingly king
>   With gold-dust on her hair.
> Now these are poppies in her locks,

White poppies she must wear;
Must wear a veil to shroud her face
And the want graven there:

My guess is that both Gabriel and Christina knew, if they did not state, that *The Prince's Progress* was in part about Elizabeth's fate, just as *Beata Beatrix* was an image of her death.

While Christina was preparing her volume for the printer, Gabriel collected together his wife's small stock of poems (unlike her painting, these were not known outside the family) and passed them to his sister with a view to their inclusion in *The Prince's Progress* volume. Initially, Christina favoured the idea but after reading the poems she returned them, suggesting they were 'almost too hopelessly sad for publication'.[6] And Gabriel, perhaps conscious that publication might prove an uncomfortable reminder of her unnatural death – several of the poems were expressive of sorrow and desire for oblivion – put the poems away. Their existence was thus concealed for many more years.

He did succeed, however, in recording a large part of Elizabeth's work as an artist. In 1866 he arranged for her surviving drawings and sketches to be photographed, printed and pasted into folio volumes as a memorial of her art. At least four of these portfolios were compiled and distributed to friends; some survive, complete or in bits, others may have disappeared over the years. The glass negatives for the photographs were preserved, apparently by chance, since little value seems to have been placed on them, but most have never since been reprinted.[7]

Into the portfolios were pasted two drawings by Rossetti himself, to represent the artist in the absence of a portrait photograph. Personal portraits were in great demand at this date, as the elaborate albums of Victorian *cartes-de-visite* testify, and the lack of a 'real-life' image was regretted. When Georgiana Burne-Jones, a friend of Elizabeth's married years, asked for a photo as a keepsake, Gabriel replied that no photo of Lizzie had been preserved, since none had ever been satisfactory; he offered instead a photo of one of his drawings.[8] In fact, at least two tiny photos did survive, again seemingly by chance.

On receiving his portfolio, the poet William Allingham, who

13

had known Lizzie in the early 1850s, noted down his memories. 'Short, sad and strange her life; it must have seemed to her like a troubled dream,' he wrote in his diary. 'She was sweet, gentle and kindly, and sympathetic to art and poetry . . . Her pale face, abundant red hair and long thin limbs were strange and affecting – never beautiful in my eyes.'[9]

So Elizabeth Siddal faded from people's minds, like a dim, troubled dream herself. In 1870, her existence was brought back into view, with the completion of *Beata Beatrix* – head uplifted, eyes closed, long throat extended, the poppy of death dropping into her hands. This proved one of Rossetti's most popular compositions, and over the next ten years a total of six replicas were produced by the artist and his studio assistant.[10] A mawkish but haunting image, disquieting in its mixture of sensuous and funereal feeling, it became the best-known portrait of Elizabeth Siddal, interpreted as the Romantic expression of the artist's inconsolable grief at the death of his beloved.

Also in 1870, Rossetti's first original poetic collection, simply entitled *Poems*, was published. This contained a number of 'amorous' or erotic poems, with titles like 'Nuptial Sleep', 'Bridal Birth', 'Supreme Surrender' and 'The Kiss', unmistakably expressive of physical passion. Since the writer was known to be a widower, these were assumed to refer to his marital relationship, and unfortunately stimulated a rather too personal interest in the deceased Mrs Rossetti, whose memory was sullied – according to some – by such public display of sexual feeling (the terms 'nuptial' and 'bridal' being used and interpreted in this sense). The hostile critic Robert Buchanan, attacking the 'fleshly' nature of Rossetti's verse, wrote disgustedly that it was as if the author had wheeled his marriage bed into the street, for everyone to witness the act. This was an insult to poor Mrs Rossetti and, he implied, smacked of necrophilia.[11]

In fact, as later became apparent, the erotic verses in *Poems* were largely inspired by and addressed to other women, but these complications – and indeed the whole issue of Rossetti's deliberate misdating of his poems, which has caused many scholarly difficulties – were not evident in 1870. On the face of it, sexual desires for the poet's beloved were easily read as sentiments addressed to the author's deceased wife. Perhaps, within the restricted circle of literary London, Buchanan had heard rumours; if not, he unwittingly hit Rossetti on a vulnerable spot. Subsequently, he was accused of vile and unfair attacks on Rossetti's moral integrity, but the text of his article suggests that his boldness consisted largely in printing, with whatever degree of disingenuousness, a frank and open response to the verses as published.

One poem in particular, 'Life-in-Love', was assumed to refer directly to the poet's late wife, since despite – or indeed because of – the rather obscure construction, the beloved appears to be dead:

> Not in thy body is thy life at all,
> But in this lady's lips and hands and eyes;
> Through these she yields thee life that vivifies
> What else were sorrow's servant and death's thrall.
> Look on thyself without her, and recall
> The waste remembrance and forlorn sunrise
> That lived but in a dead-drawn breath of sighs
> O'er vanished hours and hours eventual.
>   Even so much life hath this poor tress of hair
>   Which, stored apart, is all love hath to show
>   For heart-beats and for fire-heats long ago;
>   Even so much life endures unknown, even where
>   'Mid change the changeless night environeth,
>   Lies all that golden hair undimmed in death.

Buchanan's attack on *Poems*, amid an otherwise favourable critical reception, was widely believed to have caused, during the early summer of 1872, the nervous collapse from which Rossetti never fully recovered and into which he regularly relapsed. As a result of this breakdown, for the remaining ten years of his life Gabriel lived as a virtual recluse, first at Kelmscott Manor and then at Cheyne Walk. The nature and severity of his condition were successfully concealed by his family and friends for many years and the nature of his affliction is still not widely understood or accepted. From its symptoms – hearing voices, delusions of persecution, insomnia and acute but fluctuating mental agitation – the condition was a classic form of schizophrenia, accompanied by paranoid suspicions of a hostile conspiracy; in his worst moments, Gabriel heard whispers in the walls and believed them those of enemies scheming to destroy him. The condition was not always so severe, but in addition to the collapse in 1872 there were other relapses when he could neither paint nor write, and barely sleep. Those former friends whom he did not alienate by his suspicions were dismayed at the utter change in one they had known as the most charming and generous of men. Edward Burne-Jones, who owed his artistic career to Rossetti's encouragement, later wrote sorrowfully of visiting the silent and morose Gabriel in Cheyne Walk during the late 1870s.

Whether from ignorance or concealment, Rossetti's behaviour was described as 'artistic nerves' or 'acute sensibility' and variously ascribed to insomnia, chloral (a narcotic taken to combat insomnia) or simply to an overstrained artistic imagination. Later, it was inferred that grief and guilt connected with his wife had aggravated if not caused Rossetti's collapse; certainly sorrow and tragedy were seen as closely wound in with the intense sensibility displayed in his poems and paintings, and linked to what little was known of his personal life.

Thus it was that, during her husband's lifetime, the story of Elizabeth Siddal – who retained her own name in the histories, as if she had died unwed like Christina's neglected Princess – was effectively obscured by the dark silence surrounding both her death and Gabriel's derangement. Indeed, her own history scarcely existed, for her ghostly presence served chiefly to offset the tragic mystery of Rossetti's life and work – an exemplar of the tormented genius of the Romantic artist.

In April 1882, twenty years after Elizabeth Rossetti was buried, her husband also went to his grave – leaving strict instructions that he was 'on no account to be buried at Highgate' – and the legend began to unfold.

'One of the most rarely gifted men of our time has just died', announced a solemn obituary in the *Athenaeum* by Theodore Watts-Dunton. This placed Rossetti firmly within the Romantic tradition of the great artist whose fervid imagination was 'his blessing and his bane', and whose doom was 'to see too vividly, to love too intensely, to suffer and enjoy too acutely'. Rossetti was an undisputed genius: 'wonderful as an artist and poet, yet still more wonderful as a man'.[12]

Watts-Dunton was a lawyer and literary man whose life was

given meaning by close association with geniuses – first with Rossetti and subsequently with Swinburne – whom he regarded as brilliant but depraved and in need of protection. With his obituary, he laid claim to ownership of Rossetti the man; even more than the body of poems or pictures, this was the possession worth having, for the strange private life of this 'rarely gifted' figure gave added value to his art. The words therefore celebrated the uniqueness of the reclusive genius, now available only through the memories of a favoured few.

In Watts-Dunton's account, Rossetti's marriage was accorded three sentences:

> In the spring of 1860 he married Elizabeth Eleanor Siddall, who, being very beautiful, was constantly painted and drawn by him. She had one stillborn child in 1861 and died in February 1862. He felt her death very acutely and for a time ceased to write or take any interest in his own poetry. Like Prospero indeed he literally buried his wand . . .[13]

These few phrases obliquely but firmly fixed beauty and pathos as the frame within which Elizabeth Siddal was inscribed. And, encoded in the reference to Prospero and the literal burial of his poetry, was the hint of a sacrifice yet to be made public.

Gossip was already gathering momentum. Within weeks of Rossetti's death a book appeared, entitled *Dante Gabriel Rossetti: His Work and Influence*, written by William Tirebuck. Without quoting a single poem or citing a single painting, this biographically worthless volume stressed Rossetti's notoriety without explaining it. 'Tales were told of him and his seclusive personality,' it hinted, suggesting decadence if not insanity. 'True or untrue, these winkings and noddings . . . these buzzings of flies' combined to create around Rossetti's name 'the halo of mystery'. Elizabeth Siddal did not appear in these pages except perhaps as a shadow invoked in the description of Rossetti's paintings of women as 'abstractions, dreams, musings, lethargic spirits coming to the borderland of matter and keeping aloof from it in spiritual pride . . .'[14]

Perhaps fearful of more substantive disclosure, the Rossetti family assisted a second account by William Sharp, entitled *Dante Gabriel Rossetti: A Record and a Study*, which also appeared with indecent haste in the year of his death. This devoted 450 pages to promoting Rossetti as uniquely gifted – 'a poet and artist such as the world does not often see' – and leader of the famous Pre-Raphaelite Brotherhood or 'PRB', the group of young artists who in 1848–53 had initiated a new style of painting. It concluded with a list of paintings and drawings, an impressive canon of nearly four hundred works with the aim of deterring forgeries and spurious attributions. This was desirable because, following Rossetti's death, the contents of his studio were being sold and it was important for family and patrons to maintain the monetary values of the work, since the cult of the genius had financial as well as historical implications: the 'greater' the artist, the higher the prices his works would fetch.

Hence, too, the extraordinary delicacy with which Rossetti's reputation was protected. In this respect, it is important to recognize that the quality of his art was not beyond question; its lack of variety and sometimes slipshod technique compared unfavourably with more prestigious contemporary artists such as Frederick Leighton and G. F. Watts, to say nothing of Rossetti's erstwhile Pre-Raphaelite Brothers John Everett Millais and William Holman Hunt, who were still producing large and important works. An unfriendly critic itemized Rossetti's faults: inaccurate anatomy – 'wonderful malformation of neck' – coupled with monotony of subject – 'same face, same stare, nearly the same attitude on every wall' – and the same faults endlessly repeated, as the artist 'shut himself off in a corner and dwelt upon one idea'. He was only protected by those 'who assert they have been behind the veil and know the mysteries; he has been made into an idol'.[15] This was fair comment, for a small industry was devoted to the promotion of 'Dante Rossetti' – the name favoured by several commentators and eventually adopted by William Rossetti when writing of his brother's career – rejecting any hint of insanity but emphasizing the aura of mystery and personal tragedy that lent an undeniable glamour to his art. Genius could not be too near allied to madness nor creativity openly linked to deviance (as the sad careers of Richard Dadd, certified insane after killing his father, and Simeon Solomon, ostracized on account of homosexuality and alcoholism, showed) but hints of excess added spice to the story. The 'true artist' did not lead a dull bourgeois life.

In William Sharp's narrative, Elizabeth Siddal's entry into the Pre-Raphaelite circle took place rather abruptly when, in 1860,

> Rossetti made great changes at 14 Chatham Place, enlarging the accommodation and adding in other ways to the comfort of his residence; and here 'in the mating time o' the year' he brought home his wife Elizabeth Eleanor Siddall. This lady, who was very beautiful and who showed brilliant promise as a colourist, he had known for a considerable time . . .[16]

Whether or not Sharp was aware of the facts, this was a considerable distortion, suggesting a lengthy engagement and careful preparations for marriage. As is now clear, there was no engagement, and the alterations to Chatham Place were undertaken several months after the wedding. The aim, however, was to present a straightforward romantic attachment and a happy though brief marriage, which Sharp specifically compared with that of Elizabeth Barrett and Robert Browning, that most popular of all real-life Victorian romances.

Sharp referred to Elizabeth's 'brilliant promise as a colourist', giving her own art equal emphasis with her beauty, but neither he nor Watts-Dunton made any mention of her being a model. This was from either ignorance or delicacy, since modelling was not considered a respectable occupation. Both also spelled her surname 'Siddall'. This is an index of the uncertainty surrounding her status, which continually recurs, some writers favouring 'Siddall', as the family name was commonly spelt, and some 'Siddal', which is the spelling she herself adopted, apparently at Rossetti's suggestion. For the sake of such consistency as can be obtained, my own choice is now 'Siddal', but variant spellings have, of course, their own symbolic meanings.

Of her appearance, Sharp identified the best likeness as 'the pathetically faithful face of Beatrice' in *Beata Beatrix* and also some pencil studies 'as she appeared before her husband in daily life' in which 'there is to be traced the artist lover's gaze as it caught pose after pose and expression after expression . . . varying more in shades of sadness, for it seemed as if a premonition of early death overshadowed her life'.

In this account, her sudden death was 'exceptionally terrible' to her husband. Thus:

19

In the impulse of his grief it came about that before the coffin-lid was closed on the face he should not see on earth again, he hastily gathered together the manuscripts of the greater number of the poems now so familiar . . . and laid them as a last gift on his wife's breast . . .[17]

Four pages later, the mystery of how the buried poems could be now 'so familiar' was dramatically explained, in the first official account of the exhumation. In the autumn of 1868, Sharp explained, Rossetti, at the behest of friends, came to a decision regarding the buried manuscript. As author, he

could not be insensible to the fact that much good work had been put away in a manner that no 'creator' had a right to do . . . His still reluctant consent having been once obtained, there was no further delay . . . accordingly one night two of Rossetti's friends were present at the grave of Mrs Rossetti in Highgate Cemetery, when the coffin was opened and the packet removed.[18]

Sharp's express intention, presumably authorized by the family – who by this time must have been aware of the exhumation, although it had taken place without the knowledge of Gabriel's mother, the official owner of the grave-plot – was to quell rumours. 'The matter is too painful to dwell upon,' he confessed. 'Indeed I might not have referred to it at all had not the story been often repeated of late and with varying accounts.' His version was, he claimed, 'exactly all that happened' (although he mistook the date, which was 1869 not, as he stated, 1868). The frankness was disingenuous, however, for in order to justify Rossetti's decision, the divine rights of the artist had been invoked, overriding the normal taboos on tomb violation.

It is clear that, from the beginning as still today, the exhumation has been perceived as a deeply disturbing act, transgressing the strong Western tradition of the grave as a hallowed resting place where the dead 'sleep' peacefully, and debasing the Victorian significance of mourning, whereby part of the survivor's soul was buried with the beloved, not to be reclaimed. It overturned Romantic ideals of artistic sacrifice and renunciation for the sake of undying Love, and for over a hundred years now the opening of Elizabeth's coffin has been a symbol of religious, poetic and personal violation. Those who admire Rossetti are obliged to excuse and explain it; those who dislike him see in it an emblem of arrogance and hypocrisy. This is not the place to debate the issue a priori, but Rossetti's own ambiguous justification is worth noting. Shortly after the event, he wrote to Swinburne, hoping he would 'think none the worse of my feeling for the memory of one for whom I know you had a true regard', and explaining that the arrangements had all been made by their mutual friend Charles Howell. He continued:

> The truth is, no one so much as herself would have approved of my doing this . . . Had it been possible to her I should have found the book on my pillow the night she was buried; and could she have opened the grave, no other hand would have been needed.[19]

Swinburne concurred, citing Elizabeth's love of art. Yet, notwithstanding the probable truth of this, the symbolic meaning of the sacrificed pages and the disturbance of her body, of which Rossetti was well aware, remains predominant. His gruesome image of the corpse lifting her own coffin lid to return the book was an oblique acknowledgement that her soul had not been left to rest peacefully.

Naturally, the exhumation added a frisson of morbid fascination to Rossetti's life-story, making him into a character from a Gothick tale. While this might backfire and threaten his place in the pantheon of great artists being erected in the late nineteenth century, the carefully handled story of his poems, rescued from such a site, could only enhance his Romantic stature. And it was soon clear that Rossetti was an exceptionally valuable biographical property, for another book swiftly appeared, written by Thomas Hall Caine, and entitled *Recollections of Dante Gabriel Rossetti* (1882). As Oscar Wilde remarked with scorn, 'When a great man dies, Hall Caine and William Sharp go in with the undertakers.'[20] Paying lip service to Watts-Dunton's superior claim to intimacy – he was known to be preparing an official 'Life' – Hall Caine, a young man with aspirations to literary fame whom Rossetti had befriended during his last months, presented his text ostensibly as a simple account of the artist 'exactly as I found him in each stage of our friendship', but covertly offered revelations. Caine was the first, for example, to acknowledge Rossetti's mental derangement, referring to his obsessional belief in an organized conspiracy of persecution, although attributing this to the effects of chloral, taken to combat insomnia, the 'curse of the literary and artistic temperament.'[21]

Elizabeth Siddal again appeared in the text only on her marriage – of which 'it is necessary to treat as briefly as tenderly' – but was now revealed to have originally been Rossetti's model. Described as a 'young lady of great personal beauty, in whom he discovered a natural genius for painting and a noticeable love of the higher poetic literature', she soon became 'as much his pupil as his model' and the watercolours 'done under his tuition gave proof of a wonderful eye for colour'. Shared interests led to friendship and finally love.

However, soon after their marriage,

> the lady's health began to fail and she became the victim of neuralgia. To meet this dread enemy she resorted to laudanum, taking it at first in small quantities but eventually to excess. Her spirits drooped, her art was laid aside, and much of the cheerfulness of home was lost to her. There was a child, but it was stillborn and not long after this disaster it was found that Mrs Rossetti had taken an overdose of her accustomed sleeping potion and was lying dead in her bed . . .

The blow was a terrible one to Rossetti and his grief knew no bounds:

> The poems he had written, in so far as they were poems of love, were chiefly inspired by and addressed to her. At her request he had copied them into a little book presented to him for that purpose and on the day of the funeral he walked into the room where the body lay and, unmindful of the presence of friends, he spoke to his dead wife as though she heard, saying, as he held the book, that the words it contained were written to her and for her, and she must take them with her for they could not remain when she had gone. Then he put the volume into the coffin between her cheek and beautiful hair, and it was that day buried with her in Highgate Cemetery.[22]

The loss 'changed the whole course' of Rossetti's life. On leaving Chatham Place he burnt a great number of letters, in order to destroy all that reminded him of his wife. Grief made him morose and solitary, victim of the evil power of chloral. His finest art – here identified as the late painting of *Dante's Dream on the Anniversary of the Death of Beatrice* – was an expression of his loss:

> As if just fallen back in sleep, the beautiful lady lies in death, her hands folded across her breast and a glory of golden hair flowing over her shoulders. With measured tread Dante approaches the couch . . . and takes the kiss that he himself might never have. In life they must needs be apart but thus in death they are united . . . The floor is strewn with poppies – emblems of the sleep in which the lover walks and the sleep that is the sleep of death. The may-bloom in the pall, the apple-blossom in the hand of Love, the violets and roses in the frieze of the alcove, symbolize purity and virginity, the life that is cut off in its spring, the love that is consummated in death before the coming of fruit . . . [23]

Caine's purple prose here disclosed his direction, which was to introduce the story of the exhumation with intimations of necro-philiac desire – the 'love that is consummated in death'. With less affection, he wrote, Rossetti would not have buried his notebook; 'with more strength of will he had not done so; or, having done so, he had never wished to undo what he had done; or, having undone it, he would never have tormented himself with the memory of it as a deed of sacrilege'. Getting the date right, he continued: 'One night seven and a half years after the burial, a fire was built by the side of the grave and then the coffin was raised and opened. The body is described as perfect upon coming to light.'[24]

The first direct glimpse of Elizabeth Siddal presented in these books of 1882 was that of her corpse, seven years buried yet miraculously preserved, as befitted the beloved of a mystical lover, poet, painter and Romantic hero.

3

Icon of Decadence

As is to be expected, in these early narratives Elizabeth Siddal is defined in simple dependent relation to Rossetti. She herself has no status, no definition or meaning except as his beloved. And, specifically, as his lost beloved, for she is even more strongly characterized in terms of absence and loss. She has no parentage, no occupation, virtually no identity before marriage; as a living figure she is almost missing from the narrative, evoked briefly only to be lamented as a vanishing image, a departed vision, a phantom of grief and pain. Literally invisible, since there are no illustrations in these books, her only attributes, as given, are 'great personal beauty' and 'unusual poetic feeling'. Together with pathos and illness these shape her being, but all is shadowy compared to her role as lost love object.

However, this presence as loss is closely linked to culpability, for her death is given as the reason for her husband's decline, and for all his subsequent sorrows. 'At her request' he had copied out the poems she had inspired; her loss caused his poetic output to fail and threatened the life and sanity of a great artist. Any blame that might otherwise attach to Rossetti for the violation of her grave is thus subtly and indirectly transferred: the male genius is shown to be tormented for the rest of his life by an invisible female ghost. Haunted by her lost beauty, his grief can never be assuaged.

Beauty is too transitory a possession – especially in a long dead lady – to retain much meaning beyond that which reinforces the sense of loss and sorrow; indeed, the decay of female beauty is one of the great poetic tropes for regret and sadness. Yet it is the dominant meaning ascribed to Elizabeth Siddal, as both the inspiration of Gabriel Rossetti's art and the cause of his decline: his destruction the consequence of hers. Her beauty – paradoxically untouched by death – lies in his art, nestling between her cheek and shining hair, visible for ever in his pictures and poems, while she herself is absent, unseen except in or indeed as the work, the creation of the Romantic artist and emblem of his genius.

Within twelve months of Rossetti's death, however, almost as if predicted by Hall Caine, the face of Elizabeth Siddal became newly visible through the veils of death. As part of the process of artistic canonization, Rossetti's pictures were twice exhibited in 1883, first at the Royal Academy and then at the Burlington Fine Arts Club.

Elizabeth Siddal was not the only subject on display. Indeed, in the Royal Academy, the majority of the seventy works were the typical three-quarter-length female figures of Rossetti's later years, mostly modelled on Fanny Cornforth, Janey Morris or Alexa Wilding, none of whom resembled the artist's wife. But *Beata Beatrix* was on view for the first time to the general public and the catalogue contained an explication of subject and symbols, with the information that 'Beatrice is a portrait of the painter's wife, done after her death'. It was (mis)dated 1863, strongly suggesting a memorial of conjugal grief and piety.

Her face was also seen in a pencil study entitled 'Portrait of Miss Siddall afterwards Mrs Dante Gabriel Rossetti', and, somewhat prettified, in 'A Parable of Love', a drawing depicting 'a lady seated in front of a canvas on which she has been painting her own portrait' under the tuition of her lover. At the time this picture was owned by the poet Coventry Patmore, author of the Victorian hymn to married love *Angel in the House*. Elizabeth's features were also visible as a Lady visiting Dante, as the Virgin Mary and, most strikingly, in the detailed ink drawing *How They Met Themselves*, inscribed with the dates 1851–60, showing two lovers confronted with their own apparitions – a *doppelgänger* or ghost theme. The catalogue explained how 'the lady sinking to the ground, stretches out her arms as if appealing for mercy'.[1]

If interpreted biographically, both *Beata Beatrix* and *How They Met Themselves* may be seen to confirm the atmosphere of tragedy and distress that permeated the literary accounts of Elizabeth and Gabriel's relationship at this date, both pictures conveying a powerful sense of premonition and fate that complements the personal story. Both seem to catch Elizabeth Siddal at the approach of death, as she passes from living being to unquiet shade.

The second exhibition, at the Burlington Fine Arts Club, was larger and comprehensive. Its catalogue of 150 works included an essay by Henry Virtue Tebbs (the solicitor present, according to legal requirements, at the exhumation) who praised Rossetti's 'mystic imagination' combined with the 'ardent temperament of the South'. This referred briefly to Elizabeth's death – the artist 'had, in February 1862, the sorrow to lose his wife' – and not at all to the exhumation or nervous collapse, stating firmly that it was 'uneccessary to refer further to the facts of Rossetti's life which of late years became very secluded'.[2]

The selection of pictures mirrored Tebbs's preference for the 'early asceticism' with its mystic and spiritual elements over 'the large and luxurious type of female beauty' in Rossetti's later work, so images of Elizabeth Siddal were seen on all sides. These included four portraits, several early works including *Paolo and Francesca*, *Rachel and Leah*, *Hamlet and Ophelia*, and *St Catherine*, and no fewer than three versions of *Beata Beatrix*.

And so, at last, those who had heard of the sad tale of the artist's poor wife, the tragic event of her death and the exhumation of her coffin, were vouchsafed a visual impression. Though not without touches of humour, as in an early ink sketch of Gabriel sitting stiffly to be drawn by Elizabeth, this was an undeniably Romantic view of a pale, demure young girl who had inspired his genius, a beloved but spectral figure whose early death was a fatal blow. The subjects of several pictures reinforced the message: the lovers Paolo and Francesca in hell, La Belle Dame sans Merci, the pathetic Ophelia, the estrangement and death of Beatrice. In these images, the hitherto invisible Elizabeth Siddal was made manifest.

This was the high period of Aestheticism as an artistic and cultural fashion, with its promotion of decorative beauty and art-for-art's-sake rather than sacred or storytelling subjects. Increasingly, through the 1880s and 1890s, strands of Aestheticism developed through contact with the Symboliste movement in Europe into the poetic and pictorial cult of Decadence, with its representations of perverse desire for pleasurable pain, usually at the hands of a pale woman, 'perfect and poisonous', who is a figure of Death. From the work of Baudelaire, Gautier, Huysmans and Wilde, through to that of Moreau, Redon and Beardsley, sensual depictions of death in female shape became a recurrent artistic motif – images not of regret but of destructive lust: erotic visions of mortality that destroy what they desire.

In Britain, Swinburne evoked 'the love that caught strange flight from death's own eyes/And filled death's lips', in homage to Gautier's *La Morte Amoureuse*, and in *Ave atque Vale* imagined Baudelaire, after death, at the feet of 'some pale Titan-woman like a lover' or the grave as 'fatal mother, With sadder than the Niobean womb, And in the hollow of her breasts a tomb'. Whether phantoms or sorceresses, wraiths or sensual whores, Swinburne's females are symbols of decay, who cast a cold spell on the artist, as invoked in the *Hymn to Proserpine*:

> Thou art more than the gods who number the days of our
>   temporal breath;
> For these give labour and slumber; but thou, Proserpina, death.

and in *The Garden of Proserpine*:

> Pale, beyond porch and portal,
>   Crowned with calm leaves, she stands
> Who gathers all things mortal
>   With cold immortal hands;
> Her languid lips are sweeter
>   Than love's who fears to greet her
> To men that mix and meet her
>   From many times and lands.

In cruel guise, she is Faustine and Dolores, Our Lady of Pain. She is also Burne-Jones's Circe, Oscar Wilde's sadistic Salome, Flaubert's Salammbô, and rendition after rendition of Medusa, whose snake-entwined gaze turned men to stone. She is the Venus of the Tannhäuser tale, who holds men captive through sexual enchantment; or the mermaid, whose cold flesh lures them to drown in the depths of the sensual sea. She is a dangerous allegory of fleshly snares, whose destructive power is infinitely desirable. Sometimes a literal lady of death, she brings sweet seductive oblivion, as in Arthur Symons's 'Pale Woman' from *Images of Good and Evil:*

> I spoke to the pale and heavy-lidded woman, and said:
> O pale and heavy-lidded woman, why is your cheek
> Pale as the dead, and what are your eyes afraid lest they
>   speak?
> And the woman answered me: I am pale as the dead
> For the dead have loved me, and I dream of the dead.

Or she is the same poet's pale phantom, who kills through copulation, and his 'Laus Mortis' or death-wish:

> Most comfortable Death, mother of many dreams,
> And gatherer of many dreams of me,
> Dreams that come desolately flying back again,
> With soiled and quivering wings, from undisclosed streams.

There are evident similarities between this image of a pale, death-like woman and that of the ghostly figure of Elizabeth Siddal, particularly in the much-reproduced image of the heavy-lidded *Beata Beatrix*, whom 'the dead have loved', and who was presented in the histories as the beautiful and fatal influence on Rossetti's life. And for the sake of both his paintings of languorous *femmes fatales* such as Proserpine and Astarte (which had in truth nothing to do with Elizabeth Siddal) and for his dark, drugged soul, Rossetti was adopted into the Symboliste circle and revered as a precursor and prophet of Decadence. The women of his art were then worshipped as holy images.

Elizabeth Siddal was thus transformed into an icon of Decadence, around whom legends grew. When her grave was opened, it was claimed (probably by the notorious Charles Howell, whose career was built on lies) that her red hair had grown in death until it filled the coffin, retaining all its glowing colour. Fiery strands were said to have come away with the notebook, forming relics keenly but vainly sought by collectors, along with the worm-eaten, damp-stained pages of the notebook which had lain by her undecaying cheek. No proven locks of hair are known to have existed, but three supposed leaves from the exhumed notebook survive, one of which is in the British Library.[3] It contains several notes, one relating to the key of a safe, another to a projected painting of Virgin and Child, one on Rossetti's juvenile poem 'Sir Hugh The Heron' (which he described as 'evincing absolutely no promise at all') and the draft of a sonnet concluding

> Alas for all
> The loves that from his hands proud Youth lets fall
> Even as the beads of a told rosary!

In all the myth-making around the exhumation, a distinct erotic charge is palpable, as in Caine's invocation of 'the love that is consummated in death'. And a curious cult of Elizabeth Siddal as a fantasy sex object can be glimpsed in the literature and memoirs of the 1880s and '90s. Swinburne, who had dined with Gabriel and Elizabeth on the night of her death and gave evidence at the inquest, was a passionate if incoherent devotee of 'the incomparable Miss Siddal . . . a wonderful as well as most lovable creature'[4] who encouraged younger artists to worship at the shrine of her memory. Oscar Wilde was an admirer, praising her poetry and defending both Rossetti and his wife against vulgar biographers in a review entitled 'A Cheap Edition of a Great Man'.[5] The *fin-de-siècle* couple Charles Ricketts and Charles Shannon cultivated an artistic devotion to her image, and their picture collection included two portraits, done at Hastings in the early summer of 1854. 'We have added two charming Rossetti studies of Miss Siddal to our treasures, quite exquisite in feeling,' Ricketts rhapsodized, confessing 'but then, we have all, when young, been in love with Miss Siddal'.[6] Later he wrote:

> I have had her presence in Morris's new Red House described to me as of a delicate wraith, appearing without a word at dinner; rising from among the guests to watch the fire; gliding away silent and unobserved as she had come – a ghost in the house of the living.[7]

To these votaries, the exhumation was a topic of absorbing fascination, exemplifying the macabre conjunction of desire and death. Arthur Symons, high priest of Decadence, who identified with Rossetti (and incidentally followed him into schizophrenic insanity) composed an essay in praise of his 'Strange Soul' in which he defended the grave-opening as one element in 'the eternal tragedy of those who have loved the absolute in beauty too well and with too mortal a thirst'. And, he elaborated:

> I have never forgotten how passionately Eleanora Duse said to me, in 1900, 'Rossetti's eyes desire some feverish thing, but the mouth and chin hesitate in pursuit. All Rossetti is in that story of the manuscript buried in his wife's coffin. He could do it; he could repent of it; but he should have gone and taken it back himself; he sent his friends.'[8]

Many if not most of those who tended this cult of the ghostly Elizabeth Siddal were homosexual, although it is not immediately obvious why the figure of a dead woman should have appealed so strongly to this particular Decadent group. It was, no doubt, an extension of their admiration for Rossetti who, although primarily renowned as a lover of women on canvas and in the flesh, and a man of no apparent homoerotic inclinations, was also felt to be a kindred spirit, not only in his art but also in his private life. His reclusiveness gave rise to speculation and from about 1873 – the year after his mental collapse – it was common gossip among the clubmen and literary journalists of London, according to J. Comyns Carr, that Rossetti lacked 'manliness', not being 'virile' or 'masculine' in personality.[9] This judgement, a conflation of gender and value characteristic of the period, was circulated by male rivals and critics, and fortified not only by Rossetti's seclusion but also by his long refusal to exhibit work in public, which was viewed as an 'unmanly' fear of criticism, indicative of womanish weakness and effeminacy.

In an age fascinated and repelled by sexual inversion in equal measure – when practising homosexuality was an indictable offence – these ascribed qualities attracted gay artists of the next generation to the figure of Rossetti, so that his 'sensitive' personality exercised as strong an allure in death as in life. He was, wrote Wilde, 'a pillar of fire to the few that knew him and of cloud to many who knew him not'[10] and beyond Rossetti lay the object of his desire, the shadowy figure of Elizabeth Siddal. The perverse but powerful sense of necrophiliac attraction that pervades the Decadent cult of this pale ghost-woman may thus derive from the displaced fantasy of troilism: being 'in love with

30

Miss Siddal' was perhaps a coded signal for the love that dared not speak its name, and could prove fatally destructive.

However, cult adoration of Elizabeth Siddal was not restricted to homosexual admirers, as is illustrated by the curious history of a tiny portrait discovered in mysterious circumstances. Sometime around the end of the century the self-styled art expert Dr George C. Williamson was shown a very small picture measuring two inches by three, of a shawl-wrapped woman with loose hair. This he was told had been found in the course of charitable visiting at the home of an infirm old woman in the East End of London, who, offering it in gratitude for medical attention, said it was a portrait 'of the wife of a painter man', presented after her death as a memento to her nurse in the 1860s. This story was immediately identified with that of Rossetti, and the portrait with his ailing wife. According to Williamson, this identification was supported by William Rossetti and Charles Fairfax Murray, friend and collector of Rossetti's work, who claimed that it was the only miniature Rossetti had ever painted. In exchange, an annuity was secured for the old woman, and the object was sold to the millionaire collector J. Pierpont Morgan, who had it set in a gold Fabergé frame decorated with jade, opal and diamonds. On the back of the frame the following account was inscribed:

This represents
Elizabeth Eleanor Siddal,
who on the 23rd of May 1860 became the wife of
Dante Gabriel Rossetti.
In May 1861 she gave birth to a child,
and died on February 10th 1862,
having unhappily taken an overdose of Laudanum
in order to relieve a severe form of neuralgia
by which she was afflicted.
This Portrait was painted by her husband
between December 1860 and May 1861,
and is the only portrait the artist painted
of his wife after her marriage.
He painted her portrait numberless times
before her marriage & made many sketches of her
but afterwards made only one slight sketch in pencil
which has been lost,
and painted this Miniature.

The Legend of Elizabeth Siddal

This account is both fanciful and unverifiable. It is not known when the picture was produced; it is not a true miniature painted in watercolour on ivory but a *carte-de-visite* photograph over-painted in gouache; it is not the only image of Elizabeth Siddal after her marriage, and may indeed be neither her portrait nor Rossetti's work.[11] But the secrecy and romance surrounding the story of its discovery, together with its rich, jewelled setting, make it a reverent memorial to her: framed in gold, behind thick glass, decorated with precious stones, it resembles a holy reliquary containing a sacred fragment. Its elevation from keepsake to cult object and the accompanying tale, whereby the wealthy collector's purchase saved a poor sick widow from the workhouse, is testimony to the image's iconic power.

4

Dear Dove Divine

The Aesthetic adoration of Elizabeth Siddal was consciously based on myth rather than actuality and disdained the commonplace gossip of biography, which in Wilde's view robbed life of dignity and added to death itself a new terror. But human curiosity was stronger than high-mindedness, and there always was a ready audience for diverting tales of Pre-Raphaelite private life. Moreover, one consequence of Wilde's trial and imprisonment in 1896 was a reaction against everything associated with Aestheticism, sexual deviance and Decadent death cults, which made it expedient, as Evelyn Waugh was to remark, for biographers to emphasize the 'heartiness' of the Pre-Raphaelite Brotherhood (PRB) and their associates, in order to demonstrate the gulf that separated Reading Gaol from Red Lion Square – where Rossetti had once shared a studio.[1] As a result, the cult of Elizabeth Siddal as a beautiful wraith declined, although it was never extinguished. Even today echoes of necrophiliac fascination haunt her story, resurfacing from time to time like a troubled spirit. In the late 1890s, however, the mainstream, as it were, took a different direction, as biographers sought to put flesh on the ghostly figure and endow it with personality.

This process was promoted, from the 1880s onwards, by Rossetti's family, naturally eager to secure his status as a creative artist with the stamp of genius and therefore anxious to rescue him from association with deviance. The trouble lay not so much with accusations of 'unmanliness' as with truer, darker rumours of mental instability, drug dependence and compulsive womanizing. Admiring biographers therefore began to stress the normal aspects of Rossetti's personal life alongside their claims for the exceptional qualities of his art. And, as the collections of a number of important Pre-Raphaelite patrons came on to the market, financial con-

siderations joined family piety to produce strong practical incen-
tives for maintaining the prices of Rossetti's canvases. The cult
of genius, a marked feature of late nineteenth-century European
society, provided a livelihood not only for artists but also for a
shoal of supporters – dealers, critics, publishers, journalists – who
depended on the production and exchange of art and recognized
in Rossetti a good product, if profitable interest could be sustained. The Rossetti family, while leaning towards reticence, were
not fundamentally opposed to this exploitation.

Indeed, in several senses the family lived off Gabriel's posthumous reputation, for their substantial capital of paintings, drawings,
sketches, letters and recollections held both cultural and monetary
value. Family privacy and loyalty were, however, invaded and
compromised by the stream of inquiry and speculation, and a
chief objective was to keep some control over the flood of Rosset-
tiana, lest it swamp the market or drown the integrity of relatives
and friends. Management of the family archive was thus carefully
regulated.

After the death in 1886 of the redoubtable Mrs Rossetti, the
immediate family comprised Christina and William, together with
William's wife Lucy, and their four surviving children. Lucy was
daughter of the painter Ford Madox Brown, and the extended
Rossetti-Brown clan included Lucy's half-sister, now Catherine
Hueffer, and her sons and daughter. Outside this privileged group
lay others holding direct or indirect access and interest in the
history of Pre-Raphaelitism, from whom there issued a steady
flow of memoirs and biographies, all intent on re-creating the
early days of the PRB, now receding half a century into the
past. Alongside publication of books and articles, 'laundry list'
collecting likewise flourished, meagre scraps from members of
the movement being eagerly bought and sold as authentic relics.

The chief narrator of Elizabeth Siddal's story, mainly within
texts focusing on the great 'DGR', was William Rossetti, who
in the course of twenty years produced the accounts on which
knowledge of her life was based. This began in 1884 with three
articles for the *Art Journal* and continued with *The Collected Works
of Dante Gabriel Rossetti* in 1886, whose biographical introduction
dealt with Elizabeth's entry into the Pre-Raphaelite world. It was,
William wrote, through a fellow student named Walter Deverell
that 'Rossetti came to know Elizabeth Eleanor Siddal, daughter

of a Sheffield cutler, herself a milliner's assistant, gifted with some artistic and some poetic faculty; in the spring of 1860, after a long engagement, they married.'[2]

This was the first identification of Elizabeth's class position; hitherto she had been merely the 'lady' who became Rossetti's wife. The information, however, was not wholly accurate, for it would have been more precise to call Charles Siddall 'a Southwark ironmonger', since he ran a retail business in the Old Kent Road, where indeed his widow still resided. The ambiguities of 'Sheffield cutler', with its connotations of quality craftsmanship and provincial origin, suggested a lower or at least a more distant status. William Rossetti was well aware of the facts, for he was in contact with Elizabeth's brothers, but for some reason – he was not known as a snob – he suppressed the shopkeeping connection. The effect was to place Elizabeth socially several rungs lower than Rossetti, whose father, although an impoverished political refugee from Italy, had nevertheless held a professorship at London University. Her own occupation of milliner's assistant was consonant with a modest but genteel social position, but we may note that William avoided any reference to her being a model, despite Caine's earlier disclosure.

The following year *The Life of Dante Gabriel Rossetti*, by Joseph Knight, appeared in a 'Great Writers' series. The author had enjoyed assistance from William Rossetti and Ford Madox Brown, and been granted access to letters held by the family. He identified Elizabeth as daughter of 'a Sheffield tradesman', occupied in London as a milliner's assistant. Somewhere near 1850, he wrote, Walter Deverell was so struck with her beauty of face and form that he persuaded her to sit to him. Here, for the first time, her role as a model to others beside Rossetti was acknowledged. Rossetti, equally taken with her beauty, induced her to sit to him towards the end of 1850 or early in 1851.

> She had not been with him long before he recognized in her a strong aptitude for art . . . the position of model was soon associated with that of student. Under Rossetti's zealous tuition her progress was rapid . . . A result all but inevitable . . . ensued. The close intimacy involved in the relationship of master and pupil gave every opportunity for successful wooing and Miss Siddall became affianced to her teacher.[3]

This account reproduced a standard Victorian view of courtship: physical attraction accompanied by shared tastes, the suitor as tutor, the woman following the man's lead. Moreover, the slight social difficulty of Miss Siddal's modelling was neatly resolved by her swift translation to pupil and immediate progress towards matrimony.

Unfortunately, the long engagement mentioned by William Rossetti presented Knight with difficulties. None of the correct formalities had been observed: there was no announcement, no ring, no family introductions, no wedding preparations. The exact date of the engagement could not be fixed, Knight conceded, aware of the irregularities, but was 'probably 1853, certainly no later than 1854'. To account for this uncertainty, he offered a surprising explanation, saying that 'at Miss Siddall's request the contract was kept secret and its first publication to Rossetti's close friends seems to have been contrary to her wishes.'[4]

This unconvincing idea – perhaps contributed by Madox Brown, who had been close to the young couple during the early 1850s and understood the problem – seems to have been introduced to protect Rossetti's honour as a gentleman. As Holman Hunt once remarked, artists were often 'excused for some licentiousness' with regard to their models,[5] and Miss Siddal's social position might perhaps suggest that she had been vulnerable to seduction while working, unchaperoned, in Gabriel's studio.

To counter such unworthy suspicions, Knight stressed the evidence of Gabriel's overwhelming love and joy, documented in three pages of quotations culled from unpublished letters in which Rossetti

> speaks of her invariably as Lizzie, coupling frequently with the appellation some endearing adjective, and using at time such names, caressing or grotesque, as secure affection loves to bestow . . . Writing from Hastings he says, 'Lizzie is looking lovelier than ever', and later on, 'Everyone adores and reveres Lizzie. I made sketches of her with iris stuck in her dear hair the other day . . .' To his mother he speaks of Lizzie and himself scratching their initials on a stone . . .[6]

This exuberant lover frequently 'insists on sketching his mistress in some pose of exceptional beauty', and delights in Ruskin's description of her as 'a noble woman'. His happiness is jubilant, and the long-delayed wedding is solely the result of financial difficulties and anxiety for Elizabeth's health – both then recognized as obstacles to matrimony. As late as April 1860, when the marriage is imminent, Rossetti is once more thrown into a state of apprehension by 'a severe attack of illness on the part of Miss Siddall'. Finally, however, on 23 May, the wedding took place, when Gabriel wrote to Brown: 'All hail from Lizzie and myself, just back from church.'[7]

Rossetti's kindness as a husband was exemplary, but his wife's illness – 'the root of which was consumption' – developed into neuralgia; taking laudanum for relief led to the fatal overdose:

> One night in 1862, the Madox Browns, then living in Highgate Rise, were alarmed by a violent knocking at the door . . . Rossetti, after frantically seeking one physician after another, roused his friends to aid him in his extreme emergency. All was, however, in vain. The spirit had fled; the fair frame was tenantless and she whom Rossetti in sustained adoration had just painted as Regina Cordium had passed away for ever from his life.[8]

There followed the touching story of the coffined poems and their subsequent recovery, which Knight presented as a final act of homage: the 'buried treasure' of the poems had been 'written during the happy period of courtship and the brief honeymoon of wedded life'.[9]

This was not the truth – as William Rossetti certainly knew even if Joseph Knight did not – but the account contributed most effectively to a tale of impetuous young love and sustained affection, tragically cut short by illness and death, in the style of the best romances.

The appearance of Knight's book stimulated other recollections of the young couple in the early 1850s. In her autobiography, the writer Mary Howitt recalled living in a quaint and picturesque house called the Hermitage on Highgate West Hill, where Rossetti for a short time in 1852 had the use of a studio. 'We saw a good deal of Miss Siddall,' wrote Mrs Howitt:

She was very delicate and had certainly a marvellous influence on Rossetti; though I could never believe she possessed the artistic genius he ascribed to her, for what she produced had no originality in it. Still, she was, in her way, an interesting woman and his love for her like a passionate romantic Italian story.[10]

The next volume of fraternal piety by William Rossetti was *Dante Gabriel Rossetti as Designer and Writer* (1889), which added further fragments to his sister-in-law's story. Now, since the exact date of the momentous meeting with Elizabeth was beginning to assume some importance, William laid claim to an early year that suggested love at first sight, stating that Gabriel 'had been in love with her since 1851 or thereabouts'. Thereafter, the 'always delicate and often perilous condition of her health' had protracted the engagement. He also explained how John Ruskin, the Pre-Raphaelites' critical champion, had shown a sympathetic interest in Miss Siddal's 'limited but refined artistic faculty', by means of 'more than one munificent act'. This was a circumlocutory way of saying that Ruskin had provided a financial allowance which, strictly speaking, it would have been improper (as William Rossetti was no doubt aware) for Ruskin to make to another man's fiancée. Also revealed was Ruskin's bestowal on Miss Siddal of the 'fancy-name' of Ida after Tennyson's independent-minded Princess, an illustration of his high regard.[11]

In 1891 William issued a compact edition of his brother's poems in one volume, whose preface was 'condensed from that which appeared in the *Collected Works*' and added nothing to the portrait of Miss Siddall but, unexpectedly, changed her occupation to that of 'dressmaker's assistant'.[12] This alteration was not explained and went unremarked but, as we shall see, it has a small but significant role to play in the unravelling of her history, although this did not become evident for a long time. William's reasons for making the change are unknown; one can only speculate that he had, perhaps, received a 'correction' from a member of the Siddall family.

Each new publication thus added its details to the hitherto shadowy figure, although the portrait that began to emerge was little more than a conventional picture of Victorian femininity, defined in terms of beauty and pathos as the passive object of male admiration. But in 1892 the touching tale of young love was dealt a damaging blow with the appearance of the memoirs of William Bell Scott, an early associate of the Pre-Raphaelite circle and himself a poet and painter. Bell Scott had never received the recognition he felt he deserved, and his somewhat embittered and ungenerous – though also candid – memoirs, edited and published after his death, caused a considerable stir.

One evening in 1852, Scott related, he arrived in London from Newcastle and called on Rossetti in the ivy-covered studio at the Hermitage, where

> I found myself in the romantic dusk of the apartment face to face with Rossetti and a lady whom I did not recognize and could scarcely see. He did not introduce her; she rose to go. I made a little bow, which she did not acknowledge; and she left. This was Miss Siddal. Why he did not introduce me to her I cannot say. Perhaps the maid should have called him instead of allowing me to invade the studio without warning . . . for myself, I had not yet heard of such a person as Miss Siddal.[13]

This disingenuous recollection both hinted that something improper was going on and cast doubt on the whole story of an engagement. Why did Gabriel not introduce his betrothed? Perhaps, Scott went on to suggest, 'Rossetti was already beginning to revise his intention of marriage'. Meanwhile Miss Siddal came in for some disparagement: 'She began to think herself a genius too and did small quasi-poetical imitations of his work . . . then, her health not being good, by Ruskin's assistance she went to Mentone . . .'

The most serious allegation, however, was Scott's claim that Rossetti's professed belief that women and flowers were the only subjects worth painting had been occasioned by 'other ladies besides Miss Siddal coming within his orbit'. Here was the first public hint that Rossetti's affection for his beloved was not undivided. Indeed, it strongly implied infidelity. It was, in fact, the earliest reference to the most important of these 'other ladies', who, according to Scott, 'must have had some overpowering attractions . . . although I could never see what they were'. As yet unidentified, she was seen in the Strand, 'cracking nuts with her teeth and throwing the shells about; seeing Rossetti staring at her, she threw some at him. Delighted with this brilliant naïveté, he forthwith accosted her and carried her off to sit to him for her portrait.'[14] This evidently was no lady; as every sophisticated reader would understand, she was a prostitute, soliciting custom in the street, who was carried off for more than a portrait.

Not all Scott's memories were so compromising. He also quoted a letter from the sculptor Alexander Munro written in 1855 after a meeting in Paris – Elizabeth being *en route* for the south on Ruskin's advice – which described Gabriel as a 'foolishly fond lover'. But even this image of unmixed affection was promptly questioned by a quotation from a letter to Scott from William Rossetti in 1860, informing him that the announcement of Gabriel's forthcoming marriage had taken the Rossetti family by surprise. Compounding the disclosure, Scott continued with a letter from his own wife Letitia, relaying the gossip of the same summer to the effect that, on return from honeymoon, the new Mrs Rossetti had not visited her in-laws. Scott added his own comment that Elizabeth was a poor wife and housekeeper, being 'little accustomed to the cares and habits of domestic life'.[15]

These revelations met a hostile reception from Rossetti's family and friends. Reviewing the book, Sharp challenged the insinuations of Scott's account of how Rossetti 'in his innocent adolescence' had fallen in love with Miss Siddal, and called the references to Ruskin's financial assistance tactless. Swinburne, who privately called Scott 'that villainous old viper',[16] publicly complained that the calumnies 'cast a slur on the memory of that incomparable lady whose maiden name was Siddal'. He added, as one 'who knew her better than most of her husband's friends', that 'the memory of all her marvellous charms of mind and person – her matchless grace, loveliness, courage, endurance, wit, humour, heroism and sweetness – is too dear and sacred to be profaned by any attempt at expression'. With dignity Scott's editor confessed himself baffled; the vile innuendoes imputed to Scott, he claimed, existed only in the minds of his critics.[17]

He was right, for there were many tales circulating about Rossetti's irregular affairs which all Swinburne's indignation could not dispel and which cast doubt on any simple story of romantic love, and it was probably because they were unlikely to remain secret that William Rossetti adopted a policy of controlled disclosure, to minimize the threat to the family name.

In the wake of Scott's unwelcome intervention, there thus appeared two new, authorized accounts of Rossetti's life. The first was from F. G. Stephens, an original member of the PRB who had good claim to first-hand knowledge, although he did not actually state that he had known Elizabeth Siddal personally. Stephens's account of her entry into the Pre-Raphaelite circle has formed the basis for all subsequent versions:

> Some time in 1850 Walter Deverell, going with his mother to a then-renowned bonnet-maker's 'establishment' in Cranbourne Street (then called an 'alley') and being dreadfully bored while the lady discussed a new purchase . . . happened in his boyish and restless mood to glance wearily along the counter to where, in the background of the shop, a group of assistants could be seen diligently building headgear of the latest mode. Among these damsels sat one conspicuous by a rare sort of comeliness, tall, elegant, lithe, slim waisted . . . her abundant hair was of a darkish auburn-brown with golden threads entwined, and bound compactly about her rather small and well-shaped head, which nature poised in graceful ease upon the 'neck like a tower' . . . Her carnations, 'rather pale than wan', were not without freckles Deverell at a distance did not see but, under these spots of the sun, her fine skin was even-tinted and smooth, while her features were as choicely modelled as those of an Italian cinquecento bronze of the purest kind. In a moment, 'our dear boy', as all his friends called Deverell, was on fire to paint this strangely favoured beauty as Viola . . . for whom the model must needs be filled with an inward and spiritual grace and modesty. For Walter, to ask was to command his mother, and that lady exerted herself so successfully with the bonnet-maker, the damsel and her father – who was a watchmaker originally from Sheffield and then settled somewhere in the Newington Butts region – that the desired sittings were granted to Deverell who, poor fellow, dying young, never did the maiden justice nor quite carried out his meaning in the picture. Soon after this Rossetti persuaded Miss Siddall to sit to him in turn and thus began a close relationship, including Rossetti's falling in love with his model, their engagement in or about 1853, and his marrying her in 1860 . . .[18]

The source of Stephens's information about the Cranbourne Street shop and Mrs Deverell's involvement in the discovery of this prodigy is not known and was not corroborated. By 1894 both Deverell and his mother were long since dead, and it is unlikely that the story came from the Rossettis, for although like everyone else, William Rossetti later incorporated the tale into his own version, he offered no substantive confirmation; nor has any subsequently appeared. The whole reconstructed drama of the bonnet shop must thus derive either from Stephens's own exclusive knowledge – shared with no other members of the Brotherhood, improbable as that seems – or from his imagination, based purely on the earlier identification of Lizzie as a milliner's assistant. In the mid-century, 'Cranbourne Street' was as much a generic term for milliners as 'Carnaby Street' or 'Kings Road' for fashion boutiques in the 1960s, and there is no supporting evidence that Lizzie actually worked there.

The importance of this incident, however, lies not with its veracity but with its contribution to the romantic legend of a humble Cinderella discovered by her Pre-Raphaelite prince. Stephens's account further plays up this aspect with its description of her charms – the slim waist, well-shaped head and long neck – which to the modern ear sound unpleasantly like points in a beauty contest. Their purpose, however, was to praise her refinement and stress her beauty. The coy mention of freckles, then regarded as blemishes, suggests that she had originally been regarded as a rather plain young woman. Red hair, too, was considered ugly, which perhaps explained Stephens's euphemistic 'darkish auburn-brown'. The freckles, incidentally, were subsequently omitted from the histories, lest they undermine the picture of rare beauty.

Geographically, Stephens located the Siddall family more or less correctly in Southwark, Newington Butts being close to the Elephant and Castle and thus not far from the family shop. Socially, however, he altered their status by making his heroine's father a watchmaker. This was what Ruskin had been told, too, in 1855, and the whole occupational issue, which has since become a minor area of contention, is aggravated by the fact that on her marriage certificate Elizabeth described her father as an optician. These varying assertions are, in my view, indicative only of the shopkeeper's uncertain social position, poised between the manual trades and petit-bourgeois gentility, and of the anxiety of both

Elizabeth and her husband to 'improve' her class position; hence, in part, the repeated claims that Miss Siddal was inherently lady-like despite the deficiencies of her background.

Stephens's account was followed within the year by a memoir written by William Rossetti to accompany a selection of his brother's letters. Carefully edited, the texts omitted more than they revealed. William frankly admitted as much in the preface. Anticipating the question, 'Have you told everything of a substantial kind that you know about your deceased brother?' he gave the answer, 'No; I have told what I choose to tell and have left untold what I do not choose to tell; if you want more, be pleased to consult some other informant.'[19]

As the younger Rossetti brother, William had worked as a civil-service clerk during the family's straitened years in the late 1840s, while Gabriel enjoyed art-student freedom. But he had shared in the heady excitement of the PRB, joining his brother, John Everett Millais, William Holman Hunt, Fred Stephens and the rest as a member and contributor to *The Germ* and also the one responsible for chronicling events in the 'Pre-Raphaelite Journal'. From this he subsequently derived a good deal of reflected glory, although his own artistic aspirations, nourished during the years of the Brotherhood, had soon been sacrificed to a duller reputation as editor and critic, while he continued in government service. At a personal level, he had suffered under the strain of Gabriel's attacks of insanity, and the burden of financial and emotional responsibility. He was also aware that many of Gabriel's friends regarded him as a bore.

In considering his various accounts, we therefore need to recognise that his fraternal feelings were ambivalent, combining fervent admiration and loyalty to his brother with distress at the course of his life and its unremitting demands for affection and support, extending beyond the grave. William's work as archivist was thus defined by competing impulses of accuracy and reticence. On the one hand, he refused to make false claims – as an editor and biographer himself he detested the sanitized contemporary accounts of Shelley and Byron – but on the other he could never be altogether frank, for fear of seeming unkind, envious or lacking in familial respect. His *Memoir* was thus deliberately restricted to family affairs, enabling the more disreputable aspects of Gabriel's life to be obscured.

Towards his sister-in-law, William's feelings were not warm. By his own account he had not known her well, either in the early days – when he had partly shared the tenancy of the Chatham Place apartment – or during the brief married years, when Lizzie was too 'unwell' or dependent on laudanum to pay or receive visits. The lack of direct communication within the family suggests coolness on both sides, an impression William's early, curtailed references had done nothing to dispel. In the *Memoir*, however, he gave her a fairer hearing, partly to counter Bell Scott's slurs but also perhaps to reassert his own status as the chief fount of Pre-Raphaelite knowledge, which Stephens had implicitly challenged. By marshalling pedantic detail, William now sought to establish a definitive picture of his brother's wife. In this, he silently dropped his earlier description of her as a dressmaker in favour of Stephens's dramatic account of her discovery in the bonnet shop. He went on to add his own details.

First, her name was given as 'Siddal', on the basis that 'my brother always spelled the name thus', even though members of the family wrote 'Siddall'. Second, her age was fixed, more or less. When first seen by Deverell, wrote William, 'she was, I believe, not fully seventeen years of age'.[20] This statement meant that Elizabeth must have been born around 1834 and was thus at least five years younger than Gabriel. This was no doubt written in good faith, but subsequently proved untrue; William Rossetti clearly did not know her precise age. In any case, the effect of his guess was to establish Elizabeth Siddal as an extremely young, sixteen-year-old girl of virginal innocence when 'in 1850' (the dating of this momentous event grew ever earlier) Dante Gabriel Rossetti for the first time 'fell seriously in love'. She was, William went on,

a most beautiful creature with an air between dignity and sweetness with something that exceeded modest self-respect and partook of disdainful reserve; tall, finely formed with a lofty neck and regular yet somewhat uncommon features, greenish-blue unsparkling eyes, large perfect eyelids, brilliant complexion and a lavish heavy wealth of coppery-golden hair . . .[21]

Dissected, this did not make a wholly flattering description. The sweetness was outweighed by the disdain and the glory of 'coppery-golden' was at once modified with 'what many people call red hair and abuse under that name'. Furthermore, her voice, although 'clear and low', had 'a certain sibilant tendency which reduced its attractiveness'. In other words, she lisped.

Her social position was also definitively clarified as the daughter of 'a Sheffield cutler who had removed to the neighbourhood of Newington Butts (Mr Stephens says a watchmaker but I hardly suppose that to be correct)' and who was dead, William wrote, by 1856. He confessed to never having met Mrs Siddall but had once or twice seen Lizzie's younger sister and a brother, 'a sensible well-conducted young man'. He also recalled the existence of a youngest brother, 'said to be somewhat weakminded'.[22] This was substantially accurate if incomplete. As was later discovered, there were several more siblings, and Mr Siddall had died in 1859.[23] And it was coy: when the *Memoir* appeared, Lizzie's sister Lydia and her brothers James and Harry were still alive. William Rossetti was indeed in touch with the two men, who called occasionally at the house, as his daughter recalled. Yet the impression given was that the tenuous contacts between the Rossetti and Siddall families had long ceased.

Of Elizabeth's modelling, William confirmed her role as Viola in Walter Deverell's *Twelfth Night* (1850), and identified her as Sylvia in Holman Hunt's *Two Gentlemen of Verona* (1851) as well as Millais's celebrated *Ophelia* (1851). The last had become a famous image, hung in important exhibitions and reproduced as an engraving. But, according to the *Memoir*, it had not been long before Lizzie sat only to Rossetti, who first painted her in 1850 as *Rossovestita*, and thereafter as Beatrice, the Virgin Mary and other noble and saintly figures.

Writing of her childhood, William revealed that a neighbouring shopkeeper in Southwark had been the notorious murderer James Greenacre, who had sometimes helped her 'toddling steps over a muddy or crowded crossing'. Of this curious incident, presumably related by Lizzie herself – the Greenacre murder of the 1830s long retained a place in the popular imagination – William commented: 'such is the difference in "environment".' Then, apparently fearful lest this harmless detail suggest that his brother's wife had mixed with the criminal classes, 'let me say here once for all', he hastily added, 'Miss Siddal was a graceful ladylike person, knowing how to behave in company. She had received an ordinary education and committed no faults of speech. In our circle she was always termed "Lizzie".'[24]

The unconfirmed engagement remained a greater problem. William admitted that he did not know the exact date – an unlikely lapse of memory if such a formal event had indeed taken place – but asserted that it occurred around the end of 1851. This was a much earlier date than any given previously. Somewhat superfluously, he added 'that she was sincerely in love with him – he being most deeply and profusely in love with her – is readily to be presumed'. He then turned with characteristic scrupulousness to Lizzie's 'somewhat singular' personality:

> I hardly think that I ever heard her say a single thing indicative of her own character or her own underlying thought. All her talk was of a 'chaffy' kind – its tone sarcastic, its substance lightsome. It was like the speech of a person who wanted to turn off the conversation.

However, she was 'not ill-natured in talk, still less was she scandalmongering or chargeable with volatility or levity personal to herself; but she seemed to say, "My mind and my feelings are my own, and no outsider is expected to pry into them." ' Finally, he commented, she appeared to have no religion.[25]

All in all, although it does not appear hostile or inaccurate, this account was not over-friendly. Certain gratuitous remarks suggest underlying ambivalence. At one point William blamed Lizzie's presence in the years 1850–4 as a contributing factor in the collapse of the PRB, though he must have known that its dissolution was well advanced long before Gabriel first declared his love. He also commented on a degree of coolness between Lizzie and Christina, at which Gabriel was 'a little put out, thinking [his sister's] appreciation of Lizzie not up to the mark'.[26] A few years later, however, William denied his own inference, saying that the incident illustrated only Gabriel's enthusiasm, not any sisterly discord.[27] Christina Rossetti had died the year before the *Memoir* was published; in the decades following Lizzie's death her few recorded comments were compassionately phrased, as in her response in 1893 to William's suggestion that their sister-in-law's work be featured in an exhibition. 'I shall be really pleased if our poor Lizzie's name and fame can be brought forward,' she wrote, 'and will gladly lend my St Agnes which is such a beauty.'[28] Of her earlier feelings nothing now remains but a remark by Madox Brown, quoting Gabriel, to the effect that Christina and Lizzie 'do not agree'.[29] Certainly they were not close.

The first reference to Lizzie in the *Family Letters* that accompanied the *Memoir* came in a letter written by Gabriel to Christina in August 1852, while she and their parents were living in Somerset, in which he warned his sister 'not to rival the Sid' in drawing, and continued: 'Since you went away, I have had sent me, among my things from Highgate, a lock of hair shorn from the beloved head of that dear, and radiant as the tresses of Aurora, a sight of which may perhaps dazzle you on your return.'[30]

Here, William identified 'the Sid' as Miss Siddal without further comment on the disrespectful nature of the nickname. Later, he noted that in his letters Gabriel often referred to his beloved with a little drawing of a dove in place of her name, illustrative of both his affection – Victorian culture frequently associated young women with pet birds, doves or pigeons – and her modesty. In a Valentine verse, Gabriel called Lizzie his 'dear dove divine'. For no evident reason, however, William omitted the remainder of this letter with its account of two dresses in grey and black that Lizzie had recently made for herself, the first 'bringing out her characteristics as a "meek unconscious dove" ' and the second making her resemble, according to Gabriel, quoting Juvenal's sixth Satire, that rare bird, a black swan.

This letter is in fact the earliest proof of any declaration of affection by Gabriel. And scrutiny of all the evidence, as opposed to the assertions, suggests that his feeling for Lizzie was not a matter of love at first sight. Rather, it was not until the summer of 1852, with his parents' absence from London, together with the freedom of the studio at the Hermitage, that Gabriel fell in love. He was not earning, however, and in no position to propose marriage – which would, incidentally, explain his failure to introduce Lizzie to Scott at this date. When convenient, she could still be treated as an anonymous model.

A year later Gabriel had his own studio at Blackfriars. Here, as he informed William in a letter from Newcastle, Lizzie was painting during his absence; he added 'she will probably sleep there sometimes.'[31] This was clear, if still equivocal, evidence of growing intimacy. But by the early summer of 1854 the situation was unmistakable: the young couple were together at Hastings where, Gabriel reported, everyone admired Lizzie, and 'no one thinks it at all odd my going into the Gug's room to sit there'.[32]

In his notes William identified 'Gug' or 'Guggums' as pet names that Gabriel used for his beloved, adding that Lizzie used the term reciprocally, 'perhaps as a sort of short for Gabriel'. Yet he left unexplained the other puzzling references. Was there not, in truth, something improper about a lady sleeping in a young man's apartment, even during his absence? And in his unchaperoned presence in her room at Hastings? Even engaged couples were seldom permitted such freedoms.

Overall, however, the dominant impression of the relationship given in the *Family Letters* was one of secure and sustained affection, as was no doubt intended by the selection and editing of the texts (in which both Christina and her mother had assisted before their deaths). This was supported by a facsimile illustration of Gabriel's letter to his mother in 1860 announcing the imminent wedding 'at last in as few days as possible'.[33] All the doubts raised by Bell Scott's unkind words thus seemed to be dispelled.

Moving rather swiftly to the years of marriage – the reader searches in vain for detailed references to Lizzie during the later 1850s – William conceded that Gabriel's artistic temperament led to an unconventional lifestyle. But, he claimed, Lizzie 'was perfectly accustomed to his habits, had much of a tendency and feeling in the same direction . . . and was very little in the way of polite visiting'.[34] Moreover, he added, 'married life cannot be happy when one of the spouses is perpetually and grievously ill'. He described Lizzie's acute suffering from phthisis and neuralgia, for which stimulants and opiates were alternately prescribed, and outlined the melancholy circumstances of her death.

How informative and reliable is William Rossetti's account to be judged? There seems no reason to quarrel with his characterization of Elizabeth Siddal's personality, since it was based on first-hand experience and offered as a necessarily subjective view. And his factual information, however incomplete, provided her with a fuller biography on which later researches could be built. Yet the account is perhaps less straightforward than it appears, for the presentation of factual detail is held in tension between William's personal view of this reserved yet 'chaffy' woman, who claimed to be too unwell to visit her mother-in-law but frequently accompanied her husband to a public dining room (as he noted primly), and his desire to present an acceptable picture of innocent young love leading in the normal manner to affectionate marriage. The critique of Elizabeth's personality is therefore interfolded with affirmations of Gabriel's 'boundless fondness' to construct a picture of sustained devotion – the tenderness of the artist-lover towards his ailing beauty – that is sometimes at odds with the other evidence.

As with Stephens's account, however, the keynote is romance. After the inquest, William recalled a moment of great agitation, when Gabriel was seen 'standing by the corpse crying out: "Oh Lizzie, Lizzie, come back to me!" ' He had placed the notebook in the coffin privately, saying later, 'I have often been writing these poems when Lizzie was ill and suffering and I might have been attending to her, and now they shall go.'[35] It was a touching image of a loving husband and his patient, dying dove.

5

Pre-Raphaelite Mascot

In these early accounts, Elizabeth Siddal has all the lineaments of femininity according to the cultural definitions of the age. The image portrayed owes more to ideas of how she ought to have been – as the beloved of a romantic poet and painter – than to any inquiry as to what she was actually like, so that she is simply defined as beautiful, young, innocent, modest, patient and loving. Her role was to be looked at and adored, the object of masculine admiration, and to be drawn and painted. The pictures are, indeed, a visual manifestation of her symbolic meaning within the Victorian ideology of separate spheres and gender difference; their subject is the complementary figure in a repeating sequence of dualities: male/female; artist/model; lover/beloved; husband/-wife; health/sickness; strength/weakness; active/passive; living/-dead. On all counts, she fulfils her allotted function of defining Rossetti's fame. Even her own talent – and William Rossetti devoted a good deal of space in the *Memoir* to this, giving the titles of several pictures and quoting her poem 'A Year and a Day' – is presented as the product of Gabriel's encouragement and affection.

When these narratives were being composed, contemporary definitions of gender difference and approved relations between the sexes – seldom static – were under great stress. From the 1880s onwards, the 'New Woman' was a cultural slogan similar to 'Women's Lib' in the 1970s, indicative of challenge to patriarchal thought and practice. The New Woman sought professional, economic, social and sexual equality – and above all the vote to guarantee equal rights. In Britain, the male establishment resisted such demands; debates became heated and even violent, culminating in penal attacks on suffragette campaigns. In this context, the presentation of a 'meek unconscious dove', lovely and submissive in the shadow of the great artists of the PRB, was both an historical account and a simultaneous message to the audience of the time. It is not simply that those who wrote about Elizabeth Siddal were mainly men – many women shared the same views – but that, whether or not William Rossetti and Fred Stephens were aware of it, their image of Miss Siddal, either demure or 'chaffy', did not simply present the facts, but also expressed the nostalgia of the old men of the Brotherhood for a past era when relations between the sexes were perceived as more harmonious and when women, in memory at least, were less troublesome. This implicitly functioned as an indirect rebuke to those in the present who demanded equality. The truly feminine or 'womanly woman', in the phrase of the time, was the sweet, weak heroine of Pre-Raphaelitism, aspiring to do no more than lovingly emulate her husband's art and to inspire his noblest achievements.

It is true that the memoirs do not present Elizabeth Siddal entirely without blemishes. In addition to her freckles, she was accused of 'disdainful reserve', which suggested a lack of maidenly meekness. But this was hardly a criticism within the context of a beloved worthy to stand beside Dante's Beatrice. And if she had no 'houswifely' virtues, this was easily pardoned in one so frail and sick. Illness indeed becomes her dominant feature, in keeping with medical definitions of inherent feminine weakness. Wasting disease and youthful death added poignancy to her tale, while implying that this was but a natural aspect of womanhood.

A greater deficiency, in an age when young women were ideally obedient and devout, was her apparent lack of religion. This was strange when, as William Rossetti (himself an atheist) pointed out, his brother 'had no sort of liking for irreligion in women, and even a prejudice against women who would not believe'.[1] This was a serious criticism, and it is interesting to note the emergence of a minor counter-current among Lizzie's supporters, asserting that he must be mistaken. The young Bessie Parkes, friend of the Howitt family, had first met Elizabeth Siddal in 1854 when with Barbara Leigh Smith she had helped Gabriel find suitable lodgings for his 'love and pupil' in Hastings. Now Madame Belloc and a Catholic convert, Bessie's volume of reminiscences published in 1897 recalled a girl of 'unworldly simplicity' who 'had the look of one who read her bible and said her prayers every night, which she probably did'.[2]

The Legend of Elizabeth Siddal

With or without such details, the story of Elizabeth Siddal and Dante Gabriel Rossetti took shape in the popular imagination as one of the great romances of all time, and was included in sentimental anthologies – significant only as mirrors of the time – such as Richard le Gallienne's *Loves of the Poets*, where the chapter devoted to Elizabeth and Gabriel claimed to 'come near the legend in the making . . . to see the lovers before they escape entirely into mythology . . . and the personal history becomes a universal symbol.' Here Rossetti was 'high priest' of Pre-Raphaelitism and Elizabeth Siddal was its 'young madonna' with a 'romantic destiny'.[3]

At the end of the century, other members of the Pre-Raphaelite group were prompted to publish their own recollections, as the last survivors of a golden age. Their chief aim was to promote the reputation of the famed Brotherhood – now a historic band – and stake a position in history for each individual artist. The cult of the genius, reaching its zenith in this period, laid increasing emphasis on artistic originality and innovation: to have been the first was as important as to have been the best. Consequently, the Brothers and their supporters laid rival claims to the creation of Pre-Raphaelitism, and to its mascot Elizabeth Siddal. Appearing in quick succession, the volumes of biography and memoirs demonstrate how the survivors responded to the growing myth of the Pre-Raphaelite heroine, each supplying their own ornament to the bracelet of legend. She became a talisman or touchstone – having known her was authentic proof of membership of the charmed group in the bright circle of the PRB before it was darkened by defection and death. In this process, incidental nuggets of new information were offered as facts, but their prime function was not biographical; rather, they were certificates of historic authenticity.

Her very name acquired charisma. The new seven-volume edition of Rossetti's poems, produced from 1898 under William Rossetti's indefatigable editorship, was given, for no very clear reason, the evocative title of 'The Siddal Edition', trading on the glamour of her reputation as muse.

Recollections began to multiply. Several can be traced to the same source: the painter Arthur Hughes, who in the early 1850s shared a studio with Millais and who was later associated with the 'jovial campaign' in 1857 to paint murals in the Oxford University

Union debating chamber, under Rossetti's high-spirited leadership. Hughes has not hitherto been credited with contributions to Elizabeth Siddal's story, largely because his reminiscences are contained in other men's books, but he was the originator of several significant episodes. In 1897, Rossetti's letters to William Allingham were published (with editorial commentary by G. B. Hill, whose sole connection with Pre-Raphaelitism was having witnessed the irreverent behaviour of the mural painters in Oxford), covering Allingham's friendship with Gabriel and Elizabeth in the early 1850s. In April 1854, for example, Gabriel wrote to say that he had taken 'Miss S to Hastings'. He had also 'told Ruskin of my pupil and he yearneth'.[4] An editorial note, identifying the pupil as 'Miss Siddal, with whom Rossetti had fallen in love so early as 1850, though it was not till 1860 that he married her', introduced a verbatim account by Arthur Hughes, which largely repeated the now-familiar tale, and added a new detail:

> Deverell accompanied his mother one day to a milliner's. Through an open door he saw a girl working with her needle; he got his mother to ask her to sit to him. She was the future Mrs Rossetti. Millais painted her for his Ophelia – wonderfully like her. She was tall and slender, with red coppery hair and bright consumptive complexion, though in these early years she had no striking signs of ill health. She was exceedingly quiet, speaking very little. She had read Tennyson, having first come to know something about him by finding one or two of his poems on a piece of paper which she brought home to her mother wrapped round a pat of butter. Rossetti taught her to draw. She used to be drawing while sitting to him. Her drawings were beautiful, but without force. They were feminine likenesses of his own.[5]

Hughes supplied another anecdote, nowhere else recorded, when he told Hill that 'it was from [Alexander] Munro that I had the story' of how on their return from honeymoon in Paris, the newly-married couple heard of the sudden death of writer Robert Brough and went instantly to pawn Elizabeth's jewellery in order to make a gift of money to the widow.[6] Other cameos were offered: 'All the Ruskins were most delighted with Guggum . . . John Ruskin said she was a noble glorious creature and his father said by her look and manner she might have been a countess.'

At another time, 'a child one day overheard [Rossetti], as he stood before his easel, utter to himself over and over again the words "Guggum, Guggum".'[7]

As evidence of Allingham's authentic knowledge of this strangely-named creature, the volume included two illustrations of her own work: an ink drawing entitled *Lovers Listening to Egyptian Girls* and an illustration to Scene iv of Browning's dramatic poem *Pippa Passes*, showing the innocent Italian silk-winder passing the Loose Women.

Arthur Hughes was also the source of the most celebrated incident in Elizabeth Siddal's story, that of her modelling for Millais's drowning Ophelia. Millais, whose career became conventional and commonplace after he seceded from Pre-Raphaelitism in the late 1850s, was honoured by a retrospective exhibition in 1898, two years after his death, in which *Ophelia* had pride of place and the artist was praised for capturing the 'unwordly simplicity and purity of aspect' that characterized his model.[8] This was followed by the two-volume *Life and Letters of John Everett Millais*, in which Hughes's account of the painting of Ophelia in Millais's Gower Street studio in the early weeks of 1852 was published 'as told':

> Miss Siddal had a trying experience whilst acting as model for 'Ophelia'. In order that the artist might get the proper set of the garments in water and the right atmosphere and aqueous effects, she had to lie in a large bath filled with water, which was kept at an even temperature by lamps placed beneath. One day, just as the picture was nearly finished, the lamps went out unnoticed by the artist, who was so intently absorbed in his work that he thought of nothing else, and the poor lady kept floating in the cold water till she was quite benumbed. She herself never complained of this, but the result was that she contracted a severe cold, and her father . . . wrote to Millais, threatening him with an action for £50 damages for his carelessness. Eventually the matter was satisfactorily compromised.[9]

This incident was not corroborated, it may be noted, by any account given by Millais himself (who seems not to have recorded his own recollections of his erstwhile model) nor by any other contemporary or subsequent source. It appears to have been previously unknown to William Rossetti. There is, however, no obvious reason to doubt it. Hughes is unlikely to have invented the story which can be regarded as substantially true, if perhaps embroidered. More significant is the manner in which it rapidly entered the developing legend of the young milliner turned model, and soon came to stand as an emblem or foreshadowing of her fate. (In later accounts, the 'severe cold' was sometimes transmuted into pneumonia and other life-threatening ailments.) As Ophelia, Elizabeth Siddal became a figure sacrificed to the cause of art.

Mr Siddall's threat of legal action, however, was less often repeated. It suggested a rather mercenary vulgarity out of keeping with the image of sacrificial pathos, and has only recently returned to the tale, as my Highgate Cemetery guide demonstrated. As far as the Rossetti family was concerned, the whole bath-tub episode was somewhat unfortunate: too close examination of the details would reveal that, when Millais was painting Ophelia in the water, early in 1852, Elizabeth and Gabriel were supposedly already engaged and she posing for none but her beloved. For the Millais family, however, it was an undoubted scoop: a true-life story of the Pre-Raphaelite heroine never before told.

Elizabeth Siddal's value in this regard is illustrated by an unpublished manuscript prepared early in 1899 when surviving members of the Deverell family were prompted to try for their own share in the glory of the PRB. Frances Deverell, wife of Walter's youngest brother, proposed a short memoir to accompany the family's collection of letters to Walter from Rossetti, which would naturally enhance his reputation as the first to discover the rare beauty of Miss Siddal. William Rossetti confirmed that such 'relics' were worthy of attention and assisted with the preparation of a text entitled 'The PRB and Walter Deverell: Letters from Dante Gabriel Rossetti and others with a narrative and illustrations', now in the Huntingdon Library, California.

Those hoping for an unpublished first-hand account of the momentous encounter, however, will be disappointed. There were no contemporary references to Lizzie in the correspondence, nor any recollections of her from family members; the manuscript contains only the already-familiar tales given by Stephens and Hughes and embellished by Frances Deverell's additions from imagination. Discreetly, William Rossetti corrected the text, deleting the statement that Walter introduced his discovery to

Rossetti and others 'with triumph', and the whole of a dramatic account of Elizabeth posing for the scene from *Twelfth Night* (exhibited 1850) in the studio of a house in Kew to which the Deverells did not move until 1853. Other parts were substantially revised. 'Financial difficulties prevented the marriage from taking place for many years,' wrote Frances. 'Not to speak of other obstacles,' inserted William pedantically. 'Rossetti's devotion never wavered,' wrote Frances romantically, only to have the entire sentence crossed through. Her final flourish that 'the romance was ever more pathetic in its tragic ending to all who knew Rossetti's deeply affectionate disposition' was similarly erased.[10]

Thus amended, the memoir possessed neither new information nor sufficient romance, which probably explains why it was never published. Nevertheless, the attempt illustrates the glamour which by now attached itself to the name of Siddal. Deverell's own claim to fame – his life and work long forgotten except by association with the PRB – was dependent on his main exploit, the discovery of the Pre-Raphaelite mascot.

The promotion of Rossetti as high priest of Pre-Raphaelitism continued. Another exhibition of his work was held at the New Gallery during the winter of 1897–8, when platinotype reproductions of eighty-seven paintings were put on sale.[11] These gave the general public new access to pictures such as *Beata Beatrix, How They Met Themselves*, and *The Salutation of Beatrice*, which constituted widely available images of Elizabeth Siddal, comparable to posters of movie stars like Marilyn Monroe in a later age. Of these *Beata Beatrix* formed a particularly powerful element in the growing legend of the beautiful woman discovered and indeed created by art, first transfigured and then destroyed.

The following year, a comprehensive catalogue of Rossetti's painting by H. C. Marillier, *Dante Gabriel Rossetti: An Illustrated Memorial of His Art and Life*, had as epigraph Christina Rossetti's poem 'In an Artist's Studio'. This was dated December 1856, but first published in 1896:

> One face looks out from all his canvases,
> One selfsame figure sits or walks or leans:
> We found her hidden just behind those screens,
> That mirror gave back all her loveliness.
> A queen in opal or in ruby dress,

A nameless girl in freshest summer greens,
A saint, an angel – every canvas means
That same one meaning, neither more nor less.
He feeds upon her face by day and night,
And she with true kind eyes looks back on him,
Fair as the moon and joyful as the light:
Not wan with waiting, not with sorrow dim;
Not as she is, but was when hope shone bright;
Not as she is, but as she fills his dream.[12]

Whatever might have been true when the lines were written, this
is not an accurate account of Rossetti's whole *oeuvre*, as the other
canvases reproduced in the volume showed. Nor was it a complete account of Elizabeth Siddal's life. But it set the tone for the
biographical story of the artist's beloved. 'Both on account of her
romantic history and her individual attractions, the personality of
Miss Siddal has always exercised a delicate charm over those who
love Rossetti,' wrote Marillier, alluding discreetly to the *fin-de-
siècle* cult; the studio at Blackfriars was sweetened by the gracious
presence of the frail and beautiful figure depicted in the
drawings.[13]

Despite her own artistic gifts – demonstrated in three illustrations: a drawing by Rossetti of Elizabeth at the easel, a watercolour entitled 'Quest of the Grail' attributed to Miss Siddal, and
her detailed drawing 'The Woeful Victory' – failing health soon
'put an end to her productiveness'. Moreover,

> her life, so much as we know of it, was passive and singularly free
> from adventure. Wrapped up in Rossetti, as he was in her, she varied
> the monotony of her confined existence by occasional changes of
> air . . . During the intervals she worked in Rossetti's studio . . . or
> sat to him for endless studies.[14]

Silence, beauty and passivity were thus still her hallmarks.

According to the American collector Samuel Bancroft, when
Nathaniel Hawthorne's children ran out of cash, they would say
'Come, let's dig up father!' and William Rossetti had done the
same with the corpse of his brother in each succeeding volume
from the family archive.[15] (The allusion, incidentally, illustrates
how closely the idea of exhumation stuck to Gabriel's name.)

William was aware of such criticism: in his preface to the facsimile reprint of *The Germ* in 1901, he noted that 'few people living now know, or ever knew, so much as I' about the early days of the PRB, on which 'of late years it has been my fate or whim to write a good deal'. Critics who considered this unnecessary or ill-judged were welcome to their opinions, he continued, 'while I pursue my own course none the less'.[16]

Between the *Memoir* and *The Germ*, he had published two further volumes, *Ruskin: Rossetti: Preraphaelitism, Papers 1854 to 1862*, (1899) containing correspondence possessed by the family, and *Preraphaelite Diaries and Letters* (1900) containing extracts from Madox Brown's diary and the original PRB Journal. These were followed by *Rossetti Papers 1862–1870* (1903) and *Some Reminiscences* (1906), together with further editions of Dante Gabriel's literary works, and an extended article in the *Burlington Magazine* (1903) dealing exclusively with Elizabeth Siddal's life and work. From these, it is clear that there was a good deal of curiosity about the still enigmatic figure who had aroused Rossetti's devotion and whose death had dealt him such a blow; in adding details William was responding to demand.

To catalogue the information in order of its appearance over such a short span would be tedious: what follows here is a summary of the whole story William presented in this period. 'Her life was short and her performances restricted in both quantity and development', he wrote; 'but they were far from undeserving of notice, even apart from her relation to Dante Rossetti and the other leaders in the Pre-Raphaelite movement.'[17]

Born 'in or about 1834', Elizabeth 'received an ordinary education conformable with her condition in life' and became an apprentice in a bonnet shop in Cranborne Alley. It was probably in Deverell's studio that Rossetti first met his future wife and asked her to sit to him also. 'To fall in love with Elizabeth Siddal was a very easy performance, and Dante Gabriel transacted it at an early date – I suppose before 1850 was far advanced,' William stated boldly, admitting that for some months she nevertheless continued to sit to Millais and Holman Hunt. The engagement took place 'before the end of 1851', from which time Lizzie was continually in Gabriel's studio, for actual or supposed sittings:

After a while 'Guggum' became so much of a settled institution in the Chatham Place chambers that other people understood that they were not wanted . . . [This] may have gone beyond the conventional fence-line [but] had nothing in it suspicious or ambiguous . . . they chose to be together because of mutual attachment.[18]

This anxious defence of moral rectitude was perhaps prompted by imputations of sexual impropriety – in certain respects ideas about correct behaviour and chaperones had become more rather than less strait-laced in the half-century since 1850 – which William no doubt knew to be untrue. There is in fact no evidence of a physical relationship between the lovers before marriage,[19] and their companionship was indeed explained as unconventional but not immoral.

Nor was Lizzie's position as Gabriel's pupil a fiction: William listed a total of twenty-four works by her including a self-portrait which he twice reproduced and described as one of the pictures he 'would be sorriest to lose'. Although 'it may be admitted at once that she never attained to anything like masterliness', he praised her imagination and sentiment, 'facility of invention and composition, with eminent purity of feeling, dignified simplicity and grace'. Professionally she participated in an exhibition of Pre-Raphaelite work held at Russell Place in 1857, and in a selection of British Art that visited North America later the same year. But she possessed no independent strength, and her painting was but a pale reflection of her husband's: 'he had his defects and she had the deficiencies of those defects'. Moreover, her 'woefully bad' health prevented serious application and study. Nevertheless, the drawing room at Chatham Place was, in 1862, entirely hung with her watercolours on poetic subjects.[20]

She had other admirers besides Gabriel. In October 1854 Ford Madox Brown recorded a visit to the studio:

Called on Dante Rossetti, saw Miss Siddall looking thinner and more deathlike and more beautiful and more ragged than ever, a real artist, a woman without parallel for many a long year. Gabriel as usual diffuse and inconsequent in his work. Drawing wonderful and lovely 'Guggums' one after another, each one a fresh charm, each one stamped with immortality.[21]

Ruskin was likewise a firm friend. He called Lizzie 'Ida' after the feminist heroine of Tennyson's *The Princess*, and invited her to meet his parents. Mrs Ruskin advised on health matters, and presented her son's protegée with some valued ivory dust or gelatine powder with which to make a restorative jelly. The elder Ruskins were both charmed by Miss Siddal's demeanour. The son urged 'Ida' to accept his quarterly allowance. 'I think you have genius,' he argued, and 'I should simply do what I do . . . as I should try to save a beautiful tree from being cut down or a bit of Gothic cathedral whose strength was failing.' He asked if she would 'be so good as to consider yourself as a piece of wood or Gothic for a few months . . .'[22] He suggested she leave London for the country and told Rossetti that it would be best for them to marry, 'for the sake of giving Miss Siddal complete protection and care'.[23] He sent her to be examined by his friend, the eminent physician Henry Acland, in Oxford, brushing aside her doubts: 'You shall be *quite* independent. You shall see no one. Only once put out your tongue and let him feel your pulse . . .'[24] To Acland, Ruskin explained that Rossetti 'first got her to sit for his higher female faces and thus found out her talent for drawing . . . now she is dying unless the rest and change of scene can change her. She is five and twenty.'[25] This, it may be noted, was a different version of her age than William Rossetti's, by whose reckoning she would have been no more than twenty-one in 1855.

In the autumn of that year, Ruskin persuaded Ida to go south for the winter. With a distant relative of Gabriel's mother named Mrs Kincaid Lizzie went to Paris and then on to the Riviera. Of this excursion, nothing was recorded except the fragment of a letter from Lizzie in Nice to Gabriel, which William printed in full:

On leaving your boat, your passport is taken from you to the Police Station, and there taken charge of till you leave Nice. If a letter is sent to you containing money, the letter is detained at the Post Office, and another written to you by the postmaster ordering you to present yourself and passport for his inspection. You have then to go to the Police Station and beg the loan of your passport for half-an-hour, and are again looked upon as a felon of the first order before passport is returned to you. Looking very much like a transport, you make your way to the Post Office, and there present yourself before a grating, which makes the man behind it look like an overdone mutton-chop sticking to a gridiron. On asking for a letter containing money, Mutton-chop sees at once that you are a murderer, and makes up its mind not to let you off alive; and, treating you as Cain and Alice Gray [a notorious swindler] in one, demands your passport. After glaring at this and your face (which has by this time become scarlet, and is taken at once as a token of guilt) a book is pushed through the bars of the gridiron, and you are expected to sign your death warrant by writing something that does not answer to the writing on your passport. Meanwhile Mutton-chop has been looking as much like doom as overdone mutton can look, and fizzing in French, not one word of which is understood by Alice Gray. But now comes the reward of merit. Mutton sees at once that no two people living and at large could write so badly as the writing on the passport and that in the book, so takes me for Alice, but gives me the money, and wonders whether I shall be let off from hard labour the next time I am taken, on account of my thinness. When you enter the Police Station to return the passport, you are glared at through wooden bars with marked surprise at not returning in company of two cocked-hats, and your fainting look is put down to your having been found out in something.[26]

In February Gabriel sent a disconsolate poetic Valentine to Nice:

> Yesterday was St Valentine,
> Thought you at all, dear dove divine,
> Upon the beard in sorry trim
> And rueful countenance of him
> That Orson who's your Valentine?
>
> . . .
>
> Come back, dear Liz, and, looking wise,
> In that armchair which suits your size,
> Through some fresh drawing scrape a hole,
> Your Valentine and Orson's soul
> Is sad for those two friendly eyes.[27]

William admitted that Lizzie's relationship with the Rossetti family was not close; her 'first interview' with her future mother-in-law took place only in April 1855. But through Gabriel her circle of friends widened to include Edward and Georgie Burne-Jones and William and Janey Morris as well as Algernon Swinburne. Her intimate friend, however, was Emma Madox Brown, with whose family the Siddalls were said to be previously acquainted.

She also wrote poetry; this was perhaps William's major contribution to her story, for although he thought her verses were excessively melancholy, he reprinted a total of thirteen poems – the titles supplied by himself – noting that 'she used to take a great deal of pains and I fancy was seldom or never satisfied'. The final draft of 'Lord, May I Come?', he noted, was written 'in a very shaky and straggling way' evidently under the influence of laudanum; in it there was 'a wail of pang and pathos not readily forgettable'.[28]

'Without overrating her actual performances in either painting or poetry,' he concluded, 'one must fairly pronounce her to have been a woman of unusual capacities, and worthy of being espoused to a painter and poet.'[29] This was, evidently, the highest praise that could be offered to a woman.

Set against this relatively positive picture, however, was the obverse side of Elizabeth Siddal's story, in which weakness and disease predominated. The letters published in these volumes contain repeated references to her poor health and medical consultations, with seldom favourable bulletins. In 1854, curvature of the spine was diagnosed by Dr Garth Wilkinson, a Swedenborgian, and Lizzie was urged to enter the Harley Street sanatorium run by Florence Nightingale. In 1855 Acland gave a more favourable opinion, finding no symptoms of organic disease and attributing her weakness to 'mental power long pent up and overtaxed' – a contemporary definition of stress. The journey to the Riviera was intended to benefit her health, and in 1857 she 'tried the hydropathic cure' at the spa of Matlock in the Peak District. No treatment had the desired effect, however, and in April 1860, as they awaited the long-deferred wedding ceremony, Gabriel was near to despair. 'You will be grieved to hear that poor dear Lizzie's health has been in such a broken and failing state for the last few days as to render me more miserable than I can possibly say,' he wrote to William from Hastings:

She gets no nourishment, and what can be reasonably hoped when this is added to her dreadful state of health in other respects? If I were to lose her now, I do not know what effect it might have on my mind, added to the responsibility of much work, commissioned and already paid for, which still has to be done. The ordinary licence we already have, and I trust to God we may be enabled to use it. If not, I should have so much to grieve for, and (what is worse) so much to reproach myself with, that I do not know how it might end for me.[30]

In marriage, her health improved a little, and after being confined of a stillborn daughter, her recovery was 'rapid enough'. But the 'consumptive malady, accompanied by wearing neuralgia, continued its fatal course and her days could at best . . . have only been prolonged for some very few years'.[31]

In these accounts, ill-health carries symbolic meanings, functioning both as a manifestation of inherent female frailty in accord with contemporary medical opinion within the context of gender difference, and as the validation of Rossetti's masculine tenderness and concern for his ailing beloved. She is sickly and dependent; he is strong and protective, just as her art is a feeble but loving imitation setting in relief his greater genius. Yet, outside these metaphorical meanings, the subject is far from simple, since there is no evidence that Elizabeth Siddal suffered from any specific physical complaint. Commonly described as tall and elegant, she never exhibited a sign of spinal curvature, nor any of the well-defined and recognizable symptoms of tuberculosis. Neuralgia – a term coined in the nineteenth century to describe intense intermittent headaches such as migraine – is a rather vague condition, not a disease. Nor, despite the anxieties expressed, did she die of any natural cause. Indeed, as her friend Georgiana Burne-Jones later wondered with some puzzlement, 'How was it possible for her to suffer so much without developing a specific disease?'[32]

It is not possible to attempt a retrospective medical diagnosis, but one suspects that many contemporary references to ill-health, by Lizzie herself, her husband and friends, were exaggerated, or mistaken, or even wishful. Others were euphemisms for mental distress and – certainly during her last years – drug dependence. This is not to accuse Gabriel or William and the rest of deliberate concealment: the letters published certainly convey a persistent picture of sickness, and her friends' anxiety was genuine. But neither their fears nor her untimely death prove that she suffered from physical disease. Nor, if examined closely, does the correspondence: it is clear that, until the last months of her life, illness as such seldom prevented Lizzie from going out, or travelling, or seeing friends. 'Her habits were not those of a recluse,' as William noted.[33] She did not pay or receive calls, but this was from choice not infirmity.

Georgiana Burne-Jones's *Memorials of Edward Burne-Jones*, in which she pondered this problem, appeared in 1904, with her own first-hand recollections of the long distant days. The first mention of Miss Siddal related to the autumn of 1857 when, according to the diary kept by Ned's friend Crom Price, Gabriel departed abruptly from Oxford to join her in Derbyshire, but Georgie did not meet Lizzie until after their respective marriages in 1860, and her first memory was of London Zoo, where

> Lizzie's slender, elegant figure – tall for those days, but I never knew her actual height – comes back to me, in a graceful and simple dress, the incarnate opposite of the 'tailor-made' young lady. We went home with them to their rooms in Hampstead and . . . I see her in the little upstairs bedroom, with its lattice window, to which she carried me when we arrived, and the mass of her beautiful deep-red hair as she took off her bonnet: she wore her hair very loosely fastened up, so that it fell in soft heavy wings. Her complexion looked as if a rose tint lay beneath the dark skin, producing a more soft and delicate pink for the darkest flesh tones, her eyes were of a kind of golden brown – agate colour is the only word I can find to describe them – and wonderfully luminous: in all Gabriel's drawings of her and in the type she created in his mind this is to be seen, her eyelids were deep, but without any languor or drowsiness and had the peculiarity of seeming scarcely to veil the light in her eyes when looking down.[34]

Thereafter the couples met frequently, and Georgie later treasured a brief note from Lizzie inviting 'My dear little Georgie' to Chatham Place, since 'it seems so long since I saw you, dear'; with an affectionate reference to the blue-and-white china passion of the time it was signed: 'With a willow-pattern dish full of love to you and Ned – Lizzie.'

Yet there were disturbing signs. While the men were in the studio, Lizzie 'did not talk happily when we were alone, but was excited and melancholy, though with much humour and tenderness . . . Gabriel's presence seemed needed to set her jarring nerves straight.' With hindsight, Lady Burne-Jones might have attributed these symptoms to drug addiction; as it was she decided that her friend's suffering was due to the sudden intensity of

'Gabriel's genius and love, under which her whole inner nature had quickened and expanded until her bodily strength gave way'.[35]

These observations represent the first major biographical contribution to the story of Elizabeth Siddal from a woman. Like the brief comments by Mary Howitt and Bessie Parkes Belloc, it was based on personal recollection rather than hearsay and was shaped by sympathy. Here, for example, was the only description of Lizzie's grief over her stillborn baby, when Georgie and her husband visited Chatham Place, to find Lizzie sitting in a low chair rocking the empty cradle and looking like a distracted Ophelia. 'She cried with a kind of soft wildness as we came in, "Hush, Ned, you'll waken it!"' [36]

Soon after her own child was born in the autumn of 1861, however, Georgie received a visit from Lizzie with Janey Morris, both looking well, and not all her recollections were poignant. There was, for example, a plan for Lizzie and herself to produce an illustrated collection of nursery folk tales, and other cheerful moments, including a lively visit to the theatre when, Georgie remembered,

> Dear Lizzie Rossetti laughed to find that she and Swinburne had such shocks of the same coloured hair, and one night when we went in our thousands to see 'Colleen Bawn' she declared that as she sat at one end of the row we filled and he at the other, a boy selling books of the play looked at Swinburne and took fright and then, when he came round to where she was, started again with terror, muttering to himself, 'There's another of 'em!'[37]

This reaction, incidentally, illustrates the common response to 'unlucky' red hair in the mid-century.

Georgie also recalled their shared enjoyment of Gabriel's passion for personal limericks, citing Lizzie's 'great satisfaction' at the following:

> There is a poor creature named Lizzie,
> Whose pictures are dear at a tizzy [*sixpence*]
>   And of this the great proof
>   Is that all stand aloof
> From paying that sum unto Lizzie.

This picture of humour and intelligence is more in keeping with that retained by Lizzie's old champion Swinburne, who repeatedly complained that William Rossetti's image of sickness and sadness gave a misleading impression. Eventually, William gave in to the protests and in his final volume *Some Reminiscences* (1906) reproduced in full Swinburne's 'noble and touching eulogium' of 'dear Lizzie' ('I hope I may now speak of her as I should of a sister') whom he remembered as a brilliant and appreciative woman. She was 'quick to see and so keen to enjoy that rare and delightful fusion of wit, humour, character-painting and dramatic poetry' in Elizabethan drama, he wrote; 'I used to come and read to her sometimes when she was well enough, at Chatham Place, and I shall never forget her delight in Fletcher's magnificent comedy *The Spanish Curate* . . . there was not much need for a Bowdler [and] she thought it "better than Shakespeare".' She was wonderful as well as lovable, Swinburne concluded; and in art her 'own independence and freshness of inspiration' were at least equal to her husband's.[38]

Her death came as a shock to these friends. Georgie Burne-Jones quoted from her own correspondence the day after Lizzie's death. 'I scarcely believe the words as I write them, but yesterday I saw her poor body laid in the very bed where I have seen her lie and laugh in the midst of illness,' she told her sister. 'The evening before she was in good health (for her) and very good spirits – Gabriel took her home, saw her prepare for bed, went out to the Working Men's College, and on his return found her insensible from the effects of laudanum – which she used to take medicinally.[39]

As the last survivor of the three giants of the PRB, Holman Hunt had long grumbled against Rossetti's dominance of Pre-Raphaelite history, overshadowing his own role in the movement, and let it be known that he was preparing his own account of those far-off years. The long-awaited study – in effect Hunt's autobiography and claim to enduring importance in the history of British painting – was published in two volumes in 1905 under the title *Pre-Raphaelitism and the Pre-Raphaelite Brotherhood*. In bidding for retrospective leadership of the PRB, it also staked a claim to the Brotherhood's icon and inspiration, Miss Elizabeth Eleanor Siddal.

Hunt's description of Lizzie's looks and entry into the charmed circle has so often been quoted as an authentic, first-hand account, in conjunction with other synoptic versions, that the contradictions have rarely been remarked or, if noticed, ascribed to the vagaries of individual recollection; more generally, they have been absorbed into one seamless story, in the manner of a folk tale. Yet Hunt aimed to make his account original and definitive, in support of his own role as the mainspring of the movement, and to do so he challenged Rossetti's pre-eminence in the matter of Elizabeth Siddal by giving himself a central role.

Her story was 'a romance upon which I should remain dumb had not other versions of it already been made public', he announced. 'I therefore invite my reader into my studio when first Gabriel Dante Rossetti heard the name of Eleanor Siddal.' The use of her middle name was pointed: with it Hunt laid claim to unexpected, privileged access; to others she was merely 'Lizzie', to him she was 'Eleanor'.

In 1849, when Hunt shared his studio with Rossetti, Deverell arrived with the news:

He bounded up, marching or rather dancing to and fro about the room and, stopping emphatically, he whispered, 'You fellows can't tell what a stupendously beautiful creature I have found. By Jove! she's like a queen, magnificently tall, with a lovely figure, a stately neck, and a face of the most delicate and finished modelling; the flow of surface from the temples over the cheeks is exactly like the carving of a Pheidean [sic] goddess . . . she has grey eyes and her hair is like dazzling copper and shimmers with lustre as she waves it down. And now, where do you think I lighted on this paragon of beauty? Why, in a milliner's back workroom when I went out with my mother shopping . . . I peered over the blind of a glass door at the back of the shop, and there was this unexpected jewel. I got my mother to persuade this miraculous creature to sit for my Viola in *Twelfth Night* and today I have been trying to paint her . . . Tomorrow she's coming again; and you two should come down and see her; she's really quite a wonder; for while her friends, of course, are quite humble, she behaves like a real lady, by clear commonsense and without any affectation, knowing perfectly, too, how to keep people at a respectful distance.'[40]

Hunt declined the invitation, he said, but later employed Miss

Siddal as a model for 'a fair Celt with red hair' in his picture of the Christian priest escaping Druid persecution, and for Sylvia, the Duke's daughter in *Two Gentlemen of Verona*, his Royal Academy entry for 1851; he also used her hair for elements in his picture of Christ as *The Light of the World*.

Despite its air of immediacy, Hunt's dramatic and much-quoted narrative of Elizabeth Siddal's discovery contains more atmosphere than factual information; even without the implausibly verbatim recall of Deverell's supposed words, it reads as an imaginative extrapolation from previously published accounts. Indeed, the only new items are the now-ignored information that despite his admiration for Lizzie's looks, Rossetti 'did not for a full year profess any strong personal feeling for her',[41] and Hunt's recollection that she had once made a special trip to his Chelsea studio to tell him of a picture in a religious bookshop she thought similar to *The Light of the World*. He also recalled the private view of the 1857 exhibition in Russell Place where on his arrival Rossetti 'called me to come and see "the stunning drawings" that the Sid (the name by which Miss Siddal went) had sent. I complimented them fully and said that had I come upon them without explanation I should have assumed they were happy designs by Walter Deverell.' At this, which Hunt intended as praise, Gabriel exclaimed: 'They are a thousand times better than anything he ever did!'[42]

Carefully analysed, Hunt's claims to privileged personal knowledge of the Pre-Raphaelite mascot amounted to little more than a few trivial additions to the familiar story.

6

Sheffield Siddalites

Despite the accumulation of anecdotal detail, the figure of Elizabeth Siddal retained a certain mystery, and her image remained shadowy except where refracted through the Pre-Raphaelite prism. Thus, when in 1911 Ford Madox Brown's grandson, the writer Ford Madox Hueffer, published a lightweight book entitled *Ancient Lights and Certain New Reflections*, based on his family connections with the Victorian artistic world, now imbued with a patina of nostalgia for its bohemian glamour, he simply referred in passing to 'the almost legendary Miss Siddal',[1] as if her history were too distant to recover. This phrase prompted a curious and now wholly forgotten episode in Elizabeth Siddal's biographical story which reflects not contemporary attitudes towards gender roles but the similarly unequal relation between metropolis and provinces in British cultural life.

The last decades of the nineteenth century saw the development of strong local loyalties, accompanying the growth of economic and political strength in Britain's industrial cities that aroused civic pride and provincial patriotism. One effect of this confidence was to stimulate interest in local history and personalities. From the brief references to her father's place of origin, Elizabeth Siddal was identified and adopted in Sheffield as a 'local girl' who had made good, or at least found fame through her connection with national figures such as Rossetti and, especially, Ruskin, whose patronage of Sheffield made him a respected figure in the city.

When *Ancient Lights* came into the hands of a local historian named W. G. Wells, therefore, his 'first instinct was to look up in the index any reference to Miss E. E. Siddall'. The result was disappointing: only two brief mentions and the epithet 'legendary'. This 'just seems about the position of the memory of that beautiful, interesting but unfortunate lady who, the daughter of

The Legend of Elizabeth Siddal

Sheffield parents, stands related to one of the most interesting artistic movements in this country'. Giving a fair summary of the popular image, Wells continued: 'The nature of her story, so far as I have been able to trace it from book to book, all helps the suggestion of the legendary idea. Romance, pathos and tragedy were all gathered up in that short career.' He concluded by asking for further information from 'living people in Sheffield who knew the Siddall family prior to their removal to London'.[2]

Within a few days his request was answered by a letter to the Sheffield *Daily Telegraph* from a correspondent signing herself 'A.S.', who offered some 'personal information concerning Miss Siddall which is certainly not legendary':

> I was a fellow student with her at the Sheffield School of Art in 185- I forget the exact date at this moment, but it was the year of the Art Exhibition in Manchester.
>
> She was, I believe, in Sheffield on a visit and was staying in the neighbourhood of St George's Church. She attended the School regularly and worked in the 'Figure Room'. She remained after class hours; so did I, and as I ate my luncheon and wandered through the rooms, I met with her and we talked sometimes, or if Mr Young Mitchell, our headmaster, joined us, I listened to them, and it was then I first heard of Ruskin and the Pre-Raphaelites.
>
> Her dress was uncommon and pleased me, but the girl students generally considered it unbecoming and absurd, and made it and Miss Siddall the subject of joke and caricature. One of these latter fell into the hands of Mr Mitchell and well do I remember how his black eyes glared around the class and the sarcastic words he threw at us.

'A.S.' then recounted how Miss Siddall had invited her to join in a party on a special excursion train to the Manchester exhibition (which took place in 1857) and how on the journey she wore a beautiful silk dress in the height of prevailing fashion, as if to silence her critics. 'The acquaintance I had with her was slight,' A.S. concluded, 'but it made a lasting impression on my memory.'[3]

This clear and concise recollection – never previously quoted, to my knowledge – was quickly supported by another correspondent, Charles Green, who had also attended the art school in 1857 and was now a respected local artist; he also remembered Miss Siddal as a member of the group travelling to Manchester and as

70

a student at the school, citing Young Mitchell's policy of allowing artists and students visiting Sheffield to use the facilities while in the city.[4]

This correspondence and the information it adds to Elizabeth Siddal's history is extremely interesting, supplying the first substantive facts about her life outside the Pre-Raphaelite circle. Hitherto, her visit to Sheffield had been unrecorded, all that was known of her movements in the latter part of 1857 being the visit to Matlock in Derbyshire, apparently for health reasons, whither Rossetti had been summoned from Oxford. The Sheffield correspondents, with their recollections of attendance at art classes and a rail excursion to Manchester – where, incidentally, a number of Pre-Raphaelite paintings were on display – gave a glimpse of a more independent existence. Curiously, however, these useful anecdotes, which add much to our knowledge of her life and were published while the witnesses were still alive, were not pursued, nor subsequently incorporated in her story. Indeed, it is as if they were never written, or certainly never read by anyone outside Sheffield. Their provincial origin evidently made it difficult if not impossible for the material to reach a wider audience.

Yet the information was transmitted to London. As a result of the correspondence, another Sheffield resident who had been 'endeavouring to acquire information on the career of this lady' for many years, wrote to William Rossetti for confirmation. He then published a short article which stated 'unquestionably' (but erroneously) that Elizabeth's father had migrated to London about 1851, when she was sixteen years old. Morever, he claimed authority for flatly contradicting the recollections of 'A.S.': There appears to be considerable doubt whether she ever attended the Sheffield School of Art for the purposes of study. Mr W. M. Rossetti tells me he thinks it improbable, and adds, "Nor do I think she had any knowledge of art, apart from what she received from my brother."'[5] The authority of the metropolis was thus preferred to that of provincial and personal experience.

The following year another local historian took up the Siddal cause, producing a new biographical account in the form of a lantern lecture. Speaking in 1912 to the Sheffield Literary and Philosophical Society on 'Miss Siddal: Her Associations with Sheffield,' W. T. Freemantle proffered the truth, as opposed to the 'numerous stories' which were 'all pure romance', by tracing the Siddall ancestry back, in the genealogical manner characteristic of the time, to a Christopher Siddal of Hope Hall in Derbyshire – and a family supposedly possessed of a crest and 'Honour' as their motto. The son of a flax dresser apprenticed to a scissor-maker in 1783 was somewhat improbably identified as grandson to this gentleman, and as grandfather to Elizabeth Eleanor; her father, Charles Crookes Siddall, was trained as a Sheffield cutler and moved to London as a young man in the 1820s. Freemantle showed his audience Charles Siddall's photograph and his marriage certificate, dated 1824, which he explained had been given him in recognition of his researches into family history. He concluded that Elizabeth Eleanor was one of Charles Siddall's seven children, and had been born 'in 1832 or 1833'. She was therefore 'descended from gentle stock and from a family belonging to Sheffield. Her father founded a cutlery business in London and died in 1859 . . . The mother lived until 1892.'[6]

Repeating his talk to the Hunter Archaeological Society at the university next year, Freemantle was gratified to announce 'that he had the previous day received a visiting card discoloured with age' bearing Miss Siddall's name and giving her address as 1, Weymouth Street, Portland Place. She had visited Sheffield in the summer of 1857, he continued, when

> she was accompanied by one of her sisters and her visit was of sufficient length to induce her to fill up her time by attending the Sheffield School of Art presumably to take the opportunity for practice and study . . . There was also trace of her visting Hope, Haddon Hall and Matlock while in the neighbourhood.[7]

Again, this was new documentary evidence. The photo, marriage certificate and other details had been acquired from James Siddall (whose address had been supplied by William Rossetti, as Freemantle explained in a dramatic account of his research methods), and who before his death in 1912 had given his own version of being summoned to his sister's death-bed where 'he took [her] hand and pressed it gently – but there was no response!'[8]

Freemantle's eagerness to prove that Elizabeth Siddal was descended from the gentry illustrates a common preoccupation of his class-conscious age, when assertions of upper-class origin were frequently falsely contended, in order to lay claim to lost social status. Despite his assurance, Freemantle's genealogical evidence was in fact inconclusive: Siddall is a common name in Derbyshire and south Yorkshire, especially in the neighbourhood of Hope (where a firm of auctioneers still bears the name) and the Hope Hall connection remains unproven. The endeavour, however, illustrates a combination of provincial and class pride, aiming to prove that the 'legendary Miss Siddall' had both local and socially superior antecedents. It was a claim that perhaps arose from anxiety: the image of a cutler's daughter turned artist's model, combined with Rossetti's reputation as a woman-worshipper and the general moral laxity of the artistic world in London, all indicated a career that would not add to Sheffield's lustre.

Unfortunately, this account of Elizabeth Siddal's Sheffield personality is fragmentary, and now survives only in the form of fragile yellow press clippings loosely pasted into foolscap scrapbooks held in Sheffield Local Studies Library. These scrapbooks were filled by unidentified individuals in Sheffield, who in the early years of this century selected items of interest from the local press (usually without noting date or source), and thereby preserved, mixed with much other material on other subjects, the articles and correspondence quoted here for the first time. Locally, however, the matter was not entirely forgotten, for the centenary of Rossetti's birth in 1928 led to a revival of interest in his wife, and another group of newspaper clippings.

In May of that year the chief librarian of the city wrote to the *Sheffield Daily Telegraph* asking local citizens to record and deposit their memories as the 'raw materials of history' for the future fame of Sheffield. He instanced a recent request for assistance in tracing the Siddall family for a proposed biography of Rossetti, to coincide with the centenary. Although fruitless, the inquiry rearoused interest. 'It will greatly add to the interest of Congregationalist readers to know that Miss E. E. Siddal, who became the devoted and beloved wife of Dante Gabriel Rossetti the famous painter and poet, was prior to their marriage a member of the Queen Street Congregational church in Sheffield,' wrote the editor of the Sheffield *Congregational Year Book*. This information, he stated, came from a historical sketch of the Queen

Street chapel, and 'means much more than that she was casual worshipper or even a member of the congregation. Being a member of the church means that she was an avowed follower of the Lord Jesus Christ.'[9]

This rather unexpected piece of information – indicating serious and active participation in non-conformist observance – was not so surprising if, as may be conjectured, the Siddall family were Congregationalists in London, for the low-church communities formed a nationwide network of social contact and support for those moving from place to place; in Sheffield Lizzie would have found in the chapel a ready-made community of friends, no doubt including old acquaintances of her father.

Hitherto, however, her visit to the city, in so far as it was recognized, had been assumed to be brief; formal membership of a church suggested longer residence. Some doubt was thrown on the statement, too, by another correspondent signing himself 'Senex', who wrote that the information 'that Miss Siddal was connected with Queen Street Chapel was news to me', since his parents, distantly related to Miss Siddal, had been Methodists. He went on:

> My father's uncle, Mr William Ibbitt, of Broad Lane, artist and town councillor, once actually brought Miss Siddal to my parents' house in Brighton Terrace, Pitsmoor [a district of Sheffield]. My father and mother were not at home, and I have often heard them express regret that they missed the only opportunity of meeting their interesting relative.[10]

The bathos of this non-event only increased the writer's curiosity, and subsequent correspondence reveals evidence of a 'Siddal' faction in the city. Senex agreed with the Congregationalist editor's view that further information not coming from Lizzie's husband's family would be of most value, since 'all we know of her is told from the Rossetti point of view'. Moreover, whenever he mentioned his own interest, 'people shrug their shoulders and observe coldly that she was only a shop girl, then a model, then – '.

William Rossetti's efforts to establish Elizabeth's respectability had clearly failed. A century after her birth, the popular view was that, as a milliner, artist's model and mistress, she deserved no admiration from Sheffield's God-fearing citizenry.

Other correspondents claimed a distant connection. Emma Dunham wrote to say that her mother, Margaret Siddall, now aged eighty-nine, had been born at Hope in 1840 and 'feels sure she is the last of the family to which [Elizabeth] belonged'. Florence Wallis possessed the family tree of Christopher Siddall of Hope, and believed William Ibbitt to be first cousin to the Pre-Raphaelite muse, since 'Miss Ibbitt often spoke to me of Elizabeth Siddal's visits to her father's home'.

Senex welcomed all such communications for their potential 'in the mosaic one seeks to construct'. Yet a veil of mystery still surrounded this undoubtedly clever and fascinating woman. He challenged the Rossetti version, stating boldly: 'For myself I should welcome a veracious memoir of this Sheffield girl more than any number of eulogies of the gifted, unpleasant man whose wife she became.'

What a monstrous injustice to the poet and painter! rejoined 'Fountain Pen'. Whether his beloved attended a Congregational or a Methodist chapel was unimportant beside her 'real title to remembrance – how Rossetti loved her and after nine years' engagement married her, immortalized her beauty and enshrined her memory on many a wonderful canvas and in many beautiful sonnets.'

'I am not taking part in a literary controversy but in an interesting local inquiry,' Senex replied crustily; 'and the contention that Miss Siddal only deserves mention as a little bit of fluff that the great Rossetti happened to fancy is the very thing that the Siddalites resent.'

This championship would have delighted Swinburne and it is unfortunate that the real names of the Sheffield 'Siddalites' are unknown and their views so briefly recorded. Their existence is evidence, however, of the persistent partisanship her story has aroused over the years. More than most, moreover, the Sheffield inquirers sought and found historical information relating to their heroine, rather than simply reproducing others' accounts; the local patriotism that motivated their research was effectively translated into knowledge. It remains fragmentary, however; no confirmation of a family connection between Ibbitts and Siddalls has as yet been found.

The Legend of Elizabeth Siddal

Summarizing the new state of knowledge as a result of this renewal of interest, in 1928 the now aged W. G. Wells went so far as to accuse the Rossetti family of suppressing all details of Lizzie's early life on account of their shame at her origins. Tantalizingly, he referred to a neighbour, niece to William Ibbitt, who possessed her uncle's sketchbook containing an unfinished drawing of Miss Siddal's head. But, he concluded, there was now little more to be discovered; too much had vanished with the years. And in general, as with the earlier material from Sheffield informants, this new knowledge made little impact. The legendary, London-based version of her life story remained dominant, and in time, the whole history of her stay in Sheffield sank into oblivion, from which it is only now emerging.

II

Redefinitions

7

Suicide and the Sex War

William Rossetti died in 1919. He had spent the last years of his life shielding his brother's reputation, but knew that the full story had not been told and that it was only a matter of time before his picture of Gabriel and his dear dove divine would be radically altered. And so it proved.

This was not just a matter of new information. After the traumatic experience of World War I, the post-war years saw a conscious break with the past, now increasingly characterized as the archaic, pompous and hypocritical 'Victorian age', regarded without admiration or nostalgia. In art, too, the period witnessed the establishment of Modernist styles and tastes, turning on Pre-Raphaelite painting with amusement and scorn. In 1925 the critic Clive Bell declared that the Pre-Raphaelites' output was 'worthless' and their technique 'tedious and insignificant.'[1] Of equal importance was the development and popularization of modern psychology, with its emphasis on sexuality, the unconscious and conflicting instinctual drives. Taken together, these cultural changes profoundly influenced the way in which the Pre-Raphaelite tales were told and received during the 1920s and '30s, in the course of which Elizabeth Siddal's story took on a new shape and a new focus, and her personality underwent a startling change.

The major new facts were brought to light precisely because of changing cultural concerns, and began with a new participant in the drama, who now emerged from behind the dark curtains of gossip on to the open stage. As we have already seen, her existence was known: Bell Scott had described her cracking nuts in the Strand and in response William Rossetti had cautiously identified her in his *Memoir* as 'Mrs H—, which was the correct initial at, or soon after, the time my brother first met her.' He added whimsically 'I cannot recollect hearing anything about the nuts,' but disclosed that she was a fine-looking woman, 'with regular and sweet features, and a mass of the most lovely blonde hair'; the painting *Bocca Baciata* was a faithful portrait of her physical attractions. However, he insisted, she had 'no charm of breeding, education or intellect.'[2]

The model for *Bocca Baciata* ('the mouth that has been kissed'), according to Marillier's illustrated catalogue, was 'Miss Fanny Cornforth, a favourite model who sat to Rossetti until almost the end of his life'. She appeared as 'F' in the text and 'Fanny' in the index to William Allingham's *Diary* (1907), where she was recorded in June 1864 at Rossetti's house in Chelsea, remarking on Bell Scott's baldness in a strong Cockney accent: 'He ain't got a hyebrow or a hye-lash – not a 'air on his 'ead!', and lying on the grass in the garden wearing a white dress.[3] The index identified her as 'housekeeper', a euphemism that neither deceived those who guessed at the truth nor enlightened those who did not, although it has subsequently confused many, for Fanny did not share Rossetti's house either as employee or mistress, but had her own home and servants, for which Gabriel paid, a few streets away.

As a former prostitute she remained socially unmentionable despite her marriages, first to Mr Hughes and later to Mr Schott, but she was known, at least by reputation, to many on the fringes of Pre-Raphaelite society, for she had kept in contact with Rossetti until a few months before his death, and was proud of his friendship despite being spurned and ostracized by most of his friends, who followed the family in regarding her as a vulgar harpy. Thus, at the retrospective Rossetti exhibition in 1883 when she was observed standing beside *The Blue Bower*, for which she had also sat, Jeannette Marshall, daughter of Rossetti's physician, had no difficulty in identifying her. This was ' "Fanny", who lived with Rossetti', she noted in her diary.[4] And up to her own death around 1905, Fanny continued to capitalize on what proved a lucrative relationship, as collectors sought out Rossetti's remaining works of art and memorabilia. Over the years, Charles Fairfax Murray bought a large proportion of the art works she possessed, and in 1892 Samuel Bancroft, a businessman from Wilmington, Delaware, began to purchase paintings, manuscript letters and photographs. His correspondence indicates how openly – in private at least – Fanny's role in Rossetti's life was discussed at this date.

'By the way, just how old is she?' Bancroft asked in January 1893. 'I suspect she was born about 1838 because she looks quite twenty in the *Bocca Baciata* of 1858–59,' replied Murray.[5] After corresponding with Fanny's stepson, Bancroft pronounced authoritatively that: ' "Cornforth" was but an assumed name . . . her maiden name was Cox. She married Hughes, and when she first set up as a model she assumed an art-name, which was that of Hughes's mother – Cornforth.'[6]

Fanny had thus been waiting in the wings for some time.

In 1904 A. C. Benson published a short book on Rossetti which rehearsed the popular view of romantic young love: 'In 1850 the star of Rossetti's life rose suddenly into the clear heaven . . . a tall dignified girl of extraordinary beauty, with a brilliant complexion, pale blue eyes and a mass of coppery-golden hair. . . . Rossetti fell at once deeply in love.' Although 'untaught and ignorant,' his beloved had 'real nobility of spirit'. Tragically, 'her life was one prolonged struggle with mortal illness'.[7]

So far, so standard. But a surprise was in store, for Benson went on to describe the relationship after marriage as 'an imperfect partnership', based on class difference, educational disadvantage, and a religious gulf between Miss Siddal's simple beliefs and Rossetti's scepticism. Even more ominous were Gabriel's wayward impulses, which caused his beloved jealous pangs, for 'Rossetti loved swiftly and almost unscrupulously . . . his faults were the faults of passion, not restrained by the ordinary social code . . .'[8] He pursued potential models, one of whom 'made his acquaintance first by finding him running out of a confectioner's with a half-bitten tart in his hand to stare in her face'; another 'felt as she sat in a restaurant, her hair suddenly seized and untied . . . a few minutes after, such was his personal fascination, she had made an appointment to sit for a picture . . .'[9] This behaviour naturally gave Mrs Rossetti 'much cause for unhappiness', as Benson deduced from her poems. Taken as expressions of personal feeling, these showed deep unhappiness, sadness and anguish for lost love, expressed with bitter words on lovers' inconstancy.

This introduced a new note into a hitherto simple story, adding substance to Bell Scott's waspish remarks. And it was followed by the publication of Hall Caine's autobiography, *My Story* (1908) which, although largely a rehash of his earlier *Recollections of Rossetti*, also offered new revelations. In this Miss Siddal was 'young and beautiful and clever' when Rossetti fell in love. But the idyll did not last:

> Then came a separation, and it is not easy for me to say what it was due to – so conflicting are the stories of those who claim to know. I have heard that, beautiful and brilliant as Elizabeth Siddal was, she was not (as is natural) in the conventional sense an educated woman and that at her own suggestion and by Ruskin's help she went away to school. I have also heard that at a moment of some difference Ruskin again interposed with certain delicate overtures which enabled her to return for further study at her native place. At all events she left London and was away for a considerable time.[10]

This garbled hearsay contained a core of truth, for there was certainly a break of some two years in the relationship, at which William Rossetti had delicately hinted in his *Burlington Magazine* article, with a conjunction of phrases that has seldom been analysed:

> It appears to me – but I speak with uncertainty – that during the rest of 1858 and the whole of 1859 he did not see her so constantly as in preceding years. For this, apart from anything savouring of neglectfulness on his part, there may have been various causes, dubious for me to estimate at the present distance of time. Her own ill-health would have been partly accountable for such a result; and, again, the fact that Rossetti, increasingly employed as a painter, had by this time some other sitters for his pictures . . .

– including the model for *Bocca Baciata*.[11] This disclosure of an estrangement, it may be noted, was not incorporated in the legend, which continued to regard the relationship as unbroken, if by now increasingly troubled.

Picking up Benson's reference to other entanglements, Caine then cited certain of Rossetti's poems expressing 'a sense of a great passion too late and above all a struggle between love and duty which augured less than well for the happiness of the marriage which was to come'.[12] Stirring the brew further, he then protested against certain 'evil rumours' that Rossetti was neglectful of his wife. This, of course, put a different construction on his earlier account of Lizzie's melancholy during her married months, when her spirits drooped and 'much of the cheerfulness of home was lost to both of them'. Now she took laudanum to excess, and Caine reported hearing Madox Brown say that 'she would sit for long hours, with her feet inside the fender, looking fixedly into the fire'. All this made the domestic hearth unattractive to Rossetti, and 'if he escaped from it as often as possible it is perhaps only natural and it is no less natural if his absence was misunderstood.' Slyly, Caine added: 'I express no opinion but the facts appear to point that way'.[13]

The inference was clear: far from being Gabriel's cherished, ailing wife, Lizzie was a morose and slatternly addict. Not surprisingly, lack of conjugal comfort drove Gabriel elsewhere.

Sexual betrayal was a step away, but only later in the book did Caine introduce Fanny, with an oblique reference to 'almost fatal flirtations on that borderland of Bohemia' when Rossetti met a 'bouncing young girl fresh from the country . . . cracking nuts with her white teeth and throwing the shells at him'.[14] Further on, however, and even more sensationally, he related how Rossetti had once confided in him that: 'To marry one woman and then find out, when it is too late, that you love another, is the deepest tragedy that can enter into a man's life.'[15]

This gnomic statement was confusing: it could hardly be taken to refer to Fanny or any similar vulgar diversions. It pointed, in fact, towards another beloved, another Beatrice in the shape of Mrs William Morris, whose dark hair, long neck and melancholy gaze had filled Rossetti's later paintings. Indeed, it was well-known that he had worshipped Janey Morris's beauty in a manner that suggested passionate as well as aesthetic admiration. It was also known that Gabriel had met Janey at Oxford in 1857. On all sides his fidelity to Lizzie was in doubt.

Caine also claimed that in the last year of his life, on a long night journey, Rossetti had confessed, in 'burning words of self-reproach', his remorse at having violated the sanctity of his wife's grave, and his guilt over her death, 'as an event that had been due in some degree to failure of duty on his part, or perhaps to something still graver, although in no way criminal'. This utterance, which appeared to say that Gabriel was both guilty and innocent of killing his wife, was perhaps too obscure to be taken literally (and many readers were already rightly suspicious of Caine's veracity) but it certainly added a new and sinister aspect to the tale. And it plausibly explained why Rossetti's life had been overwhelmed by remorse, not for any unkindness nor 'any act of infidelity' but simply for 'the far deeper wrong of failure of affection for the one being to whom affection was most due'.[16]

When these sentences were written, the term 'infidelity' carried other, more general meanings besides that of adultery. But that was the sense smoking-room rumours attached to Rossetti's name. And there were many besides Caine who revelled in uncovering the seamy side to the famous Pre-Raphaelite woman-worshipper, soon changing him from a spiritual to a lustful lover of beauty, and from a devoted into a faithless husband. It difficult to judge exactly how much was known or guessed by how many, but the view of Rossetti as a hot-blooded womanizer steadily gained ground, especially among the gossiping intelligentsia. A typical example is the inquiry by Bernard Shaw, who in 1928 asked Caine about rumours of 'raging red-haired trollops' in Rossetti's life, among whom he alleged 'there was a Fanny or some such name' much given to tantrums.[17] Privately, Swinburne had referred to Fanny as 'the bitch', while Ruskin was reputed to have remarked: 'I don't object to Rossetti having sixteen mistresses, but I won't have Fanny.'[18] Fairfax Murray and Samuel Bancroft were amused, and made lists of the other supposed mistresses' names.[19]

A keen stoker of these gossipy embers was Thomas Wise, described in the *Dictionary of National Biography* as 'book collector, forger and literary heir to the Pre-Raphaelite movement', whose acquisitive desires and dishonesty were matched by prurient curiosity into the sexual irregularities of his heroes – Shelley, Byron, Rossetti and Swinburne. Ostensibly motivated by admiration for these great Romantic figures, by dwelling on their private behaviour Wise effectively reduced their stature, in a manner that complemented Lytton Strachey's open critique of hypocrisy in *Eminent Victorians* (1918); both contributed to the twentieth century's oedipal process of 'killing the father' in order to destroy the power of the past.

In his pursuit, Wise bought up letters and manuscript fragments which, with his first editions and forgeries, were later sold to the British Museum under the dignified title of the Ashley Library.

Beata Beatrix, Dante Gabriel Rossetti. Tate Gallery, London

How They Met Themselves, Dante Gabriel Rossetti. Courtesy of
Fitzwilliam Museum, Cambridge

Elizabeth Eleanor Siddal, possibly by Dante
Gabriel Rossetti. Walters Art Gallery,
Baltimore

Elizabeth Eleanor Siddal, Dante Gabriel
Rossetti. Victoria and Albert Museum,
London

Ophelia, John Everett Millais. Tate Gallery, London

Elizabeth Siddal (1855), Dante Gabriel
Rossetti. Ashmolean Museum, Oxford

Writing on the Sand (watercolour), Dante Gabriel Rossetti. Reproduced by courtesy of the Trustees of the British Museum

Viola and Olivia from Twelfth Night
(engraving in *The Germ*), W.H. Deverell

Love's Mirror, Dante Gabriel Rossetti.
Birmingham City Council Museum and
Art Gallery

Rossetti Sitting to Elizabeth Siddal, Dante Gabriel Rossetti. Birmingham
City Council Museum and Art Gallery

Lady at the Easel, Dante Gabriel Rossetti
Courtauld Institute Galleries, London

Photograph of Elizabeth Siddal (*c.* 1854–5)

Elizabeth Eleanor Siddal (1861), Dante
Gabriel Rossetti, Whereabouts unknown

This includes, incidentally, the single, damp-spotted page said to be a leaf from the notebook buried with Lizzie. It also contains a packet of items relating to Fanny, among which are letters to William from Gabriel at the time of his mental collapse in 1872, when Fanny's welfare was a major concern; William's calculations as to the amounts of cash obtained from Gabriel by Fanny and her second husband; a letter from Fanny to Gabriel; and a fine photo of her, posed against a mirror. Also in the packet are some notes, apparently made by Wise in the mid–1920s, attempting to piece together Fanny's provenance, and a letter from Edmund Gosse objecting in strong terms to Wise's proposal to include the items in his private catalogue. 'About putting in the entry about F[anny] S[chott]'s letters,' wrote Gosse, 'I must say that personally I think it would be quite dreadful to do so. We have no more right to drag the sordid frailties of a great man into the light than to recount dirty tittle tattle about our neighbours.'[20]

But the process was already well under way. With a more delicate wit, Max Beerbohm published in 1922 a sequence of caricatures, featuring among other scenes a vision of Rossetti introducing Fanny to Ruskin, as Lizzie looks coolly down from a portrait frame. Fanny is large and blowsy, with Cockney pretensions to gentility. 'Very pleased to meet you, I'm sure,' she says, as the great critic disdains to take her hand.[21]

In 1928 Evelyn Waugh was at the beginning of his career. He had personal Pre-Raphaelite connections, being collaterally related to the successful pharmacist who fathered Holman Hunt's two wives, Fanny and Edith Waugh, and while at Oxford had written an essay on the PRB. Observing the forthcoming centenary of Rossetti's birth, he obtained a commission for a new biography, which was to be informed by a new scepticism. Lytton Strachey had demolished the credibility of hagiography and in the modern age, Waugh announced, now that Rossetti's painting no longer commanded admiration and his life scandalized no one, the aim was 'to clear away all traces of legend' and offer a plain account of Rossetti's life and work.

Free from the fear of offending Rossetti's family, Waugh's assessment was refreshingly level-headed, if somewhat brisk. He quoted the scattered information succinctly, adding new snippets from unidentified informants, and comments of his own, in contemporary style. Thus: Lizzie's 'younger brother . . . was slightly dotty. She seems to have been attached to her sister, whom the Pre-Raphaelites called "the Roman", on account of her nose.' Lizzie's own character was difficult to discern; she 'used her wit to turn aside the attempts at intimacy she feared', and her 'pathetic little life' was aptly reflected in her sad little drawings, which had 'so little artistic merit and so much of what one's governess called "feeling" '.[22] Her verse, too, was full of unrelieved melancholy.

Rossetti, by contrast, was 'exuberant, slangy, expansive, buoyant, widely educated and of some reputation, conscious of untried strength and unexplored potentiality'. It was a tragedy that he met 'Guggum' when he did: she was 'wan and prim, already crushed by the difficulties of life, her strength failing daily, practically uneducated and entirely unknown, with only her fading beauty bearing the taint of underlying decay . . .' To the vigour of youth, she brought Rossetti' 'the icy breath of corruption and mortality'. From the start their relationship was doomed.[23]

And there was the new evidence of infidelity and neglect to evaluate. Naturally, Gabriel had been unfaithful – he was a 'man of the south', passionate and 'insistent of satisfaction'. But these affairs were merely swift, unscrupulous and insignificant. Evidently influenced by Ruskin's reference to 'sixteen mistresses', Waugh dismissed such philandering as normal; casual infidelity was no matter for censure.

Like Waugh's harsh judgements on his subject's wife, this somewhat surprising attitude to Rossetti's supposed sexual laxity derived only in part from the hitherto suppressed rumours, being more closely connected with the cultural tenor of the post-war period. In the 1920s, marital infidelity was a public concern in a way that it had not been in the Victorian age. Then, despite scandals and attempts at divorce reform, the prevailing practice had been to maintain a facade of propriety. A common solution was for adulterous men to maintain two households – one illegitimate – without disrepute as long as a respectable silence was sustained. Now, however, adultery, although still associated with scandal, had become an acknowledged and common event, publicized weekly in divorce-court proceedings. Moreover, it was regarded in some circles less as an issue of morality than as a practical way to relinquish a spouse whose charms had faded.

Increasingly, the advanced view was that when love died it was best to discard the shell; partners were entitled to seek other relationships, and mistakes were better rectified than endured. Waugh himself, who married in the same year as his *Rossetti* was published, was deserted by his wife within a matter of months when their basic incompatibility became clear to her (an event which may have coloured his attitude towards Lizzie).

Overall, such notions, reflected in contemporary divorce legislation, undoubtedly benefited husbands more than wives, who were likely to suffer economically through divorce. They served, too, to defend and justify casual sexual infidelities of the kind that were attributed to Rossetti, by legitimizing the idea of 'natural' sexual appetite. Hence Waugh's characterization of Gabriel as an indolent and sensual 'Latin' type, whose life was devoted to the physical beauty of woman in both painting and seduction. Such a stereotype, indeed, was increasingly common in contemporary fiction and drama and in large measure the alteration in Rossetti's character was a direct reflection of the age.

Within this perspective, Waugh's belief in the basic incompatibility of Gabriel and Guggum naturally led him to emphasize the evidence of conflict between the couple, and to view the delayed marriage as a sign that the relationship was fundamentally flawed. He therefore drew attention to a serious quarrel described by Rossetti to Madox Brown in 1857, over a proposal for a phalanstery or artistic college or commune with studio and living accommodation, which the Browns hoped to share with various painters and their wives. Waugh quoted Gabriel's letter at length:

Last night a misunderstanding occurred between Lizzy and me about what passed when you were there, concerning the scheme of a college. She seems under the impression that you came there in great surprise at hearing that I had not consulted her on the matter, and with the wish to speak to her yourself . . . I cannot but imagine that, as my friend, you would have preferred first asking me what had passed between us, before speaking to her . . . seeing that on the night when Morris, Jones and I came to you, and we were discussing the scheme, I expressly said I should be married by the time it came into operation, and require space accordingly in the building. When you spoke . . . of two married couples as beginning the scheme . . . I refrained from saying anything, simply because Lizzy has sometimes shown such displeasure at my mentioning our engagement . . . that I could not

87

tell how far her mother was aware of it, or how Lizzy would take my mentioning it before her.

I had spoken of the scheme to her some days ago, but she seemed to take little interest in it . . . She now says she understood only a range of studios, and would strongly object to living where 'G' was, of which objection of hers I had no idea . . . I have myself wished to keep her and him apart hitherto, as I do not think he has acted lately as a friend towards me in her regard . . . However, my wishes as to this scheme would entirely depend on hers . . . As it is, she seemed last night quite embittered and estranged from me on this account, whether for the moment or permanently I cannot yet tell, and it has made me most unhappy ever since, more so than anything else could make me.[24]

Biographically, this was indeed an important letter. It had been first printed in 1899, when William Rossetti had sought to play down its significance by excusing Gabriel's 'irregular habits' and denying these had any sexual basis. The identity of the mysterious 'G' to whom Lizzie objected had been concealed behind this initial, which William acknowledged was not correct. In the new climate, however, the significance of the 'misunderstanding' was obvious: 'embittered and estranged' became the keynotes of Waugh's analysis of the doomed marriage. Following the loss of her child, he claimed, Lizzie 'gave way to melancholy, which often took the form of resentment and jealousy against her husband'.

And there was worse to come, with Lizzie's death. 'The few people who could have told the full story of that last evening together are now in their graves,' wrote Waugh, 'and nothing beyond the orthodox account found in the official biographies has ever been authoritatively recorded. Perhaps there is no more to recount.' But:

There are however two stories that were widely circulated at the time and widely believed . . .

The first is that on the night of his wife's death, Rossetti was not at the Working Men's College but in the company of another woman, with whom he was carrying on an intrigue. He returned to find his wife unconscious and was left with an insatiable suspicion that she had known of his betrayal and had taken her own life in consequence.

The second and more convincing version is that Rossetti was, as was stated at the inquest, innocently engaged at the Working Men's College, but that his wife was now in a condition when she construed every absence as an infidelity; she took her own life, leaving beside her bed a letter for Rossetti reproaching him with his cruelty towards her.[25]

This was sensational stuff, offering a serious challenge to the pre-war accounts so carefully constructed by William Rossetti.

Hall Caine had, indeed, hinted at the possibility of suicide, while Swinburne, in a letter to his mother after the inquest, privately printed in 1917, had said that 'happily there was no difficulty in proving that illness had quite deranged her mind so that the worst chance of all was escaped', which also seemed to cast doubt on the official verdict.[26] But neither allegation had made much impact, since Caine was notoriously unreliable and Swinburne's remark seemed merely lurid, for the inquest had not proved that Mrs Rossetti's mind was deranged but that her death was accidental. Boldly, Waugh was going public with the gossip.

His revelations, which he was careful to call 'stories', came from Thomas Wise, and might well have been dismissed along with Wise's other inventions, had it not been for the fact that the idea of Lizzie's suicide already possessed a long history. 'No doubt he had a wretched life since his wife's death fr. poison she took herself!' Jeannette Marshall had written in her diary on hearing of Rossetti's death. 'They had only been married 2 years, & she found herself superseded, & took laudanum.' Later, seeing Fanny before *The Blue Bower*, she added that this was the 'nasty, common-looking creature . . . because of whom his poor wife committed suicide'.[27] Furthermore, a suppressed passage in the manuscript of Bell Scott's *Autobiographical Notes* – which perhaps helps explain the hostility with which the book was greeted – claimed that on the night of her death Mrs Rossetti 'had pinned a written statement on the breast of her night-shirt and put an end to her troubles, real or imaginary'.[28] Waugh's words were therefore justified, although, as his own biographer was to note, they were 'deliberately elaborated to add colour and dash' to his story.[29]

Hall Caine was not to be outdone, and at once revised and reissued his *Recollections of Rossetti* (1928) with additional speculations on Lizzie's death. 'What happened to her during the hours in which she was alone, what impulse led her to the act she committed, whether it was due to an innocent accident . . . or to dark if delusive broodings?' he asked melodramatically.[30] The answer came in his amended account of the overnight rail journey with Rossetti in 1881:

> I will no longer hesitate to say that during the painful journey from Cumberland, he told me that on the night of his wife's death, when he returned to her room from his walk he found a letter or message addressed to himself lying on the table by her side. I think he said he had not shown that letter to anyone, and that he had never mentioned it before. Of this last fact I cannot be certain, but sure I am that he said that the message had left such a scar on his heart as would never be healed.[31]

Like infidelity, suicide was by this date no longer the scandal it had once been, when those dying by their own hands had been refused burial in consecrated ground and families were tainted by association with self-murder. Nevertheless, it was still a source of shame, and blame. And, as it were on behalf of the phantom woman he had loved when young, Charles Ricketts rose to Lizzie's defence in his review of Caine's book. 'Many years ago this tragedy was hinted at in Bell Scott's reminiscences and publicly denied by Swinburne,' he wrote. 'Madox Brown, questioned by my friend Shannon, told him of Rossetti's frantic appearance at his house on that tragic night still in his socks, for he had removed his boots on returning home not to awaken his wife.' And like other close friends, Madox Brown had denied both the suicide and the rumoured letter.[32]

The year closed with another centenary biography, *Dante Gabriel Rossetti: Painter Poet of Heaven in Earth* by R. L. Megroz, whose book was dedicated to Thomas Wise. Megroz was much troubled by his hero's unkind neglect of his dear dove's health and welfare. Why was the engagement so long and uncertain? As early as 1854 Madox Brown had wondered in his diary 'Why does he not marry her?' and the question had not been answered. To Megroz, to profess love and fail to marry was not the action of an honourable man, painter and poet of heaven on earth.

His solution was to blame the lady (whom he also inexplicably chose to call 'Eleanor Siddal') for her unfitness as the wife of such a genius. In his view, the Pre-Raphaelite atmosphere was too intense for the 'insufficiently cultured but proud working girl', whose poor health was compounded by morbid psychology. 'It might have been well for both of them if they had never married,' Megroz commented morosely; for it was not lack of money that delayed the wedding but the bride's spirit, 'morbid at the core'. Lizzie was inherently 'doomed to nervous instability and excessive irritation'. To blame Rossetti was 'to go laboriously out of the obvious path of truth in judging a man who . . . can never be seen in too favourable a light'.[33] Having thus rather brutally transferred Gabriel's own mental instability to his wife, Megroz described her poems as 'uniformly painful' and melancholy, 'harping monotonously upon the theme of betrayed and disillusioned love'. Had Rossetti therefore behaved callously? The truth could not be so simple. In addition to her psychological and physical sickness, Lizzie had been the object of romantic advances from Ruskin, who was said to be sufficiently in love with her to arouse Rossetti's jealousy. There were also the attentions of another painter – the unidentified 'G' – leading to the notorious quarrel in 1857.

At this point, the story cut abruptly to Rossetti's meeting with the beautiful Jane Burden later the same year, with a hearsay account of how William Morris had been instructed to marry Jane 'so that such a stunner should remain in the family, as it were'. Nor was this Rossetti's first distraction during the years of his engagement to Lizzie. There was the affair with 'fair haired, solidly-built Fanny Cornforth', who was 'his mistress for more years than any other woman'. Again, however, Gabriel was not to blame for this philandering:

Rossetti would probably have married sooner than he did but for such a disorganization of his emotional life as would result from engagement to a woman who would not be entirely his before marriage, and the simultaneous intimate contact with another woman capable of satisfying his senses and content to do so.[34]

'A woman who would not be entirely his before marriage': put plainly, this meant that Lizzie, moody and resentful, had refused Gabriel sexually, and thus driven him into the arms of other, looser women. By implication, she was culpable; if he was unfaithful, her frigidity was the cause.

Similarly with her cruel suicide. In all probability Lizzie had taken the overdose 'in a hysterical moment, with the knowledge that it was fatal' in order to reproach Gabriel for his neglect.[35] And this was the true reason for his long years of seclusion and drug-induced decline.

Together, Megroz and Waugh told a very different tale from that related by the Pre-Raphaelite survivors. The new biographers, naturally, believed theirs to be the truth, which had been concealed by Victorian concern for propriety, and which they were simply uncovering now that the need for hypocrisy was past. And indeed their evidence – of bitter discord between Lizzie and Gabriel in the mid–1850s, and Fanny Cornforth's emergence on the scene around 1858 – was strong and relatively unambiguous, while the rumours as to the real cause of Lizzie's death were, as we have seen, of some antiquity.

Their conclusions that infidelity and sexual jealousy had driven Lizzie to her death were by no means certain, however. Both Allingham's diary and the evidence of Rossetti's paintings showed that the years of Fanny's ascendancy had been the mid–1860s. Although her first appearance, in *Bocca Baciata* (1858) had antedated his marriage, by the time it took place she was married herself (according to William Rossetti) to Mr Hughes, and there was no *prima facie* evidence of an affair with Gabriel during Lizzie's lifetime. The sexual scandal, such as it was, related to the years after her death, when Fanny was a frequent visitor, if not resident, at Cheyne Walk. Moreover Hall Caine's belated account of a suicide note was hardly conclusive, for his lies were legendary, and the other rumours were based on equally insecure foundations.

Yet the romantic legend had been irreparably undermined. Romance and long engagements were, of course, out of fashion, and there were other reasons why the theme of sexual conflict and betrayal dominated these biographies of the post-war period. The emergent sexual ideology of the time, contained in sex-reform propaganda, books of popular psychology and 'advanced' fiction, stressed the vital importance of vigorous heterosexuality for physical and mental health, warning of the dangers of repression and frustration. Where the Victorians had a model of sexual conduct in pecuniary terms, with profligate spending condemned in favour of the careful saving of husbandly resources, the new invoked medical metaphors of celibacy as poison and sexual intercourse as healthful and clean. Together with the rejection of everything Victorian went ridicule of shame and prudery.

In the new science of psychology, sex was defined as the primary drive, always seeking direct outlets and becoming destructive if dammed or denied. Simplified versions of the newly popularized Freudian theories of infant sexuality and neurosis-inducing repression fed into notions of sex as the motive force of human existence. Gender difference was no longer defined in terms of emotional and social 'separate spheres', but as instinctual and polarized male and female sexuality.

In this perspective, men and women had different natures, males said to be impelled by a thrusting, mobile, dominating sexual urge symbolized by penetration, females by a receptive, nurturing, submissive impulse. This distinction – in many ways merely a reformulation of separate spheres – created an ideology of gender based on ideal complementarity, but one which was also oppositional and conflicting. Electrical concepts of sexual polarity through attraction and repulsion were articulated in the texts of the new sexology (as the study of gender relations was called), in part developed from notions suggested by Havelock Ellis and associated British sex reformers but chiefly derived from the new science of psychoanalysis and the work of Freud, Jung, Adler and their followers.

One influential text was *Ideal Marriage*, which appeared in thirty-seven English impressions from 1926 to 1961 and promoted successful sexual intercourse as the foundation of marriage. Women were urged to discard fear or distaste for frequent sex in order to encourage healthy, natural relationships – a prescription accompanied by birth-control advice to facilitate unlimited sex without the repeated pregnancies that damaged women's health. Harmonious sexual relations were defined as mutually pleasurable, although the female role was still seen as traditionally passive: willingness was advocated, but not assertiveness. In *Sex Hostility in Marriage: Its Origins, Prevention and Treatment* (1931) the same author claimed that good sex was founded on female submission, where the woman 'not only accepts but desires dependence', whereas 'sex hostility' was a dangerous threat to happy marriage. Other writers warned that women who resisted sexual demands risked losing their husbands to prostitutes or the divorce courts. The male need for heterosexual congress was paramount.

From these ideas came the popular concept of the 'sex war'. *Frigidity in Woman in Relation to Her Love Life* (1931) argued that the two sexes were engaged in a permanent conflict, and that resistance to sexual intercourse was 'one of woman's weapons in this universal struggle'. Conflict arose from the fact that 'two bipolar forces struggle for mastery over human life: the will-to-power and the will-to-submission'; women ought to accept the latter and thereby learn to enjoy sex. Refusal to submit was negative and destructive. And the newly identified affliction of female frigidity was a fate worse than death. *The Poison of Prudery* (1929) denounced 'erotically impotent women' who did not enjoy intercourse as degenerate and 'a menace to civilization'; they were responsible for sex antagonism and wrecked marital happiness. Abstinence was equally dangerous: *Lysistrata or Woman's Future and Future Woman* (1927) asserted that 'a thwarted instinct does not merely subside. It seeks compensation and damages for its rebuff.' Nor were all these statements made by men: in *Motherhood and Its Enemies* (1927) Charlotte Haldane warned that the non-fulfilment of 'normal sex functions' could lead to the emergence of secondary characteristics of the opposite sex – hence the wide-spread view that spinsters were likely to grow moustaches. Pro-longed female abstinence led also to fanaticism and crankiness, anti-vivisectionism and freak religions.[36]

In this vigorous promotion of 'natural' sexuality, virginity, once a virtue, was redefined as a danger to psychological health. Cruelly, in a period when marriageable men were in short supply owing to the Great War's carnage of youth, spinsters were described as 'elderly virgins', with limited experience and a narrow outlook. They were frequently said to be therefore unsuited for responsible work in education and medicine (at the same time, owing to public policies on unemployment, married women were also being excluded from these professions). And, since sexual fulfilment through marriage and motherhood was defined as woman's natural destiny, some sex reformers seriously advocated polygamy and concubinage as a solution to the lack of husbands, enabling spinsters to be saved from a damagingly sexless existence.

Biographers like Waugh and Megroz were thus simply incorporating contemporary ideas into their accounts of Rossetti, who was credited with a healthy sexual appetite as befitted a modern hero and an artist, whose *métier* had always been viewed as licentious. His mistresses multiplied until there was, by implication, scarcely a model whom he had not bedded. As a sensualist, who sought consummation in his worship of woman, wrote Waugh, Rossetti 'was impelled by a highly passionate nature, easily roused and insistent of satisfaction'; he 'relished the adventure of promiscuity'.[37]

Conversely, Elizabeth Siddal – now no longer politely called 'Miss Siddal' but always referred to by the demeaning diminutive 'Lizzie' – was discovered to have refused sex with Gabriel though there was nothing in the sources to support this. She was redefined as 'frigid', suffering the inevitable consequences of neurosis, and it was increasingly implied that all her ailments stemmed from this frustration of her natural sexuality. No explanation was offered as to why eventual marriage and normal sexual relations did not cure all her troubles; it was evidently assumed that by this time the harmful effects of denial had eaten too deeply into her soul.

Indeed, in Waugh's account, there was a hint of the fashionable fascist notion of eugenic breeding. Lizzie was 'tainted' with corruption and morbidity: the marriage brought no joy or fruitfulness, and both her death and that of her stillborn child could be considered merciful.

Once his pure, Pre-Raphaelite inspiration, Elizabeth Siddal had now become Rossetti's incubus.

8

Violet's Elizabeth

The notions of sexual conflict and polarity current in the 1920s and '30s informed fiction as well as biography, most notably in the work of D. H. Lawrence. *Sons and Lovers*, the novel which made him famous, was published in the same year as the British Psychological Association was founded and was adopted by the psychoanalytic movement as a work exemplifying the new Freudian understanding of oedipal conflict and striving through libido. The links were later strengthened through Lawrence's relationship with Frieda von Richthofen, whose close friend Otto Gross had been analysed by both Freud and Jung and was a member of the Schwabing circle or Kosmische Runde in Munich, with progressive ideas on love as erotic union through instinct, with male and female as cosmic poles.[1]

This sexual ideology, which was probably more widely read in fictional form than in sex manuals or psychoanalytical literature, found imaginative expression in Lawrence's later novels. *The Rainbow*, for example, contained a characteristic vision of sexual attraction and repulsion in the account of the doomed love between Ursula Brangwen and Anton Skrebensky:

> . . . at such moments, when he was mad with her destroying him, when all his complacency was destroyed, all his everyday self was destroyed, and only the stripped, rudimentary, primal man remained, demented with torture, her passion to love him became love, she took him again, they came together in an overwhelming passion . . .
>
> But it all contained a developing germ of death. After each contact, her anguished desire for him or for that which she never had for him was stronger, her love was more hopeless. After each contact his mad dependence on her was deepened, his hope of standing strong and taking her in his own strength was weakened.[2]

96

Similar analyses, both reflecting and helping to shape the gender ideology of the time, were elaborated in *Women in Love* and *Lady Chatterley's Lover*.

Lawrence's talent had been recognized and his work first published in 1911 by the *English Review* under the editorship of Ford Madox Hueffer, author of *Ancient Lights*. By this date Hueffer had left his wife and was living as the common-law husband of novelist Violet Hunt who, acting as 'reader' for the *English Review*, befriended Lawrence. Like Hueffer, Violet Hunt had personal connections with Pre-Raphaelitism: her father was a landscape painter acquainted with Holman Hunt and Madox Brown and she herself had been at school with the daughters of William Morris and Burne-Jones. Over the years she had heard, retained and recirculated a good deal of gossip about the famous Brotherhood.

'Had a long talk with Holman Hunt, at Lady Seton's,' Violet recorded in her diary some time around 1900, noting down Hunt's view that Rossetti

> behaved very badly to the poor woman he married. He was engaged to her, but their engagement was not generally known, and he never owned it . . . She told some friends of hers that she was engaged to Rossetti, as she was. That friend congratulated Rossetti, who instantly said there was no truth in it. They went on in this way, growing more and more apart . . . [until Lizzie] got very ill, and was supposed to be dying. Just before her end, Rossetti came to see her. I think H. H. said that she had asked to see him to bid him goodbye, she was really dangerously ill. He was touched, and professed love for her, and said that if she would but get better, he would marry her. She did get better and he did marry her. He then lived at Blackfriars Bridge . . . They had no cook, I almost think no servant. They never dined at home, but went to a restaurant in Fleet Street, and he sent her home alone and came in late.

Holman Hunt also reputedly claimed that poor Lizzie had 'an unhappy life and died by her own hand', knowing of the affair with Fanny; when Rossetti came in on the fateful night he found her 'lying on the bed with a paper on her breast to say that her life was so miserable that she wished for no more of it. Fanny was brought into the house before twenty-four hours were over . . .'[3]

Violet Hunt gossiped too with Emily Tebbs, widow of the

lawyer who witnessed the exhumation, who told her that when Lizzie was pregnant,

> they had a violent quarrel due to his fault. He then had 'Fanny' as a mistress, and the excitement and emotion of this quarrel brought on a miscarriage. The same thing happened when the second baby was on its way. She felt what was coming then, and said, 'There, you have killed this baby, too.' She had another miscarriage, and a miserable life all the time she lived with him.[4]

No purpose is served by attempting to judge whether these allegations came from Violet's informants or her own imagination, nor whether they had any basis in truth – the obstetric details relating to Lizzie's stillborn child in 1861 indicate that this was not a miscarriage but a spontaneous haemorrhage at full term – but they testify to the wilder reaches of rumour current in the early years of this century, and to Violet Hunt's long-standing fascination with the tale of Elizabeth Siddal. This was furthered by her liaison with Madox Brown's grandson, although, in view of his reputation for elaborate lies, it is perhaps surprising that, along with the desk he inherited from Aunt Christina, 'Fordie' did not supply Violet Hunt with a more embellished account of Gabriel's marriage; the Brown-Rossetti family tradition was not sympathetic to Lizzie.

By 1920, Ford had in his own words, 'set up house with another lady', leaving Violet in the unhappy position of a discarded mistress. She seems to have turned in compensation to what she saw as the story of another ill-treated woman, and her endeavour was encouraged by Thomas Wise, who continued to fan the embers of prurient interest in the private lives of the PRB. By 1923 she was inquiring into the Sheffield connection in search of material for a biography of Elizabeth Siddal. W. T. Freemantle and W. G. Wells sent the fruits of their long-running researches, a mixed bag of true and erroneous information. Wells, for example, firmly believed that Lizzie's birthplace was either Sheffield or the ancestral Siddall village of Hope in Derbyshire. Violet Hunt, on the other hand, was convinced that Lizzie was 'a thorough Cockney', although the Southwark parish registers contained no record of her birth, as Violet found. Informed by Wells that Lizzie had attended Sheffield Art School, she queried 'how to account for the mysterious fact that a little London-born child should attend the Sheffield School of Art? Was she visiting relations? I gather so. Then she was of "some class".'5

Freemantle described his meeting with James Siddall, and furnished the marriage certificate which showed that Charles Siddall and Elizabeth Eleanor Evans were married at Hornsey in Middlesex in 1824. Hornsey parish records, however, contained no evidence of children born there, and Lizzie's birthplace and date remained elusive. Freemantle also supplied the names of five siblings: Annie, Charles jnr, James, Clara and Henry. In addition, he provided Lizzie's visiting card with the Weymouth Street address.

From her inquiries, Violet Hunt thus discovered a good deal about Elizabeth Siddal's life and background. But, perhaps because for years she had been loudly denouncing Rossetti's cruelty, she could not find a publisher for her book. In 1930 she reaffirmed her intention of 'writing a life of Mrs Rossetti' in a letter to the *Sunday Times*, and was rewarded with a reply from the granddaughter of Lizzie's sister Lydia Siddall, whose mother, now Mrs Higgins, had been born soon after her aunt's death in 1862 and named Elizabeth Eleanor after her. Her memories, transcribed in 1930, opened up for Violet Hunt's benefit a hitherto untapped vein of family information. As Mrs Higgins began:

So far as I have always understood it was in a friend's bonnet shop where Aunt Lizzie was seen . . . It was my mother [Lydia] who was first seen by my father (Joseph Wheeler) hanging up candles in Aunt Lucy's shop, and fell in love with her . . . My Aunt Lucy (Mrs Day) was Grandmother Siddall's sister, and a very pretty woman . . .

I have never heard that Grandmother Siddall had been a housemaid but judging from my remembrances of her she did not know the first thing about housework. She must have been a very good-looking woman, and as children, when she came to visit us, our greatest delight was to coax her to let down her wealth of beautiful hair which fell to her knees like a beautiful cloak.

Then there was Aunt Annie, who married a Scotsman named McCarthy . . .

Aunt Clara, my youngest Aunt usually called 'Tump', was one of the dearest and most unselfish of women.

My two Uncles, James and Harry, carried on their father's business at Old Kent Road.

As my mother always broke down when talking of her sister Lizzie

I did not hear much of her history until the poems, which were exhumed, were published. Then I heard a discussion between Aunt Clara and my Mother, Aunt insisting that they were word for word of the original manuscripts, which she had read, and my Mother saying it was impossible, as she had seen them placed under her sister's head in her coffin before it was sealed down. At that time none of the Siddall family had heard of the exhumation . . . The tress of Aunt Lizzie's hair which my Mother had was cut off before burial. So far as I know none of the Siddall family had any hair which might have been cut off after the exhumation . . .

My mother was her sister's constant companion, travelling to Bath, Matlock etc, always together. My Mother has told me how, when away, perhaps at Bath, or Matlock, or any of the other places they visited, Rossetti would be wheeled around in a bath chair, and he would wag his head from side to side and have his tongue lolling about . . .

My Grandfather Siddall had lost his all owing to a lawsuit over property in Sheffield. He lost the case, but it was reopened and decided in his favour. However, his daughter Clara was so distressed at the privations which other lawsuits would mean [that she] destroyed all the necessary papers . . . I have always understood that Hope Hall, Sheffield, should have been inherited by my Grandfather . . .

Mrs Higgins also stated that, on her own birth soon after Lizzie's death, Rossetti sent 'all the baby clothes, which had been prepared for their child which did not live' to Lydia, 'tucking a £5 note in the pocket of the baby's basket'. However, he took no further interest in his sister-in-law's family when neither the baby girl nor her subsequent sisters proved to be auburn-haired.[6]

The Wife of Rossetti, Her Life and Death, was eventually published in 1932, the centenary year of Lizzie's presumed birth. Its author was growing elderly and her faculties of memory and tact – perhaps never strong – were beginning to fail. Moreover, she was more of a novelist than a scholar, and thus primarily concerned with drama, atmosphere and the strong delineation of character. Notwithstanding its wealth of new and detailed information, her contribution to the legend resulted in what can only be described as a fictional Elizabeth. Like Violet herself, this character is a tragic woman betrayed by her lover.

'I can never forgive Rossetti,' was the melodramatic opening.

The phrase was allegedly spoken by Robert Browning but the precise indictment was not clear. Casual conjugal neglect and infidelity were again presented as ordinary vices within the bohemian world of Pre-Raphaelitism, where the painters cruised the streets searching for 'stunners'. This image, which has proved evergreen, brought the early days of the PRB vividly if inaccurately to life; it was in fact based on a misreading of the *PRB Journal* which noted the young painters' fear of speaking to an attractive girl lest they fall into the clutches of a prostitute.

The dawn of love between Gabriel and Elizabeth was described by Violet Hunt with a novelist's imagination in a manner redolent of Lawrence, whose books had just been reissued. Caught in the rain while staying with Barbara Leigh-Smith on her country estate at Scalands, the young couple

> took refuge in the dim dark wood by a little spring that welled up under a stone half-hidden by lush grass. There they cowered, shielded by the leafy screen which the arrowy death could not pierce. And, when it was quieter, making a cup out of her fair hand, she gave him to drink out of it, from the well . . . shyly, with the affectation of one who is aware that the moment has come . . .
>
> And she sang to him. They were both gay, like children on whom Doom lies.[7]

And the central drama was a Lawrencian struggle for emotional dominance between male and female.

Flourishing the Weymouth Street address, Violet Hunt reconstructed a scenario in which Lizzie lived 'in rooms by herself, spending the rest of her time in the company of one man, closeted with him alone for hours, for days, for nights, using his chambers while he was away . . . sleeping in his bed . . . yet unable to point to a ring on her third finger . . .' In this atmosphere, 'a duel, silent but to the death began'. Rossetti was alternately attentive and neglectful; to him 'women were cheap; he had no respect for them . . . but at that moment he said everything Liz wanted him to say, as he alone could say it, and soothed her. There was nothing else to do. She would have died.' Their sexual tension was innate, unalterable:

> He saw that it would be misery for both of them. He was bound to make her unhappy because his temperament demanded, and would

have, something larger, more mutable, more vicious even: his will to live, artistically speaking, would force him to see that he got it – *Bocca Baciata, The Kissed Mouth* as opposed to the reticent croonings of the 'meek unconscious dove' who would, of her nature, languidly, piously, forever frustrate the artist's imperious 'Now'.[8]

'He had never loved her more than now that he was going to betray her.' Not only with Fanny but also with Annie Miller, Holman Hunt's model. Yet the lovers were locked irrevocably together, for 'the Sid, relying on her looks (for she was still beautiful enough)' retained 'the queer, half-magical power she possessed over him'. Finally married, they

> quarrelled babyishly, bitterly, suicidally – until the very centres of life for both were involved. The Browns' hearthrug received her convulsed form, flung down, twisting, heaving, shaken in gusts of passion that nothing in the way of comfort and fine words could allay. They just threw a rug over her and crept away.[9]

Her once-bright beauty decayed. She became 'peevish, uncertain-tempered and staring-eyed', a 'sour myth' immured in Chatham Place alone with her birds and bottle of laudanum. It was an insanitary location, where the Thames at low tide revealed 'a brown, sliding plateau of liquid suet' while the Fleet ditch below the windows was nothing but a sewer, roofed over and teeming with rats.

Suicide was an appropriate climax to this increasingly sensational tale, and received its full value in Violet's narrative, imaginatively enhanced by dramatic delaying devices. After a quarrel in the cab home from the restaurant, Lizzie supposedly tried to prevent Gabriel from going out again:

> Twisting the necklace round and round in her hand she began to hint – more than hint – at Fanny, trying to keep him beside her with the threat of another miscarriage – suddenly clapping her hand to her side . . . He was convinced that she was acting . . .
>
> 'Stay with me, Gug, stay with me!' . . . Half undressed, she followed him to the landing, and stayed hanging over the banisters; any of the lodgers might have heard the frantic partner of his bed shriek as he passed down the stone stairs with his head bowed as under a storm – 'Go then, and you'll kill this baby as you killed the last!'

With dramatic skill, the *coup de grâce* – the suicide note pinned to her nightdress reading 'My life is so miserable that I wish for no more of it' – was held in reserve until discovered by Brown shortly after Lizzie finally expired.[10]

This is, of course, neither the style nor the language of orthodox biographical writing, and despite her serious intent, the emotional approach vitiated Violet Hunt's book, rendering it virtually useless as a source of information. (It has, however, been unfairly criticized for its lack of footnotes, since very few of the early biographies gave adequate references, and her practice was not exceptional.) More striking than its melodrama, however, is its analysis of gender relations. For, although written expressly to convey a woman's sympathy with its subject and her sufferings, the author more than once blamed Lizzie for her 'pensive, determined, *noli me tangere*' attitude. She, too, accused Lizzie of sexual refusal, and prim, petit-bourgeois frigidity that prevented her from yielding joyously. In this respect, and despite her own unhappy experience of sexual generosity outside marriage, Violet Hunt was firmly on the side of prevailing ideology with its masculine bias: Lizzie's tragedy, she argued, might have been averted had she been more willing to enjoy sex, especially without waiting for a wedding ring.

In this context, it is curious to note that Bessie Parkes' daughter, defending her mother's memory of Lizzie against Violet Hunt's version, claimed that this frigidity was one of many inventions. 'Violet Hunt makes a great play with her statement that Lizzie was a very cold woman, virtuous and austere, and kept poor Dante Gabriel at arm's length,' wrote Marie Belloc Lowndes to a friend. 'I wonder if you will be surprised to hear that they were living as man and wife all the time, which was the reason why his mother and sister would never go to the house at Blackfriars, for they were very narrow and extremely religious.'[11] Poor Lizzie was thus condemned whether chaste or wanton.

But, if Violet Hunt blamed Lizzie for her fate, the text also contained a strong current of sympathy for a woman whose pain derived less from her lover's infidelity than his indifference. This was of course a reflection of Violet's own position; she herself had failed to secure that ring on her third finger and been neglected and deserted by her lover, to be laughed at by others. And, although failing to register the evidence of Gabriel's great betrayal in 1858, when Lizzie was lost to the Pre-Raphaelite circle, she effectively presented her subject's distress and desolation, as she sank into addiction and despair so deep that not even marriage could save her.

Although therefore read as an anti-Rossetti manifesto, the book took no sort of feminist position. It arraigned neither the man or men in the case, nor the prevailing relations of men and women in society, but instead blamed the victim. Lizzie's problems were seen as inherent in her personality rather than her position. Like others of its age, this version of Elizabeth Siddal's story also omitted virtually all mention of her own artistic career. Her pictures were largely ignored, and her poems quoted only as evidence of her excessive, self-absorbed misery.

Why then did *The Wife of Rossetti* arouse such hostility? It was publicly and privately condemned as a tissue of scandalous imaginings and has ever since been dismissed as worthless. Yet in many ways its presentation was not dissimilar to those by Caine or Waugh or Megroz or others who came later; these also claimed that the marriage was unhappy, that Gabriel was unfaithful, and that Lizzie had killed herself. The male authors also extrapolated from the few facts a distinctly personal account of Elizabeth Siddal's character, yet it was Violet Hunt who was the chief target of abuse. She was, of course, a woman and a novelist, self-evidently lacking the authority of male biographers and critics; and although she excused Rossetti's behaviour, she did not entirely exonerate him from blame. For the most part, other writers, with the notable exception of Waugh, still venerated him as a Romantic genius.

In many instances, attacks on Violet Hunt were accompanied by grudging praise. 'I have read Violet Hunt's Rossetti book and hate it,' commented W. Graham Robertson, the *fin de siècle* artist who kept a lonely vigil for Pre-Raphaelite painting during the wilderness years of the 1920s and '30s. 'It's the more odious for being, in the main, true to facts.' 'I must confess it's a wonderful achievement,' he wrote later, 'the amount of material she has got together is simply staggering.' But he felt that, despite herself, Violet had made a good case in Gabriel's defence:

One had always heard that he was inconsiderate and neglectful of his wife, but if Lizzie was as Violet represents her, the only wonder is that he didn't murder her. The book is bitter – most painful – here and there 'touched up', I think, but it is certainly most interesting and well written.[12]

'The purely imaginative passages are, of course, particularly difficult to refute,' Robertson noted, and it was in response to these that Helen Rossetti Angeli, daughter of William Rossetti and Lucy Madox Brown, found or cast herself as defender of her uncle's reputation. Although, like her sister Olivia Rossetti Agresti, Helen Angeli had renewed the family's ancestral links with Italy through marriage (incidentally translating a collection of official statements promoting the achievements of Fascist Italy under Mussolini,[13]) she remained committed to their British interests too, representing 'the last poor remains of friends of Rossetti', who responded indignantly to Violet Hunt's version. 'Is no one left to refute it?' she asked.

Privately, Helen Angeli also conceded that *Wife of Rossetti* was better than she feared. 'I am reading Violet Hunt's book about Lizzie Siddall *et al* with less indignation than I ought to!' she reported,

'I can't help finding it distinctly entertaining. I think she might have left my poor Aunt Christina alone, but believe I know where she gets her rather venomous descriptions of her. I suppose people like this gossipy, scandalous stuff and VH's is well done. I though it would be much worse. She evidently has original sources (not all Ford as I had supposed) – how far true, how far lying, I know not.[14]

Publicly, however, she attacked the book, as a romance and work of fiction, based on the 'gleanings of the PRB waste-paper baskets, hearsay and the echo of hearsay, gossip and the reverberations of gossip'. Including in her rebuke also Evelyn Waugh's attack on Rossetti's ethical failings, she defended her uncle against allegations of infidelity and cruelty. He had inspired intense love and admiration in others, she stated, observing that his critics' own moral standards left much to be desired. And she flatly denied Violet Hunt's tale of the suicide note, being equally concerned to defend her grandfather Ford Madox Brown against accusations of having destroyed evidence in order to mislead the inquest.

'Lizzie's last message, as reported, is touching and romantic,' she told *The Times Literary Supplement*. 'But she did not write it. Nor did Madox Brown find it . . . the story told is impossible.'[15]

It may have been an implausible story, extravagantly told, but it had a provenance; Violet Hunt was not its sole begetter. Nor, it may be noted, did Helen Angeli specifically deny that Lizzie had killed herself. Like the exhumation, this was a tale that would continue to run.

9

Costume Cinema

As we are seeing, the representation of Elizabeth Siddal owed as much to its context amid the changing configuration of gender as it did to the discovery of facts. Indeed, the factual information functioned chiefly as a framework within which biographers sketched their own preoccupations. It is not therefore surprising that, although a few more nuggets of information were dug up in the 1930s and '40s, the period was notable rather for the dramatization of the myth in a manner that mirrored the popular culture of the age, and for its extension across the Atlantic.

'Poor splendid wings, so frayed and soiled and torn!' This Swinburnian epigraph set the tone and title for Frances Winwar's book, published in New York in 1933 and in London the following year, which claimed to be neither fictionalized nor Freudian, but a historical study in which 'gossip holds no place'; yet in which 'out of the dust of the dead letter the author has sought to reanimate the living spirit'. In the event, the author told a tale worthy of Hollywood in its imaginative simplicities. Indeed, one might suspect *Poor Splendid Wings* of being written with a movie adaptation in mind, for its presentation of Elizabeth Siddal is in cinematic terms:

> Before long she became Gabriel's exclusive model. More aware of her latent talents than others had been, he spent hours guiding first her pencil, gradually her brush. As he leaned over her shimmering copper hair in heavy wings about her face and closed his hand over her fingers, he learned as much as he taught – learned that here was a damozel of flesh and blood, whose hair was more fragrant than the flowers of his imagined pleasances, whose hand, warmer than the touch of dreams, set the pulses beating at his temples, whose changing blue-grey eyes were now stiller than still waters of evening, now corruscating with meanings he trembled to read.[1]

This was the literary equivalent of the slow dissolve with swirling music, preceding censored embraces. Gabriel's chaste adoration developed swiftly into physical passion, aroused by the voluptuous beauty of Fanny Cornforth, who was here cast as the sexy siren in opposition to the virtuous maiden Lizzie, in a classic battle for the hero's body and soul. In this text, however, Lizzie is not frigid but possessed of her own deep passion. She had 'no obstacles of social position or religion to overcome' and gloried in the depth of her adoration for Gabriel, as he in his desire for her. Yet she was too sickly to thrive on sex. This is the stuff of pure romance, in swooning flashbacks:

> What gladness had been hers when Gabriel, dear innocent Gabriel, had laid her head on that sweet grassy bank and spread her hair on either side . . . then she had thrilled to the warmth of his kiss, creeping up her throat to her lips, and she had known what it was to be called back to life. No, no! He had never been false. It was only her broken health oppressing her with black fancies . . . How could she be sure? . . . What certainty had she at this moment, when she was rending her heart between faith and doubt, he was not giving her a definite answer – in the arms of another? Fanny, or Hunt's pretty model – Italian, too, they said . . .[2]

The historical drama was filled out with supporting cameo parts depicting Christina's snobbish hostility and Ruskin's disapproval of the bohemian *ménage* at Chatham Place. Less conventionally, Winwar made the loss of Lizzie's baby – for which she was anachronistically admitted to hospital – the precipitating factor in her decline, driving her over the edge. Following the stillbirth, Lizzie

> sat for hours in her low chair, her feet inside the fender, her eyes fixed moodily upon the fire. Gabriel watched her, spoke, listened for a word that never came. It was like watching over a corpse. Shivering, he seized his hat and fled for a breath of air to clear his brain. Lizzie brooded on, unconscious. Why had she hoped and suffered if the fruit of her love was only to be the memory of a stillborn child? Sometimes she would sit beside the empty cradle, rocking an imaginary baby, the child that was to have made Gabriel wholly hers. So Georgie and Ned found her one day, startling her to a cry: 'Hush! Do not wake it . . .' Do not wake the spirit child of the blessed damozel.[3]

Trial by Virgins, by David Larg, also published in 1933, likewise offered an imaginative account of Rossetti's emotional life. This too has been consistently dismissed by Pre-Raphaelite scholars as a worthless 'free fantasia' – a judgement merited by the preposterous title alone – but as a work of middlebrow biography it was not significantly worse nor more inventively interpretative than other similar books. Its author was of course American, which may account for its poor reception in Britain.

His was an admittedly incomplete story, subtitled 'Fragment of a Biography', which focused on Rossetti's relations with his father, his sister and his wife, who therefore features fairly fully, and is presented, in the words of a later writer, as 'a kind of tragic villainess, with a cynicism which became bitter and a bitterness which became a torture both to herself and to Rossetti',[4] the now familiar incubus account. Among Larg's originalities, however, were verbatim dialogues between his characters – some at least partly reconstructed from contemporary letters – in the style of a screenplay. There is thus a supposed conversation at Nice between Lizzie and Mrs Kincaid, an otherwise neglected figure in the Pre-Raphaelite soap opera. Lizzie is also given direct speeches to scream at Gabriel during the quarrel over the proposed 'colony of art', when her anger 'burned everything before it like a flame':

'Take your hands off me. Not sure, are you, whether we are engaged or not? Don't know, you do, what my mother will say? Well, listen to what I say. Get out. And keep out. Want to know if we're engaged? Lovely. Well, now you know. We are not. I say we are not. Go and marry your whore at Wapping and tell your mother she can keep her great genius of a son.'[5]

There is a good deal more of this authentic 1930s dialogue, composed with sublime disregard of documentary practice. Like Violet Hunt, David Larg succumbed to the powerful desire to view the Pre-Raphaelite story as costume drama, and handle it with the gusto of fiction rather than the decorum of scholarship.

Elsewhere, using a stream-of-consciousness device, he entered into his characters' minds, giving Elizabeth – his preferred appellation – his own rather coarse authorial views disguised as her own thoughts:

After all, what was the Wapping woman to him or he to her? A convenience to both of them, perhaps, making a spiritual liaison possible where it would not have been possible. She was the ally of Elizabeth. He came back from her with a friendliness that did them both good. There was nothing in common between Elizabeth and the Wapping woman and therefore no subject for hatred. They were as distant and complementary as a lavatory and a drawing-room.[6]

The 'Wapping woman' was of course Fanny Cornforth, following Violet Hunt's fixed but unfounded belief that Fanny lived in this rough dockland quarter of East London. This was symbolic geography intended to distance her from Lizzie, whose own place of origin in Southwark had declined, socially speaking; by the 1930s the Old Kent Road was a poor slum district, yet remained slightly superior to Wapping, with its docks, brothels and criminal gangs. There is no evidence that Fanny ever resided there.

Again, the women were presented in terms of duality. Love and sex were divisible, and both a male birthright; spiritual Elizabeth and carnal Fanny were opposing aspects of femininity. This was a view of female sexuality that long shaped the classification of women in the sexological investigations of the inter-war years, and structured the classic presentation of femininity in fiction and cinema, where female representation was conceived in terms of madonna or whore, angel or slut. In addition, throughout twentieth-century popular culture a standard motif is of women as rivals for a man's affection, yet also allies in the great female cause of fulfilling male needs, spiritual and physical.

It is worth noting briefly here that several stage versions of the legend appeared in the mid–1930s. In 1934 *The Merciless Lady*, with Lizzie as Keats's cold, bewitching Belle Dame, was performed at the Birmingham Repertory Theatre, and the following year a second play written by Megroz and Herbert Duhamel was aborted before production by objections from William Rossetti's grandson. Graham Robertson's response was characteristic. 'I was delighted at the banning of the play,' he wrote 'and hope that all such plays will be squashed henceforth.' He himself had vetted a third script which he now hoped would 'perish automatically', while a friend in the theatre had turned down yet another version. *The Merciless Lady*, Robertson noted, had failed in the provinces and would be heard of no more – 'so that's splendid and a great relief'.[7] The Megroz version, however, was staged at the Arts Theatre where banned plays were privately performed. 'This is what they give as the life story of the greatest man of his century,' reported Robertson:

> All the early part of the play is concerned with his efforts to get the virtuous Miss Siddal to live with him without marriage, which she refuses to do. Then, after five years or so of 'having the affectionate side of him satisfied by Fanny', he is bullied by brother William into marrying Lizzie, who has by now worn herself into a nervous frenzy as well as having developed curvature of the spine – not very convincing reasons for marriage, one would think. He is obviously tired of her and neglects her, so she kills herself, first confiding to Swinburne what she means to do! There follows a period when Gabriel collects every streetwalker he can find to wipe away the memory of the tragedy and Fanny (living very properly with her own husband – I don't gather which one) tries to restrain him and keep the worst of the ladies away – positively Fanny's first appearance as a moralist, I should say.[8]

He added that, at the first night of this farrago, Megroz and Violet Hunt had been seen sharing a taxi.

Another theatrical – or cinematic – version was provided in 1936 by Sacheverell Sitwell, in a long essay in *The Dance of the Quick and the Dead*, which opens like a movie with a view of a man and woman dining at the Sablonniere restaurant in Leicester Square. It is written in the present tense, as a costume drama with gaslamps and horsecabs; through the window, the Victorian figures are animated but unidentified:

> When she speaks, her voice is soft and low so that it hardly carries as far as the next table . . . her companion talks as if to be overheard and has indeed something flaunting about his whole manner . . . yet, for all the physical differences in them, they are alike and the one is the counterpart of the other. Their relationship is that of brother and sister more than that of lovers. But even so, the vital difference of birth divides them. He could be nothing but aristocratic in his origin, while she had the humility of something that has been hidden for a

long time, obscured by poverty and darkened rooms. She has been brought out into the light; and this it is that is killing her.[9]

Eventually, the figures are identified as Swinburne and Miss Siddal and the artistic embellishment of the documentary record is acknowledged. As the reader watches, Rossetti joins the couple and, with a dramatic change of perspective, it is revealed that this is not fictionalized biography after all, but imaginative literary criticism. Sitwell's argument uses the device of a flashback to the Decadent days, when Miss Siddal was a beautiful wraith beloved by Aesthetes, to evoke a long-neglected era; the characters have been re-created to explain literary history. 'We may well watch them carefully,' Sitwell tells the reader, 'for one entire phase of poetry depends on them.' In short, Swinburne's early work was so influenced by his friendship with Elizabeth Siddal that it represents 'in some sense, the product of her personality, or ghost'.[10]

In this curious reversion to the 'pale woman' of the 1890s, she is a lovely shell, echoing just what Swinburne would have her say: the 'whole of the Aesthetic movement emanates out of Miss Siddal's languorous poses'. The Romanticism of Keats is linked to *fin-de-siècle* Symbolism in images from paintings (for which, incidentally, Elizabeth Siddal did not sit):

> images of the mill stream and the weir; of the long grass and blossoming orchard; of the cornfield that was like a sweet honeycomb; of a dovecote full of white doves; of a dove grey crinoline and an upturned face with sad straight hair, looking with closed eyes into a little birdcage that dangled in the sunlight; these images that mean the Pre-Raphaelites owe their creation to the poetry of Swinburne and the personality of Miss Siddal.[11]

The personality of this Miss Siddal – no discourteous familiarity here – is defined in her aesthetic nature, in the long and delicate neck, 'in the heavy lidding of her eyes and in the long folds of her dress'. Everything about her is artificially blanched with illness, and it is her destiny to be cruelly bruised by fate, and carried inexorably towards death.

Finally, however, the narrative returns to the gaslit restaurant, where two prostitutes are shown the door, and thence out into the murky London streets where Miss Siddal and Mr Rossetti – who bear their pre-marital names – travel westwards, oblivious to historical accuracy, towards Chelsea, where Gabriel did not live until widowed. There follows the squalid quarrel from the pages of *Wife of Rossetti*, complete with shrieking on the stairs and suicide note. Lizzie's pet dove – originally created by Violet Hunt out of a conflation of Gabriel's emblem for Lizzie and a bullfinch she had at Chatham Place – dies by the window and is placed reverently in the coffin with the poems. As implausible but compelling as a well-made Hollywood film, this image-packed period piece concludes with the opening of the grave, when 'Rossetti dared not look into the coffin . . . but the book was given into his hands. Her auburn hair had grown across and entwined its mildewed green binding.'

All documentary sources agree that Rossetti was not present at the exhumation, but as Sitwell had already shown, in his deft evocation of atmosphere and manipulation of history, adjustments to literal truth are often required by art, and this was an appropriate ending to a neo-Decadent drama.

Helen Angeli's gibe about the gleanings of PRB waste-paper baskets, primarily directed against Thomas Wise, was an index of the continuing interest in Pre-Raphaelite memorabilia. Anecdotes from the attics of memory still furnished regular additions to the legend. In 1931, for example, Graham Robertson's own reminiscences of life as an artist and man-about-town in the 1880s and '90s contained a conversation with the actress Nellie Farren, famous for her burlesque roles as principal boy. 'I was one day showing her a picture by Rossetti,' Robertson wrote:

> 'Rossetti', she said slowly. 'It's a long time since I heard that name. He used to be a clever sort of man. Did he get on?'
> 'My dear', I explained. 'He got off some time ago. He's been dead for years.'
> 'Rossetti'. Nellie repeated the name thoughtfully. 'I suppose it's the one I mean. A queer fellow, was going to marry a red-haired girl.'
> 'That's it,' said I.
> 'They wanted to adopt me,' said Nellie.
> 'Good gracious,' I gasped.
> 'Yes, that's what Father said,' she continued. 'He thought it an odd way to start married life – especially as they seemed to have no money. Of course he wouldn't give me up, but I often used to go

with him and sit in the painting room. Is the red-haired girl dead too?'[12]

The story cannot be checked, and it is possible that Nellie Farren was mistaken, or that Robertson put words into her mouth in his eagerness to identify her would-be adopters. But it may well be true, and if so offers an isolated glimpse of the couple during the brief years of their marriage – the incident must date from after the wedding – and sheds a pathetic light on the loss of their own child, whom if adopted Nellie was evidently intended to replace.

In the same volume, incidentally, Robertson recalled visiting the Madox Browns' house in Primrose Hill in the late 1880s, where the drawing room was hung with 'small paintings purporting to be by Elizabeth Siddal, and indeed drawn and tinted by a faltering and unskilful hand but quite obviously in all save execution fresh from the brain of her magician husband'.[13]

In 1937 the American collector Janet C. Troxell published her personal collection of correspondence and memorabilia in *Three Rossettis: Unpublished Letters to and from Dante Gabriel, Christina, William*, which contained the brief texts of two surviving letters from Lizzie. Since so few of her own words were preserved, these represented valuable additions to the documentary record, although unfortunately Janet Troxell did not reveal how she had obtained them.

The first note addressed Gabriel as 'my dearest Gug', indicating Lizzie's use of the pet name. Biographers have made much of Gabriel's use of this childish term for his beloved, and less of the fact that it was a reciprocal, mutually affectionate nickname. The letter, in contrast, was mature in tone, expressing sorrow at the death of Joanna Boyce Wells, a fellow artist and friend of the Rossettis who died in childbirth in July 1861. 'All people who are at all happy or useful seem to be taken away,' Lizzie wrote, adding that Mrs Wells' death would be 'a fearful blow to her husband for she must have been the head of the firm [i.e. marriage partnership] and most useful to him.'

Lizzie was writing from Red House in Kent, home of William and Janey Morris, where she was participating in the scheme to decorate walls and furniture with pictures and patterns. 'If you can come down here on Saturday evening, I shall be very glad indeed,' she told Gabriel. 'I want you to do something to the figure I have been trying to paint on the wall. But I fear it must all come out for I am too blind and sick to see what I am about.'[14] This was an ominous reference, although the text hardly supported the image of a bitter, suicidally jealous wife. Nor did the second note, also from Red House, written while Gabriel was in Yorkshire on a portrait commission. This commented on the low price received for a painting and reminded him to put aside or send on the money for some knives. 'I do not wish those people to think I am unable to pay for them,' she explained. Both letters were signed 'from your affectionate Lizzie'.[15]

The matter-of-factness displayed in these prosaic conjugal communications should be set beside other documented evidence from the same date (as in an agitated letter from Gabriel in Yorkshire to his mother) when Lizzie abruptly left Red House and returned alone to Chatham Place. On another occasion she left the Madox Browns' house in similar, unexplained haste. Her behaviour was evidently erratic and worrying: as well as the psychological effects of the stillbirth noted by Georgie, Lizzie was by now heavily addicted to laudanum – an alarming combination of drugs and depression that justified Gabriel's concern.

In 1940, however, circumstantial confirmation of infidelity leading to bitterness was provided by the publication of the material Samuel Bancroft had acquired from the ageing Fanny Cornforth in the 1890s, chiefly consisting of letters from Rossetti, which brought into the public domain for the first time documentary evidence of their affair. Indeed, the very existence of personal letters showed that the relationship was more than professional. Carefully analysed, the material suggested that the affair dated from after Lizzie's death – the first preserved item was a photo of Gabriel inscribed with the words 'To Fanny, D.G.R. 1863', while the first extant letter was dated April 1870. In addition, the date of Fanny's marriage to Timothy Hughes was correctly given as 11 August 1860, and the summary of Bancroft's information from Fanny and her stepson firmly stated that it was following the death of his wife that Fanny 'took charge of Rossetti's housekeeping arrangements' at Cheyne Walk, and became a favoured model.[16]

But a rather different gloss was provided by Bancroft's dating of the first meeting between Fanny and Gabriel as the summer of 1856 when, with Madox Brown and Burne-Jones, he was strolling in the Royal Surrey pleasure gardens looking for subjects and models. Attracted by Fanny's magnificent golden hair, one of the party accidentally gave it a touch so it cascaded down her back; the result was an invitation to Rossetti's studio as a model for the fallen woman in *Found*.[17] The following February came the notorious quarrels, and the clear inference that Lizzie was aware of her rival.

Although so confidently presented in this and other narratives of the period, the tales of Lizzie's jealousy caused by Gabriel's dalliance were not undisputed. Compiling a memoir of her parents, Bessie Parkes's daughter Marie Belloc Lowndes remained convinced that her mother's account of Elizabeth Siddal's life and death was correct. She recalled earlier brushes with Violet Hunt, whose determination to prove that Rossetti had a mistress before the death of his wife and that this was the reason why Lizzie killed herself was, she wrote, 'a complete invention'.[18] She also strenuously challenged the idea of suicide. Bessie had kept in touch with Lizzie all her life, and had indeed played a major part in bringing about the long-delayed wedding. She also went to see Lizzie Rossetti the day before she died, and

> found her far happier than she had been for some time, for she was again expecting a child. The theory, not raised at the time of her death, that she had taken the overdose with any thought of ending her life, was to this old and trusted friend quite untenable.[19]

Mrs Lowndes also claimed that Bessie had found Lizzie making baby clothes, and had afterwards regretted not giving evidence at the inquest, which might have helped to scotch the rumours of suicide and clear Gabriel of suspicion. 'My mother was convinced he had not been unfaithful to Lizzie during her lifetime,' she wrote firmly, 'and she knew him very well.'[20]

These comments were prompted by the publication in 1942 of William Gaunt's *The Pre-Raphaelite Tragedy* (a title immediately altered to 'The Pre-Raphaelite Dream' in deference to wartime sensitivies) which, like its predecessors, offered a 'true story' conceived in highly fictional and dramatic terms. The 'main actors' were Rossetti, Millais, Holman Hunt and Morris, with their artistic iconoclasm and delight in beautiful women. The action took place 'with many shifts of scene' and several concurrent plots, in one of which Rossetti

> falls in love with a beautiful model, discovered by one of the group, and marries her: but she takes a fatal dose of laudanum, as he thinks through his treatment of her, and in remorse he buries his poems in her grave. Later he resurrects them, though this also helps to make him a haunted man . . . [21]

The story was told in abrupt dramatic paragraphs, short scenes of two or three pages in the style of a screenplay, with sudden cuts and dissolves. Much is misty, like historical feature films of the forties, with dramatic heightened close-ups. The very large cast-list deployed deprives Elizabeth Siddal of a central role, however, and she appears as a silent enigma, the essence or emblem of Pre-Raphaelitism. 'A movement of dream must have its dream woman,' wrote Gaunt. 'If Miss Siddal had not existed it would have been necessary to invent her'. She drifts through a sequence of silent visual images:

> beautiful as the reflection of a golden mountain in a crystal lake, said Ruskin . . . 'which is what she is to him' . . . Her complexion was clear, her colour a shade too high . . . She was passive . . . Quietly and still the 'poor wretch' lay in that bath in her embroidered dress . . . Inertly she sat for long hours looking into the fire . . . [22]

The gloomy adjectives multiplied. Lizzie was a melancholy doll whom Rossetti loved because she was so unresponsive, with the prim, narrow poverty of the petit bourgeoisie. She was inscrutable as a sphinx, full of mournful beauty, natural silence, frigid apathy; she was a statue to be warmed into life, and Gabriel was both Pygmalion and Svengali. Together, his genius and passion created in her 'the mysterious agony of Pre-Raphaelite love with its droop and heavy-lidded frustration.'[23] Being thus but half-alive, Lizzie's death was a non-event.

This was in fact a bad case of constructing biography from art, deducing Elizabeth Siddal's personality from the image of *Beata Beatrix*. Gaunt, however, had other conjectures to offer, introducing into the triangle of Rossetti's emotional life not only the

117

'purely physical' Fanny, who represented no real rival to the ethereal Lizzie, but a new Beatrice in the shape of Janey Morris, whom 'oral tradition would have it that Rossetti loved', and whom he met in the autumn of 1857.[24] This inference was supported by the fact that, on her daughter's death in 1938, Jane's letters from Gabriel had been deposited in the British Museum on condition that they be closed to the public for fifty years, which suggested something worth concealing.

Lizzie's death was now due to despair at being supplanted not by a shameless whore but by a spiritual rival. Being herself but a projection of Gabriel's genius, 'fatally agitated by the expansion in the heat of his mind', Lizzie was simply extinguished when he turned elsewhere, surviving only as shadow and ghost, to haunt his imagination.

This view of woman as shadow or mirror, the creation of the artist's light, is a reminder of how in essential respects patriarchal thought still determined the perspective within which the story of Elizabeth Siddal was seen. It might be felt that the conditions and social change of World War II, which saw women of necessity entering masculine domains, would have altered traditional views of gender relations, making this image of Lizzie seem outmoded. But in various cultural fields, of which *The Pre-Raphaelite Tragedy* was but one example, the prevailing definitions of active male and passive female persisted alongside alternative representations. They were in this period particularly popular portrayals in historical fiction and films, as if functioning to identify the abnormality of the present and compensate for its difference from the imagined past. Not for the first time, the feminine image of Elizabeth Siddal carried powerful contemporary meanings that all but obliterated her historical role.

This does not mean that Gaunt himself was personally committed to patriarchal values, and indeed he specifically seems to have returned to the earlier romantic view of Miss Siddal, eschewing the misogynist accounts of hysterical squabbling in favour of a 'dream woman'. But his book belonged to its age, when traditional patterns held nostalgic value. And when the exigencies of war were over, women were withdrawn from the workforce and returned – in ideology at least – to the less active spheres allotted to them in earlier days. Beauty, gentleness and the romance of being a man's inspiration and helpmate were reinstated as feminine ideals.

10

Hysterics on the Hearthrug

The year 1948 saw the centenary of the original PRB, though there was little contemporary admiration for their painting now that neither the heightened realism of the style nor the moral subjects of nineteenth-century art found favour. Among professional painters, Modernism and abstract act were in the ascendant, while with the general public Impressionism retained its popularity. For both groups, 'Victorian' was still an adjective of insult. However, sufficient minority interest, as much for the nostalgic value of Pre-Raphaelitism as for its intrinsic merit, secured the PRB a place as rare plants in the backwaters of culture and centenary commemorations were therefore planned.

The first of these was an exhibition mounted in the summer of 1947 by Birmingham's municipal art gallery, which contained a large collection of Pre-Raphaelite paintings. Its catalogue, constrained in size owing to post-war shortages, contained a succinct summary of the movement, which invoked Elizabeth Siddal as one cause of the dissolution of the PRB and her death as the beginning of Rossetti's later style. But it also contained, in an exhibition of 280 works, three of her drawings and her self-portrait, which represented the first acknowledgement in a long while of her own artistic career. The standard potted history of her life, however, was given in the Notes on Artists:

SIDDAL, Elizabeth Eleanor (1834–1862). Born Sheffield. Sat to Deverell for 'Viola'. He introduced her to Rossetti, whom she married in 1860. She wrote poems and also painted, chiefly in watercolour. Died of an overdose of laudanum.[1]

The following year six watercolours were exhibited at the Whitechapel Art Gallery, mostly lent by Mrs Angeli and the Tate

120

Gallery, and *Clerk Saunders* was also included in an illustrated catalogue of the movement that identified her in familiar terms. 'The discovery of Elizabeth Siddal was perhaps Walter Deverell's most important contribution to the Pre-Raphaelite movement,' it stated. 'For Rossetti, Elizabeth Siddal played the part of Beatrice or the Damsel of the Holy Grail or other frail ideal presence':

> In spite of the impossibility of producing, palpably, the exquisite conditions that would have helped so decisively to purify the flame of his attachment, Rossetti succeeded . . . in casting, so to speak, a perceptible aureole about the object of his adoration.
>
> Under the spell of his attentions, Elizabeth Siddal became the muse of the Brotherhood; her earthly passage, sad and mysterious, was untimely completed, but her inspiration lingered.[2]

Slightly late for the centenary, in 1949 a massive book appeared, of the kind that seems to render further studies unnecessary. This was Oswald Doughty's long-awaited 700-page biography *Dante Gabriel Rossetti: A Victorian Romantic*, issued by Oxford University Press, which it locked into a tight template the legend of Elizabeth Siddal as a Pre-Raphaelite Muse on the one hand and quarrelsome hysteric on the other: appearance and actuality in contradictory tension.

Oswald Doughty's background was academic. Previously he had edited eighteenth-century texts and in the 1940s he was professor at the University of Cape Town in South Africa where he was known as a Rossetti enthusiast; his house was named after Kelmscott Manor. As a scholar of English literature he based his interpretation of Rossetti's life on the poems and prose writings, so neglecting pictorial art that the uninformed reader might not realize that painting formed Rossetti's main career. Whatever the limitations of the approach, however, the substantial quality of his work was undeniable: all available source material was collected, sifted, sorted and collated into a magisterial account. Moreover, as William Rossetti's editions and memoirs were now out of print, *A Victorian Romantic* provided a useful and definitive account of a figure who still occupied a prominent if isolated position in nineteenth-century studies. Finally, despite Doughty's self-confessed predilection for purplish flights of fancy writing – witness a particularly lurid final page – he kept his imagination on a strict rein, and his biography lacked only the detailed footnotes necessary to a work of enduring scholarship. Gaining also from the reputation of the OUP, *A Victorian Romantic* therefore became the standard reference book and main source book through the 1950s and '60s, being reissued in 1960, with some additional material, and again in 1963 – by which date it was complemented and in time superseded by the four-volume Oxford edition of Rossetti's *Letters*, an enterprise begun by Doughty himself.

Doughty's presentation of Elizabeth Siddal thus shaped her story for over two decades. It was essentially unsympathetic, and its judgements were harsh. Introduced as a proud, shy, slightly bewildered girl, she was said to have the 'ill-bred sarcasm of a shop-girl', whose beauty and vulnerability allowed Gabriel the pleasure of having her around, like a pet. Under his guidance she began to paint and 'turning poetess also, to write plaintive little love-sick verses, all pathos and self-pity'.[3]

In the early years of their supposed engagement – about which Doughty was rightly sceptical – Lizzie and Gabriel 'passed quiet days and evenings in Chatham Place working at their painting and poetry' – an image of seclusion that coincides with Rossetti's drawings of Lizzie reading, sketching or sewing, and one Doughty claimed to find in Gabriel's sonnets. From the start, however, the relationship was one of 'vicissitudes, stress and strain, quarrels and reconciliations, emotional ambivalences'. Their love

> had its phases, moved like the sea to the ebb and flow of tides, was chequered with storm and sunshine. To this rhythm their lives would be patterned for the next ten years, until the end. That he passionately desired Lizzie is evident. That he wished to marry her is less clear, engagement or no engagement. That Lizzie demanded marriage as the price of possession is easily divined.[4]

This diagnosis of the root trouble was of course inherited from the pre-war period – *A Victorian Romantic* had been many years in the making – with its idea of a sex-war struggle over marriage, and a ring as the price Gabriel was unwilling to pay for his beloved's virginity. But it also accorded with what was increasingly revealed as Doughty's sneering perception of Lizzie as an ambitious shop-girl – a twentieth-century occupation – intent on a better life. Asserting that the traditional legend of Lizzie as the patient, dying, gentle dove had been falsely constructed by Gabriel to exploit Ruskin's financial subsidy (which may well have been at least partly true), Doughty saw her as scheming, overwrought, ill-educated and ungracious. She was 'obstinate, primitive, stupid' in not wishing to consult Dr Acland, forcing Ruskin to 'exquisitely chivalrous epistles' which only revealed her own want of manners.

Lack of breeding was the keynote. Doughty noted Acland's view that her painting of a mountain churchyard for *We are Seven* showed remarkable imagination for one brought up 'within a street or two of the Elephant and Castle' – a district now synonymous with the worst housing in London. The surviving fragment of the letter from Nice about her encounter with the passport official was 'a lamentable exhibition of insular and ill-bred wit'. When Ruskin visited Chatham Place, he found the Browns 'always' there, with Lizzie and Emma sluttishly 'in bed or half-dressed'.[5]

Then, in a chapter simply entitled 'Strife', 'the once gentle dove turned bitter, even violent towards her lover, and quarrels between them became common'. No longer shy and submissive, she was 'poor neurotic Lizzie with her copious self-pity and love of mournful self-dramatization'. Vulgar squabbles were frequent. When, in 1856, Gabriel was discovered dining and dancing with pretty Annie Miller, 'hitherto unsuspected combative qualities' were revealed in Lizzie, who attacked Gabriel with 'noisy and violent demonstrations of disapproval deeply tinted with the local colour of her native Kennington Oval'. Amid the stress of battle the civilized manners she had acquired from the Pre-Raphaelite circle 'unconsciously gave place to the more primitive culture of the Old Kent Road'. These quarrels, in which Lizzie was aided and abetted by Emma Brown, regularly culminated in angry scenes when 'Lizzie would shriek and roll on the carpet' in the throes of hysterical rage.[6]

The careless geography of south London was a matter of class prejudice rather than place, just as Doughty's lurid imagination was coloured by snobbery as much as misogyny; in his view, Lizzie's social and educational inferiority was the chief cause of

123

discord. Once the early romance was over, Lizzie was a disastrous partner for Gabriel.

The class judgement was explicit. To earlier writers like Fred Stephens, Rossetti's love for a lowly milliner was evidence of his chivalry. To Evelyn Waugh, the prim gentility of her shopkeeping origins was the chief reason for her frigidity. Now the slums of Southwark – earmarked for clearance in the era of post-war reconstruction – were invoked to account for Lizzie's quarrelsomeness and stubborn lack of gratitude, while Rossetti's mistaken loyalty to his once-dear dove vindicated his honour as a gentleman.

The introduction of Annie Miller's name here requires some explanation. Rather like Fanny, Annie Miller had previously enjoyed a subterranean existence in the Pre-Raphaelite story, of which whispers occasionally reached the surface. Doughty had been listening for a long time, and pieced together his account from the scraps of information available. Portraits and subject pictures from Rossetti's *oeuvre* showed that Annie had been his model during the 1860s, for paintings such as *Helen of Troy*. In 1937 a careful ink drawing inscribed 'Annie Miller 1860, Aetat XXI, DGR' had been sold at Christie's, while in 1940 a fine watercolour entitled *Woman in Yellow*, taken from Annie, was acquired by the Tate Gallery. Two other portraits were bought by Janet Troxell around the same time from Annie's daughter Miss Thompson. She was also mentioned by name in the diary of George Boyce, published in edited form in 1941. Long before, William Rossetti had suggested, without naming her, that she had been the cause of a quarrel between his brother and Holman Hunt, and she had featured as an additional rival to Lizzie in *Wife of Rossetti*, where Violet Hunt hinted darkly that her full story would never be told.

Annie Miller had in fact been Holman Hunt's model for *The Awakening Conscience*, and the object of his personal attentions. 'There was the making of an intelligent woman in her,' related a friend on hearing the tale from Hunt, 'and he arranged to have her educated, possibly with a view to marrying her. But Rossetti, whose principles were exceedingly lax, beguiled the girl away from him.'[7] This had been the basis for William Rossetti's cautious account in which he stated that Gabriel had been technically but not gravely at fault for employing Annie as a model.[8] It was also the explanation for Lizzie's objections to 'living where "G" was' in the artists' commune: the initial stood for Hunt at a time when Annie was his intended bride. In a section of Madox Brown's diary omitted from the version published by William Rossetti, Lizzie's fury at Gabriel's inconstancy in 1856 had centred on an occasion when Rossetti and Boyce escorted Annie to Cremorne. Emma called on Lizzie in Weymouth Street and found her complaining about Gabriel's behaviour. 'He seems to have transferred his affections to Annie Miller and does nothing but talk of her to Miss Sid,' wrote Brown in exasperation. 'He is mad past care.'[9]

On her return from Nice, Lizzie had indeed found Gabriel seeking and praising other models, among them both Annie and the actress Ruth Herbert. His affections had in fact strayed, although there is no evidence of anything other than flirtation. As Doughty concluded, Annie Miller was never a serious rival for Gabriel's love, but she joined Fanny in the list.

In *A Victorian Romantic*, Doughty was the first writer publicly to identify Fanny as a prostitute, 'vulgar, vital, primitive', with greater physical attractions than the 'fading, neglected Lizzie', and to insist that Rossetti had had an undoubtedly adulterous affair with Janey Morris. Abruptly, however, at the opening of a chapter headed 'The Woeful Victory' (after the title of Lizzie's last picture) in 1860 Gabriel and Lizzie were 'married at last!' to Doughty's evident amazement. But the once-beautiful girl of seventeen was now a broken and embittered invalid of twenty-seven, and the marriage was dismal:

> Of Lizzie's feelings now that the long fight for legal possession of Gabriel was over we have no sign . . . in the moment of victory she remains obscure, enigmatic as ever . . . still prey to the strange nervous malady due to baffled desire for marriage and knowledge that only through illness could she obtain her end, by playing on Gabriel's anxiety and remorse.[10]

'The questions about Lizzie are many and unanswered,' Doughty concluded. The notion of Woman as essentially mysterious and unknowable was a commonplace of the gender ideology his book rehearsed. In his own life, Doughty preferred young men.

After marriage, moreover, 'Lizzie's housekeeping was more original than efficient' – a judgement taken from Bell Scott's slighting reference and William Rossetti's admission that his sister-in-law had 'very little of a housewifely turn'. This was, as with everything else, partly true: the couple occupied a service apartment in Chatham Place rather than running their own house with its usual middle-class complement of servants, and were accustomed to dine out at a time when this was largely a masculine habit. In moral terms, however, the judgement coincided with the post-1945 impulse to promote the domestication of women now that wartime conditions no longer required working wives, state-run nurseries or public restaurants. This period saw 'good housekeeping', with its attendant emphasis on cooking, cleanliness and consumer comforts, redefined as the desirable role for married women; with the marketing of modern household equipment, this heralded the image of happy wifehood in the 1950s.

According to this figuration, Elizabeth Siddal was not a good wife. Not only did she ignore her domestic duties, but a 'natural morbidity deepened into definite hysteria', and her disinclination kept Gabriel from seeing friends, so that 'his home seemed but a hospital and a prison'. Scrupulously, Doughty cited the contrary evidence, from Bessie Parkes, Elizabeth Gaskell, Georgie Burne-Jones and, above all, Swinburne, only to demolish it by citing a wild suggestion contained in the latest volume of reminiscences by Ford Madox Ford (né Hueffer) published in 1938, to the effect that Swinburne and Lizzie had planned to elope.[11] On this flimsy foundation Doughty built 'a secret adolescent passion' in Swinburne, who idolized Lizzie with calf-love.

Her death was predictable, clearly foreshadowed in her morbid verses,

full of her own sad and sentimental and self-consciously pathetic broodings . . . the expression of a tense, overstrained spirit . . . brightened only by some glimmering hope of a life beyond the grave . . . To the hereafter poor Lizzie had forwarded her soul's sentimental desires – a kind of spiritual luggage in advance; but ominous perhaps too!

On the issue of intentional or accidental death, Doughty took no partisan position, claiming that this very uncertainty was the 'intolerable ghost' that haunted the rest of Gabriel's life: 'doubt as to the unanswerable question of accident or suicide was the direct cause of Rossetti's subsequent neurosis and decline'.[12] Yet Oscar Wilde – not the most reliable informant – was quoted as the source of a rumour that Gabriel, angered on the fateful evening by his wife's demands for laudanum, had thrust the phial into her hand before leaving with the words 'There! Take the lot!'[13] Suicide was therefore strongly suspected. Indeed, Lizzie's valedictory verses 'Light and night are falling from me' were found near her body, and there was a message pinned to her nightgown, 'asking Gabriel to care for her weak-minded brother'.[14]

This, as it transpired, was not the invention it seemed, but came directly from Helen Angeli, whose own account of her uncle's life was issued in the same year and contained the newest of the 'true revelations', with the added weight of family tradition behind them.

Angeli described Lizzie as 'a girl of humble estate but great beauty, talent and refinement', who throughout her long engagement was 'a very sick woman, neurotic and inclined to melancholia, often seriously ill, with a tuberculous tendency'.[15] Her close friend Emma Brown was 'not always the wisest of counsellors', and encouraged her complaints about Gabriel. Elizabeth was intelligent and responsive but also 'shy and proud' and 'evasive in company'. Gabriel's unbounded but unwarranted faith in her genius was a heavy drain on her strength. Contrary to unkind accounts, his affection was patient and unwavering. For years, the couple 'worked and lived together at all hours of the day and night', in a romantic but platonic relationship, 'without a breath of scandal'. There was, according to Helen Angeli, defending her father's words in the *Burlington Magazine* nearly half a century before, no evidence of impropriety, nothing to indicate that Gabriel desired and was refused sex. As she correctly pointed out, long engagements were approved by 'the Victorians' and Gabriel had no quarrel with Lizzie in this regard. However (in a footnote) she was undoubtedly 'hysterical and unreasonable at times', and the scenes alleged to have taken place on the Madox Browns' hearthrug had some basis in fact. Helen Angeli's mother Lucy Madox Brown – in her teens during Lizzie's last years – 'did certainly once witness some scene of this kind (though I am not sure that a hearthrug was involved). Afterwards, 'it was made abundantly clear to her that Gabriel was not to blame'.[16]

In this book, Helen Angeli's main aim was to defend her uncle Gabriel from his critics – among whom she numbered most of his recent biographers – and in particular against the persistent inference that he had caused his wife's death through infidelity and indifference. In pursuit of this objective, she dated his sexual relationship with Fanny Cornforth to the years after Lizzie's death and emphasized his tender care for Lizzie. Much space was devoted to refuting the wild claim – from Violet Hunt out of Emily Tebbs – that Lizzie had accused Gabriel of killing her unborn child by his callous behaviour, and a ridiculous rumour emanating from Swinburne that Rossetti was in the habit of 'procuring abortions'.

Elizabeth's death was another matter. On the key question of suicide, Helen Angeli was ready, now that nearly a century had elapsed, to disclose 'the real circumstances of the tragedy', as told by Madox Brown to his daughter Lucy, and by Lucy to Helen's sister Olivia. The truth was that when Gabriel found his wife unconscious he took from her nightgown 'a briefly scribbled message with words to this effect: "Take care of Harry." Later the same night, Gabriel showed the note to Madox Brown, who immediately destroyed it.'[17]

The content of this note – Harry Siddall was Elizabeth's youngest brother – was felt to refute any notion that Lizzie's death was due to her husband's cruelty. Its claim to authenticity was supported by the disclosure that for many years payments were made to the surviving Siddall brothers James and Harry. But such private charity was as common as lengthy engagements in the Victorian age, hardly requiring death-bed instructions; had Lizzie died a natural death, the Rossettis would still have felt an obligation to assist her needy relatives. And it was irrelevant as supporting evidence, for now the family had given the 'official' account of the death-bed message, it was clear that Elizabeth Siddal had intended to die; she would hardly have left a note, whatever its import, if she had expected to wake next morning as usual. Hitherto, as in Helen Angeli's own earlier attack on *Wife of Rossetti*, the popular but unofficial verdict of suicide had been denied by the family; now it was admitted.

Helen Angeli did not evade this inference. She explained instead that Lizzie's death was inevitable, given her neurotic personality and morbid brooding; she was prone to 'sterile musing and melancholy, obsessed with the idea of death. She nurtured sorrow like a nurseling vampire at her breast,'[18] and her self-inflicted death, with her opiate phial always to hand, could hardly have been prevented. Gabriel had indeed done his utmost to save his poor, sick, deranged wife. Once again, the blame was shifted.

Five years later Helen Angeli went even further, stating in another book that those who had known Lizzie best 'knew who had been the real martyr of that foredoomed marriage. To Gabriel alone . . . did poor Lizzie's death appear an irretrievable disaster.' Helen's mother Lucy Brown heard and understood the comment of a friend who 'exclaimed aloud what others dared not whisper: "Thank God for Gabriel!" ' when he heard the news.[19]

Like other versions, this configuration of events – that Lizzie's death was not only inevitable but welcome – is by no means implausible. From his letters around the time of their marriage, it is clear that Gabriel did not expect his wife to live and in the context of drug addiction and a stillborn child his expressed anxiety for her health probably masked apprehensions as to her mental balance – as when Ned and Georgie Burne-Jones watched her rock the empty cradle – which perhaps became prophetic.

However, these modern versions of the myth proffered by Oswald Doughty and Helen Angeli, in which Elizabeth Siddal appears as a sick, neurotic, depressive, suicidal figure, happen also to coincide with the diffusion of psychological theories of neuroses and personality disorders propounding the view that women – who formed the majority of mental patients – were more naturally subject to hysterical behaviour, and that this was caused by deep-seated maladjustment to the correct forms of female identity. Through the 1940s and '50s, the term 'neurotic', first used in the 1880s for 'sensitive, zealous, managing women', was popularly applied to any woman who proved 'difficult' or unreasonable. To call a man neurotic, by the same token, was to imply a lack of appropriate masculinity. Although appearing scientific, the term was thus closely linked to definitions of gender. And one particular personality disorder, identified as a form of the fashionable idea of inferiority complex, claiming to explain how feelings of inadequacy lead to an intense struggle for self-assertion, 'which if unsuccessful, can develop into compensatory neurosis and retreat into illness as a means of obtaining prominence',[20] fits the contemporary accounts of Elizabeth Siddal's neurotic behaviour so neatly that one wonders whether the biographers were acquainted with psychoanalytic ideas, or whether they were merely echoing contemporary commonplaces. In any case, this image of a nagging, neurotic, hysterical Lizzie is matched in this period by other cultural representations in fiction and film of unhappy women locked into situations they can neither resolve nor escape except by suicide.

And the myth of radical incompatibility between Gabriel and Lizzie was current not only in middlebrow biographies but also in the high intellectual world of literary criticism. Graham Hough's study of Victorian poetics *The Last Romantics*, published in 1949, placed Rossetti's work in the context of nineteenth-century 'romantic sentimentalism'. Combined with a negative code of sexual ethics, this produced the 'ideal love' of his verse, awkwardly unable to reconcile the demands of the senses and those of the soul. To this, unashamedly mixing critical analysis with personal history, Hough related the catastrophe of Rossetti's marriage in terms of the impossibility of combining sexual and sentimental feeling, resulting in 'the mere romantic confusion of Rossetti's poetry'. It was then a simple matter to trace how Lizzie had 'failed to satisfy his senses', causing the final tragedy. So ingrained by this date was the tale of Gabriel's unfaithfulness and neglect that Hough had no hesitation in relating the sonnets of *The House of Life* (mostly in fact written during the relationship with Janey Morris) to the unhappy story of his failed marriage. The weaknesses in Rossetti's now despised and virtually unread poetry, were ascribed to his having remained shackled to a woman he had ceased to love, rather than turning robustly to a new mistress and muse as befitted a bohemian artist.[21]

Disentangled from its literary context, this analysis rehearses prevailing views on the advisability of ending flawed relationships. It is not surprising to learn that divorce reform was again under discussion.

11

Sixties Swinger

With the emergence in the 1960s of what is popularly known as
the permissive age, tolerance of sexual freedom for artists was
extended to include sexual freedom for all, and the silent justification of Rossetti's bohemian behaviour was more frankly
acknowledged. At the same time, the image of Elizabeth Siddal
as that of neurotic, bitter but clinging femininity was gradually
abandoned in favour of a new personality in keeping with changing ideas. Put briefly, in the 1960s Elizabeth Siddal lost her virginity. Marriage – rejected in this decade along with other social
conventions – ceased to be the price Rossetti paid for possession.

Once again, this altered perspective was based more on contemporary attitudes than new historical information. The new versions were constructed from existing source materials, however, and in many ways, of course, the sources supported a
'permissive' view, for the Pre-Raphaelite circle can legitimately
be seen as the counter-culture of its time: iconoclastic, unconventional, progressive, and self-confident in its artistic and social
affairs, rejecting or challenging the bourgeois lifestyle of the Victorian age. Although the truth was never so simple, the Pre-
Raphaelite world may to some degree be regarded as a forerunner
of the 'alternative society'.

The transition was not abrupt, for the older views persisted
through to the 1970s, while the newer characters were in the
process of creation from the early 1950s. Thus, to Rosalie Glynn
Grylls in *Portrait of Rossetti* (1964) Elizabeth Siddal was aloof,
chaste and sexually cold, and deliberately delayed marriage to
Rossetti in order to retain 'the virginity that tantalized him'. She
was quiet and withdrawn, yet also 'perky and flippant', given to
facetious retorts and a morbid preoccupation with death. She
grew hysterical, and her tantrums were encouraged by Emma

Brown – who now became an equal scapegoat. Emma's problem with alcohol (hitherto a family secret) was revealed, and the two women formed a delinquent pair, their quarrelsomeness exacerbated by drink and drugs. Once married, Lizzie was feckless and slatternly, resentfully suspicious of her husband's dalliance. But 'how gladly would Gabriel have come back to her as a wife if she had been ready . . . to forgive and forget – and to cook'.[1]

To Virginia Surtees in the 1970s, Elizabeth Siddal was still 'sickly and neurotic and of a morbid temperament'[2] and a 'talented, listless creature'[3] while to the editor of *Apollo* magazine in 1973, at the time of a new exhibition of Rossetti's work at the Royal Academy:

> Lizzie is a pathetic figure. She was beautiful, even though the drawings do depict a rather wishy-washy personality . . . What a strain it must have been to hold her own in his circle! . . . It was in keeping with the doomed nature of Lizzie's life that she produced a stillborn child . . . [for] Rossetti was a sensual man and Lizzie, it may be suspected, was frigid: she answered his dreams but not his needs.[4]

By this date, however, this miserable figure, alternately pathetic and sarcastic, bitter and sickly, had been superseded by a character who can best be described as a Pre-Raphaelite groupie, a child of the pop culture, with a streetwise innocence in keeping with her working-class origins.

This character first began to emerge in a sequence of texts that reflect the growing interest in Elizabeth Siddal as a figure in her own right rather than a vacuous if beautiful accessory to the PRB. With certain important exceptions – *Wife of Rossetti* and William Rossetti's *Burlington Magazine* article – virtually all the works in which she is discussed present her as a subsidiary personality. But she has always had her own following of 'Siddalites', whose chief interest in the Pre-Raphaelite drama is the elusive but fascinating young woman buried in Highgate Cemetery. Many of these followers have been women, whose own consciousness perhaps makes them more curious about the experience of a female model, muse, poetic mistress and artist's wife, as well as more willing to consider her own work in painting and poetry as a form of self-expression rather than a pale copy of her spouse's.

Thus, in a brief essay written in the early 1940s on Rossetti and the use of mystical images of truth in pictorial art, Nicolette Gray invoked 'the rare paintings of Miss Siddal' such as *Clerk Saunders* or the *Quest of the Grael*, together with a quotation from her poem 'Dim phantoms of an unknown ill' as expressive of 'an unknown world, the knight in his cockle-shell on the waters surrounded by walls and symbols and figures of unknown import, the consciousness alone with its unknown images and afraid'. More specifically, the self is 'aware of the images as a sense of reality . . . to retain which it must be kept detached from abstract ideas'. This strand Gray identified as belonging to the Romantic tradition that pointed forward from Rossetti and Siddal through Beardsley and Sturge Moore to the Surrealists.[5]

Ida Procter quoted the same verses in 1950 in another essay, devoted to 'Elizabeth Siddal: the Ghost of an Idea', and published in the *Cornhill Magazine*, citing also Lizzie's request from Brighton for her paintbox: 'although I am in constant pain and cannot sleep at nights . . . I should like to have my watercolours sent down if possible, as I am quite destitute of all means of keeping myself alive' as evidence of 'her desire to bear witness to the world'. Self-expression was her 'desperate and valiant struggle for existence in the daylight. She knew it was her inner life's blood.'[6] Explicitly comparing Elizabeth Siddal with Emily Brontë, Procter emphasized her artistic commitment:

> There was still the vision, the ideal, the artistic life to be lived: pictures must be made and poems written; and even if all were full of pathos, yearning, pain and morbidity, it could be accompanied by a certain luscious medieval flamboyance of colour. The situation was anxious but not hopeless. And paint she must.[7]

The *Cornhill*'s illustrations included *Lady Clare* and the medieval scene entitled *Lady Affixing Pennant to Knight's Spear*, and this new attention to Siddal's work was no doubt prompted by her representation in the Birmingham and Whitechapel exhibitions. Quoting judiciously and sympathetically, Ida Procter produced a model essay, clearing a modest but well-defined space for her subject in the landscape of Pre-Raphaelitism, concluding:

> And what can be said of the achievements of Elizabeth Siddal? Not more than a dozen poems and probably less than twenty pictures: and

a dead child. A woeful victory indeed when weighed in the balance of material values. But she has left us, like the moulded glove of a departed visitor discarded upon the hall table, the delicate skin of her personality, the legend of her charm and courage, the bloom of a strange lustre which was never destroyed by despair or poverty or ill-health.[8]

Within this changing perspective, Elizabeth Siddal also became a fictional heroine, by which is meant not the dramatically re-created figure in the biographies already cited, fictionalized though they be, but the chief character in a number of novels.

In the early days of its history, the Pre-Raphaelite circle had considerable appeal to novelists, the first known example being Averil Beaumont's *Magdalen Wynyard, or The Provocations of a Pre-Raphaelite* (1872), although, despite its intriguing title, this turned out to contain little about art; its conventional three-decker plot involves aristocratic snobbery, obstacles to true love, long-lost brothers and sensational death. *Miss Brown* (1884) by Vernon Lee (the pen name of Violet Paget) was more authentic, containing characters recognizably based on Millais, Rossetti, Swinburne and Jane Morris, who is the indirect inspiration for the heroine Miss Brown, a dark beauty plucked from obscurity as a servant and educated to be an artist's wife. Theodore Watts-Dunton's *Aylwin* (1898) was also partly a *roman à clef*, with the motif of a lost beloved and model, believed dead, miraculously restored to her lover.

In *Wife of Rossetti* Violet Hunt essentially rewrote Elizabeth Siddal's story in novel form, despite her biographical intentions. And the poet HD – who knew Ford Hueffer and Violet Hunt in London before World War I – used the same material for her unpublished prose work of 1948, *The White Rose and the Red*, part historical novel, part imaginative fantasy.[9] Indeed, Elizabeth Siddal's story lent itself to fiction, so many of the historical facts being uncertain, contradictory or obscure, and her personality so apparently elusive. Her role as model and muse, dying young as if symbolically destroyed by her own beauty, has made her an attractive subject for women writers, who are enabled through fiction to explore more aspects of her story than is possible in the factual form of biography. In addition, for diffident writers, fic-

134

tion has the advantage of being less authoritative and therefore less vulnerable to critical challenge on the grounds of accuracy, and it would seem that in some instances women writers have chosen to present Elizabeth Siddal's tale in novel form rather than attempt a more scholarly work. Despite the freedom of fiction, most have stuck surprisingly closely to the source material, clearly aiming at a 'true representation'.

One example is Nerina Shute's slight but inventive *Victorian Love Story* of 1954, in which the author 'set herself the task of writing stories which are true in the form of novels rather than biographies; her books are about real people but they are interpretative books'. This frank avowal makes a refreshing change from fiction in the form of biography; the interpretative licence taken by several respected biographers suggests that Shute need hardly have been so apologetic. Fiction, however, allows unashamed use of the dramatic dialogues denied to scholarly works, and the heroine of *Victorian Love Story* is Miss Sid, a sharp London girl with characteristic Cockney 'faults of speech' and a bright, ignorant boldness. She has never heard of Ophelia, and is pert enough to kiss young Johnny Millais on the cheek, a liberty never ascribed to the sad and sickly heroine of previous books. She and Emma discuss strategies for manoeuvring Gabriel into marriage, which eventually succeed – largely because Miss Sid sticks like glue to the circle she has entered. She observes with acute eye and unillusioned tongue, and likes Swinburne because he makes her laugh. 'It is ever so restful when a person stops being romantic,' she explains. 'It is like taking off your corset.' Later, she and Jane Morris discuss culture:

'If you and I were educated,' said Jane, 'do you think they would like us as much as they do now?'
'Of course not. Men like women to be beautiful and ignorant,' said Lizzie wisely.
'That's what I think,' said Jane.
'Half the time no one can understand what they are talking about,' said Lizzie. 'You should hear Gabriel when he talks about Rousseau.'
'You should hear Morris,' replied Jane.
'But if we did understand they might not like it,' said Lizzie.
Both women laughed, as though something very funny had been said.[10]

A similarly daffy personality, anticipating the 'dolly bird' of the 1960s, is presented in Paula Batchelor's novel, *Angel with Bright Hair* (1957), but appears most strikingly of all in the character of Elizabeth Siddal as a bright lower-class girl in Ken Russell's film biography *Dante's Inferno: The Private Life of Dante Gabriel Rossetti* (1969). Opposite a solid but smouldering Oliver Reed, Judith Paris played a Cockney Elizabeth Siddal as a wide-eyed but knowing Sixties Swinger, like Twiggy in crinoline and shawl, larking with Gabriel by a stream or concealed behind canvases in the studio when frosty Christina calls. She is flippant and chaffy (to use William Rossetti's word), with a sharp London voice, egalitarian in her approach, with an unrefined readiness to shriek and scrap. On her return from France she unceremoniously ejects Fanny from the studio.[11]

She is seen mending Gabriel's shirt in their untidy apartment; when he rhapsodizes on her hair – a golden veil around his heart – she stabs him ineffectually with her needle. 'I cherish you and you attack me!' he shouts. 'You should be soft.' But this girl is no meek dove: she reacts fiercely to Ruskin's gift of medicinal ivory dust: 'What does the stupid fool think I am – a sick elephant?' and says Ida is a 'stupid name'. And then, penitently, in the manner of the true groupie, she confesses that she only wants to paint in order to please Gabriel. A central image, repeated at intervals through the film, is the ghoulish shape of Lizzie's skeletal corpse rising from its coffin to haunt her husband – a Gothick motif borrowed from the contemporary horror-movie genre.

Rather surprisingly, in view of the 'drug culture' of the 1960s, Lizzie's opium-addiction is not stressed, despite its evident affinity with ideas of psychedelic mind-expansion. Such elements, including also a dramatic cut where Lizzie is seen in bed with a partner who turns out to be Emma Brown when the viewer has already imagined Gabriel, were probably precluded by the fact that the film was commissioned for television by the BBC. Nevertheless, in the chaotic unchaperoned atmosphere of the shared studio apartment, the sex-and-drugs era is an underlying, submerged motif. Russell was criticized for his melodramatic licence but (apart from the recurrent rising coffin, intended as a symbol of Gabriel's remorse) all the incidents are based on material in the Pre-Raphaelite literature; the film-maker was only a little more inventive than the biographers.

A decade later, the BBC produced a quieter dramatization of the Pre-Raphaelite myth, in the six-part series *The Love School* in which Ben Kingsley played Rossetti. Both works are a testament to the enduring power of the legend, and the fascination it exerts over each generation.

Dante's Inferno and *The Love School* were also signs of reviving interest in the Pre-Raphaelite age. After many years of neglect, the 1960s and '70s saw new exhibitions devoted to the major figures: Madox Brown in 1964, Millais in 1967, Holman Hunt in 1969, Rossetti in 1973 and Burne-Jones in 1975. The four-volume edition of Rossetti's *Letters* began appearing in 1965, alongside a comprehensive survey of the literature in *Pre-Raphaelitism: A Bibliocritical Study* by W. E. Fredeman (1965), which was followed by a full *catalogue raisonné* of Rossetti's work by Virginia Surtees in 1971. These works, soon accompanied by editions of the diaries of Ford Madox Brown and George Price Boyce, together with other scholarly studies of Victorian life and art, and the new availability of manuscript correspondence (Rossetti's letters to Jane Morris were opened to public inspection in 1964), greatly facilitated clearer assessment of the original source material on which, over the years, a vast pile of interpretation had been heaped.

The links between the revival of interest in Pre-Raphaelitism and the emerging hippie movement, which 'owed much of its imagery, manner, dress and personal appearance to the Pre-Raphaelite ideal' were remarked at the time. At a Pre-Raphaelite show at the Maas Gallery in London in 1970, members of the younger generation were seen to 'resemble the figures in the pictures they had come to see', as one critic noted:

> The young have discovered premonitions of the psychedelic experience in Pre-Raphaelite colour, and associate the introverted beauty of the feminine images with pure sexuality. Frederick Sandys's profile study of a girl sucking pensively at a sprig of blossom . . . deserves to be seen as a first-rate PR job for the Flower People.[12]

The mood of the flower-power age, with its promotion of long-haired loose-gowned sexually permissive femininity, self-indulgence and drug-taking certainly appeared to echo that of the Pre-Raphaelite era – not forgetting, too, the hippie passion for archaic, imaginary worlds such as that created in Tolkien's *Lord of the Rings*, itself partly derived from the late romances of William Morris. At the same time, academic art history was beginning to turn seriously to the study of nineteenth-century painting, which after generations of neglect and abuse was once again the subject of scholarly inquiry. The two impulses came together in a number of illustrated books on the PRB and their associates, of which Timothy Hilton's *The Pre-Raphaelites* (1970) for the World of Art Library is still a standard text. Here, Elizabeth Siddal is presented as Rossetti's beautiful beloved doll:

> In time, he came to take possession of her. He guarded her jealously and handled her preciously. He allowed her to model only for his closest friends. He never introduced her to people and least of all did he introduce her to his parents. In 1852 he moved out of his family home to live in Chatham Place near Blackfriars Bridge. There was a party a week after he moved in, but after that visitors were few and discouraged. Rossetti and Lizzy, alone, lived together, slept together and created together, for Rossetti taught her to draw and encouraged her enthusiasm for writing verse.
>
> This enclosed world of love, this *egoisme à deux*, this self-protective eccentricity, is expressed in many of the pictures of these Chatham Place years . . . There is the often-repeated motif of the touch, the caress, the encircling arm, the embrace; and then, beyond sight, the kiss, their eyes closed. The reciprocity of the artist-model relationship is now that between lover and beloved . . .[13]

In these pages, Elizabeth Siddal gazes into a canvas as if into a mirror, and she the legendary Lady of Shalott. It is a dream world of fantasy, evocative of 'Love and Peace', the slogan of the age. The less happy aspects of her tale are curtailed – this is not biography but art history – in favour of extensive treatment of Rossetti's 'best' picture, *Beata Beatrix*, 'nominally a painting about Dante's Beatrice but actually a picture about Lizzy', which is infused with erotic feeling, so that 'she looks as if she is in ecstasy; and as in Bernini's *St Theresa* it looks as much a sexual as a religious ecstasy (Rossetti used a give-away word when describing this picture, saying that she is 'rapt from earth to heaven'.)[14]

The character of Elizabeth Siddal as created by Russell and

Hilton, unlike her predecessors, does not guard her virginity – what 1960s heroine did that? And their treatments fill her story with sexual imagery, admittedly with some degree of ironic extravagance, in keeping with the tale's excesses. This Lizzie is sexually willing, although not equal; like certain archetypes from the world of popular culture she is erotically doomed to death, shining luminously in the reflected light of the famous figures in whose orbit she moves while heading for drug-induced self-destruction. Her own small talent – still defined as a pale imitation of her lover's – is not proof against the fire of Pre-Raphaelite intensity. The contemporary world is close, and one is reminded of the sad case of the singer Marianne Faithfull, her career all but destroyed for a time by drink and drugs, as well as, more poignantly, that of Marilyn Monroe, a cult heroine similarly defined and destroyed by beauty and vulnerability. Like that of Elizabeth Siddal, Monroe's death remains a tragic mystery and the life stories of both women have been similarly told and retold, as emblems of their age.

The return of Elizabeth Siddal as an icon for the sixties, when rebellious youth defied the timidity and social order of the adult world, was thus appropriate to a culture whose leading figures, rising from the working class, risked or found death through both drugs and wanton self-display. Although this does not accord with what is known of the 'real' Elizabeth Siddal, her romantic story as a milliner's assistant in Cranbourne Alley transformed into the image of the Pre-Raphaelite age chimed with the promotion of pop stars and fashion models discovered in hairdressing salons or Carnaby Street boutiques. Her supposed flirtation with death in a world of art, sex and opium, from the drowned Ophelia to the transcendant Beatrice, was an obvious prototype for the decade. In the sixties and beyond, dying young of an overdose was a glamorous, heroic gesture against the slow decay of middle age, and Lizzie easily became an archetype of reckless, beautiful, vulnerable femininity.

In 1981 *The Golden Veil*, another fictional version of Lizzie's story, was published by novelist Paddy Kitchen, in which Lizzie's love for young Walter Deverell, the first to praise her beauty and open the door to the charmed world of art, is the mainspring of the story. She is a young Cinderella with half-formed dreams, whose diffuse grief at Walter's death leads her to laudanum and

139

an always unsatisfactory relationship with Gabriel. She relinqu-
ishes her virginity in the wood at Scalands without protest,
pleased to gain a secret pledge and a lover. Gabriel is, unusually,
presented as patient and devoted, if sometimes erratic, who on
one occasion promises to give up other women if Lizzie will
abandon laudanum. But hers is the sad history of an addict with
no will of her own, rapidly losing touch with reality; her last
fragmentary thoughts summarize the sorry tale of hope and
weakness:

> It was February – exactly eight years since Walter . . . She had mur-
> dered her second baby by now – where could she possibly be incarcer-
> ated after the black, bloodless room? No wonder Saint Cecilia was
> kissed by Death, that's what involvement with art . . . The linnet,
> how could she have buried it in the sand, it wasn't stiff, perhaps it
> might have revived . . . *In the desert a fountain* . . . Gabriel – no, she
> could not think of Gabriel – his eyes – either everything or nothing.
> Harry! She had never gone to see him as promised . . . not even kept
> her promise to . . .
> She went to the bottle on the dressing table . . .[15]

The story evokes the dreamy attractions of the hippie counter-
culture, through which many girls aspired to escape from sub-
urban dullness into the reflected glamour of a bohemian world of
art and rock music, excited by the freedom from conventionality
yet without apparent ambition of their own. Paddy Kitchen has
indicated that her imaginative reconstruction of Lizzie's personality was based in part on observation of such dreamy, passive
female students at London art schools in the 1960s. The then
fashionable style of tangled hennaed hair and loose trailing gowns
with beads and flowers in profusion certainly echoed the aesthetic
look with which the Pre-Raphaelite Lizzie is associated, and numbers of young women seem indeed to have adopted her as a figure
of fantasy, around whom to weave their own dreams of love and
fame, as mistress and muse to a poet or painter or perhaps pop
singer.

This symbolic image, however, should be set against the information that modern scholarship was yielding in this same period.

Following the publication of the four-volume edition of Rossetti's letters in 1965–9, the manuscript of the original *PRB Journal* was published in 1975 in an annotated edition, showing that the drastic mutilations inflicted by Gabriel Rossetti during or after his break-down in 1872 were unlikely to have been directed against entries referring to Elizabeth Siddal, as William had maintained, since most excisions antedated her appearance on the scene. Nor did she appear until after her marriage in the surviving texts of George Boyce's diaries, which spanned the years 1851 to 1875, despite Boyce's frequent visits to Chatham Place in the early 1850s and his close acquaintance with Gabriel. This supported Georgiana Burne-Jones's statement that neither her husband nor William Morris had been introduced to Miss Siddal during the 1850s, the years of supposed engagement.

The *Letters* contained a humorous account of Lizzie's encounter with a donkey-boy on the beach in Somerset in the summer of 1855, quoted verbatim by Gabriel and endorsing the impression of a sharp, observant wit given by her description of the passport office at Nice. The donkey-boy

> opened the conversation by asking if there was any lions in the parts she comed from. Hearing *no*, he seemed disappointed, and asked her if she had ever ridden on an elephant there. He had last year when the beasteses were here [i.e. Clevedon] and on mounting the elephant for a penny, he felt so joyful that he was obliged to give the man his other twopence, so that he couldn't see the rest of the fair . . . All that could be got in an explanation of why he thought Lizzie some outlandish native was that he was sure she comed from very far, much farther than he could see.[16]

The most important of the new material was the full text of Ford Madox Brown's diary, published in 1981, which substantially amplified the picture of Elizabeth Siddal, documenting in particular her close friendship with Emma Brown but also giving a clear picture of the relationship between Lizzie and Gabriel in the mid-1850s.

In March 1855, Brown recorded Gabriel's jubilation when Ruskin agreed to purchase Miss Siddal's drawings, commenting: 'He is right to admire them. She is a stunner and no mistake.' (Brown's meaning is somewhat ambiguous in view of the later use of stunner to mean an exceptionally attractive model; it appears that here he meant simply a superlatively promising artist.) He continued: 'Rossetti once told me that when he first saw her he felt his destiny was defined. Why does he not marry her?' In April, Brown accompanied Lizzie to sundry colourmen to purchase her own paints with Ruskin's money; they then met Gabriel and went on to his mother's, for 'Miss S's first interview', after which Gabriel escorted her home. Some weeks later at Chatham Place, Gabriel showed Brown his 'drawer full of "Guggums", God knows how many, but not bad work for the six years he has known her'.[17]

This was evidence of a blossoming romance. In August Brown and Rossetti went to see the paintings in Stafford House, where they met 'Miss Siddal beautifully dressed for about £3, altogether looking like a queen'. During the summer Lizzie and Gabriel twice spent happy weekends at the Browns' home in Finchley, where Lizzie had her host's bedroom and Gabriel slept at the inn; on the second occasion they all went out in a phaeton 'and with Rossetti's assistance got through much money'. Two days later:

> Emma went into town with Miss Siddal before Rossetti was come in from his rooms at the Queen's Head, so that when he did come his rage knew no bounds at being done out of the society of Guggum and vented itself in abuse on Emma who was 'always trying to persuade Miss Sid that he was plaguing her etc etc, whereas that of course Miss Sid liked it as much as he did etc etc . . .'

Gabriel followed the women and later summoned Brown to join them at the theatre, but,

> not choosing to go and witness the conduct such as it might be of these three, at the pit of Astleys, I entered a coffee shop opposite and with a glass of negus spent the time, then walked over as the crowd came out but they were gone. So in a cheerful temper I went off to Blackfriars and there found Gabriel gone and Miss Siddall in bed, so I backed out of it and past 12 went and got a bed, Emma being gone to sleep at her mother's.[18]

On 12 September Brown was again bidden to Rossetti's 'where Emma was to meet me to dine and go with him and Miss Sid to Drury Lane by orders. When we got there he had forgotten that

after a certain hour we could not get in, so Emma and I paid 5/-
and he and Guggum went home.' The Browns and their baby
slept at Chatham Place where Brown fell ill, while both Ruskin
and Fred Stephens called, amid scenes of 'physical and moral
confusion, discomfort and untruth mixed with dirt and feeling of
reckless extravagance'.[19]

At this date Rossetti was chivalrous in defence of his beloved.
Fred Stephens was received coolly, 'owing to his speaking irrever-
entially on the subject of Guggum', while a temporary difference
between Gabriel and Christina was caused 'because she and
Guggum do not agree'.[20] Brown, it may be noted, is the only
contemporary source besides Gabriel and Lizzie, to use the familiar pet name: it was not vouchsafed to other members of the
circle.

Following this sociable if unconventional and extravagant
summer – which evokes a cheerful bohemianism unlike the general image of Victorian behaviour, with much to commend it to
the hippie generation – Lizzie departed to France, supplied with
extra cash by Brown, Gabriel having already spent £20 of her
allowance from Ruskin. Within six weeks she had spent the rest
and Gabriel hurried over to Paris to relieve her needs and put her
and Mrs Kincaid on the train to Nice. On New Year's Eve Brown
noted, 'he has sent Miss Sid in all £55 since her departure'.[21]

On her return, as the entries make plain, the emotional situation
was altered. In the first three months of 1856 – when he sent the
comic Valentine to 'dear Liz' in Nice – Rossetti had a new discovery, Brown noted: 'a certain stunner' named Ruth Herbert,
actress at the Strand Theatre. And there were other distractions.
By 14 May Lizzie was back in London, in her own lodging at
Weymouth Street, and Gabriel was again accusing Emma 'on the
grounds that she possibly puts Miss Siddall up to being discon-
tented with him, which she does not, for poor Miss Sid complains
enough of his absurd goings on not to require that sort of thing'.
At the end of May Emma and Lizzie went to Ramsgate together,
where it rained and Emma lost her purse. In July Holman Hunt
told Brown of his perplexities over Annie Miller, and 'how
Gabriel like a mad man increased them taking Annie to all sorts
of places of amusement . . . to dine at Bertolini's and to Cremorne where she danced with Boyce.' William Rossetti took
Annie boating, and Gabriel seemed quite forgetful of 'Guggum',

143

as indeed Lizzie complained to Emma later in the month. But by September, Brown reported, Gabriel had 'forsworn flirting with Annie', as 'Guggum rebelled against it', and she and Gabriel 'seem on the best of terms now, she is painting at her picture'.[22]

Over the winter Brown recorded a number of instances where Gabriel claimed to be on the point of marrying Lizzie 'at once . . . and then off to Algeria!' He was 'only waiting for the money of a picture to do so when, lo the money being paid . . . never a word more about marriage'. Lizzie, 'determined to have no more to do with him', went to Bath, where Gabriel followed and 'promised marriage immediately, when since he has again postponed all thoughts of it till about a fortnight ago when he came to me and talked seriously to me and settled all he was to do', borrowing £10 for the licence. But nothing came of it, and Brown reported that Lizzie now seemed 'to hate Gabriel in toto'.[23] There followed the notorious quarrel over the proposed artists' colony, and Lizzie's bitterness at any reference to their supposed engagement.

At this stage, unfortunately, Brown's diary tailed off; there are no further references to Miss Sid. But, as the quotations are necessary to demonstrate, the picture had become clearer: Gabriel had fallen out of love with his dear dove, but did not know how to resolve the relationship to which he was in honour bound. And Lizzie, who later the same year left for Sheffield, was in no position to hold him to his promises.

III

Reconstructions

12

Emergent Feminist

Latterly, in the 1980s, a new version of Elizabeth Siddal has been emerging, who is partly a victim of patriarchal oppression and partly a rediscovered proto-feminist, as fits the age.

Feminist art history, for example, has begun to redefine Elizabeth Siddal as the captive dove or caged bird of Pre-Raphaelitism, symbol of the confinement and exploitation of women in both society and art. In a typical essay entitled 'Deverell, Rossetti, Siddal and "the Bird in the Cage" ', the American scholar Elaine Shefer discussed the many nineteenth-century pictorial representations of women and cage birds, defining Elizabeth as Rossetti's pet:

> . . . not only the amiable dove, but the parrot who could be trained to imitate her master and the canary who could be taught to sing prettily . . . He taught her to write poetry and to paint. Before meeting Rossetti, Elizabeth had attempted neither of these things . . . Protected and sheltered by Rossetti, she painted at home, in his studio, under his auspices.

In a wide-ranging analysis of symbolic meanings that promiscuously mixes paintings, poetry, psychoanalytic and medical theories (Lizzie's sickness now ascribed to the newly fashionable female disorder of *anorexia nervosa*, as symbolic in its own way as the earlier diagnoses of consumption and neurosis), the essay concluded that 'Elizabeth was the perfect bird in the cage'. A personalized account of life and art is thus produced in support of the thesis that women in the Victorian age were psychologically enslaved. As a pet, Elizabeth is seen to require Rossetti's protection: 'weak and dependent, with strong feelings of guilt and

147

fear, she chose to stay in her cage', a victim of oppressive patri-
archy, which had conquered her soul.[1]

Today, critical responses are more likely than not to focus on
a perception of inequality, rather than on Lizzie's appearance or
personality. As Rossetti is seen to dominate the story, so he is
now accused of dominating her life, of exploiting her beauty for
his art, and of discarding her once that beauty faded. The tale of
the exhumed coffin, as I have repeatedly heard in conversation,
provokes indignation and anger on the grounds that even in death,
Rossetti could not let his dove rest in peace, but must dig up her
body to further his own career. In this context, the misapprehen-
sion about *Beata Beatrix* being posthumously painted from 'life',
quoted at the start of this book, gains a certain symbolic truth: it
is a metaphor of the current view of their relationship. Similarly,
to criticize the pictures and censure the exhumation is to protest
against the patriarchal system in which women are still abused
and exploited, still judged in terms of beauty and still defined in
subservient relation.

Other recent writers have sought instead to detach Elizabeth
Siddal from the entwining grasp of the PRB and present her with
a biography of her own, both as an artist and a woman. The tools
of social and demographic history have been used to rescue her
from oblivion at those periods of her life when she was not
'visible' through her connection with the painters, and to correct
the wilder growths of speculation that have adhered to her legend
over the past hundred years. In 1977, the longstanding mystery
of Elizabeth Siddal's date of birth was finally clarified by Marion
Edwards of the Public Record Office in London who, beginning
with the Census of 1851 (opened for public inspection in 1951)
first discovered Elizabeth Siddal's birthplace to have been Holborn. Here parish records revealed her birthdate as 25 July 1829.
Details of seven siblings, the marriages of her eldest sister Ann
in 1850 and younger sister Lydia in 1861 were also uncovered,
together with the deaths of her elder brother Charles in 1852 and
that of her father in 1859.[2]

At a stroke, this research confirmed most of the information
obtained by W. G. Freemantle from James Siddall and by Violet
Hunt from Elizabeth Eleanor Higgins. It also radically revised the
image of a young milliner 'not yet seventeen' being suddenly
translated into the Pre-Raphaelite limelight. When she first went

Lady of Shalott, Elizabeth Siddal. Courtesy of Jeremy Maas

Lady at Loom, illuminated manuscript. Courtesy of the British Library, London

Jephtha's Daughter, Elizabeth Siddal. Ashmolean Museum, Oxford

Self Portrait, Elizabeth Siddal. Photo
courtesy of Ian H. Taylor

St Cecilia Sketch, Elizabeth Siddal.
Ashmolean Museum, Oxford

Sir Galahad and the Holy Grail, Elizabeth
Siddal and Dante Gabriel Rossetti.
Whereabouts unknown

Sketch for Sir Galahad, Elizabeth Siddal.
Ashmolean Museum, Oxford

Lovers Listening to Music, Elizabeth Siddal. Ashmolean Museum, Oxford

Pippa Passing Loose Women, Elizabeth Siddal. Ashmolean Museum, Oxford

Macbeths, Elizabeth Siddal. Ashmolean Museum, Oxford

Give Me the Daggers (engraving), unknown artist

Woeful Victory, Elizabeth Siddal. The Trustees, Cecil Higgins Art Gallery, Bedford

Before the Battle, Elizabeth Siddal. Tate Gallery, London

The Ladies' Lament, Elizabeth Siddal. Tate Gallery, London

to sit to Deverell as Viola, it is now clear that Elizabeth Siddal was a young working woman twenty years of age, and only fifteen months younger than the man who became her husband.

Thus began the still incomplete process of presenting Elizabeth Siddal with a history independent of Rossetti and the PRB. Trade directories revealed her father's various commercial premises in London during the 1820s and '30s, following his marriage to Elizabeth Eleanor Evans, who is now known to have been born in Shoreditch (although her Welsh antecedents, if any, are still undiscovered). Another, as yet unpublished, strand of family history suggests that Miss Evans was of a slightly higher social class than her husband: oral tradition mentions property owned by the Evans family in Bunhill Row and Golden Lane.[3] It therefore seems possible that the marriage enabled Charles Siddall to set up in business as a shopkeeper in London's expanding economy, where Sheffield cutlery was a hallmark of high quality.

A 'Sheffield warehouse' or wholesale business off Fleet Street was registered in the name of C. Siddall in 1825. The same year his daughter Ann was born and baptized at the New Road Independent (or Congregational) Chapel, when the family were resident in Middleton Place, Clerkenwell; in 1827 a retail ironmongery shop was registered at this address. A year or so later family and business had moved to Charles Street in Hatton Garden, Holborn, where Elizabeth was born, a year after her brother Charles. By 1832 Charles Siddall had a warehouse in the Strand as well as the Hatton Garden shop, and the following year opened a new shop at 8 Kent Place, a terrace on the Old Kent Road. Here Lydia was born, followed by Mary, Clara, James and Henry, making eight children in all, born within eighteen years.

By 1841 the business comprised two shops, one in Kent Place and the other in Upper Ground, Southwark, just south of Blackfriars Bridge, where the family were resident at the time of the Census. Charles jnr, aged fourteen, was apprenticed to another cutler in the Old Kent Road. In 1844, the Siddall family moved back to Kent Place.

Other public records show that in June 1850 Elizabeth's eldest sister Ann married a Scottish-born printer, named David MacCarter. She raised six children, including a daughter named Elizabeth Eleanor. Lydia, as her daughter Mrs Elizabeth Eleanor Higgins had recorded, married Joseph Wheeler in 1861 and had seven children. In adulthood, the youngest sister Clara Siddall became mentally ill, eventually dying in an asylum in Epsom in 1902. As yet unpublished letters from Clara to Rossetti show that Gabriel continued to send money until 1880. James Siddall carried on the business at Kent Place until the end of the century; he died in 1912, four years after his younger brother Harry.[4]

The mid-century Censuses give a snapshot view of Elizabeth Siddal's life. In 1841 she was at home, aged eleven; in 1851 (when she had given up dressmaking/millinery in favour of modelling) she was still at home, aged twenty-one with no occupation listed; and in 1861 she was married, at 13 Chatham Place, aged twenty-nine (!) and like her husband listed as 'Artist:Painter'. Two visitors were staying: Emma Madox Brown and an eighteen-year-old youth with an illegible name, from Boston, USA.

This information demonstrates that Elizabeth Siddal's story did not begin with her entry into the Pre-Raphaelite circle. And these researches into her antecedents are also indicative of rising interest in local and family history as a new way of looking at the past – from below in terms of ordinary people rather than through the famous figures of political or diplomatic history. It also signals a specific concomitant interest, current during the past few years, in recovering women's lives from the oblivion and silence of most previous records, as part of a general revision of the position of women in history.

Concern with the position of women in art history has resulted, during this same period, in new prominence being given to Elizabeth Siddal's career as a painter. This may be said to have begun, tentatively, in 1978, when Mark Lasner and Roger Lewis published a limited edition of *The Poems and Drawings of Elizabeth Siddal*, printed by a small press calling itself the Wombat Press (wombats being Rossetti's favourite animals). This reproduced fifteen pictures and sixteen poems, together with a brief chronology of her life[5], and represented the first significant publication of her pictorial work, and the first republication of her verse since William Rossetti's original efforts. As such, it was indicative of growing interest in her career. However, as with most limited editions, the restricted and expensive nature of publication only partly helped to promote a new identity; in other respects it simply repeated the prevailing view of Elizabeth Siddal's work as precious but slight, a 'secluded pool' outside the Pre-Raphaelite mainstream. The men's work, of course, is everywhere reproduced on a wide scale, in books, prints, calendars, greeting cards, posters, table mats and the like.

The large Tate Gallery exhibition *The Pre-Raphaelites* held in London from March to May 1984 contained two and a half works by Elizabeth Siddal. Among thirty artists and 250 works she was the only woman represented. The 'half' picture was the watercolour *Sir Galahad and the Holy Grail* jointly inscribed as designed by 'EES' and executed by 'EES & DGR'. Although previously attributed to Elizabeth Siddal alone – as when reproduced in 1912 in *The Letters of John Ruskin* – the catalogue entry was assigned to the scholar responsible for the Rossetti entries, who noted that 'like many of her works this is weird, macabre, peopled by stiff, drawn-out figures moving through an insubstantial architectural setting'.[6]

The solo Siddal entries were allocated to the feminist art historian Deborah Cherry who, referring to the artist firmly by surname, insisted on detaching the work both from her personal history and from her dependence on Rossetti. This stressed the ideological position of the works as 'actively productive in the construction of gender difference . . . and strategically placed within historically specific discourses on women'. In this analysis, the *Lady of Shalott* was 'not offered as a victim or spectacle for the masculine gaze' and did not 'attain visibility within the relays of power'. Like *Lady Clare* it was seen to offer 'a particular and different construction of class and gender'. Above all, the standard critical judgement of the artist as weak and derivative – as implied in the entry for the *Holy Grail* – was challenged:

All too often Siddal's drawings are viewed as pale echoes of Rossetti's and said to be dependent on his. Such analysis should be resisted. It produces and reproduces patriarchal ideology, constructing the woman artist and her work as negative, and sustaining the male artist and his art in a position of dominance and privilege.[7]

This analysis was itself resisted and rejected by the art historical establishment, to whom such ideas and language were unaccept-

151

able in 1984. The accompanying article on Elizabeth Siddal by Deborah Cherry and Griselda Pollock, commissioned for the collection of scholarly papers to complement the Tate exhibition, was refused by the editor and appeared instead in the journal *Art History* in June 1984 under the title 'Woman as Sign in Pre-Raphaelite Literature: A Study of the Representation of Elizabeth Siddal'. This presented a post-structuralist version of Elizabeth Siddal, in which

> 'Siddal' functions as a sign. More than the name of a historical personage it does not simply refer to a woman, or even Woman. Its signified is masculine creativity [which] articulates the informing ideologies of art history about the personal process of artistic creation and its natural disposition between the sexes.

The authors thus used the case of Elizabeth Siddal not as a biographical adjunct to Pre-Raphaelite art, nor even as an artist in her own right, but as a means of challenging the 'masculine' valuation of art in terms of originality and ambition, and of disputing the still current assessment of women's art as weak and derivative beside the great works – masterpieces – produced by men. It concluded that

> art history is a field invested with power, and the production of knowledge is historically shaped within relations of power. The discourses on the artist and on creativity which are circulated in and by art history have ideological effects in the reproduction of socially determined definitions of masculinity and femininity, and the dominant tropes of Pre-Raphaelite literature have functioned decisively to produce and secure gender difference.[8]

This semiotic Elizabeth Siddal is, of course, not a biographical subject at all, but a figure with which to unpack the meanings and privileges contained within past and present discourses of art history. As such it relates to current intellectual investigations into the nature of representation and symbolic value, as well as to feminist theories of gendered discourse. However, it also helps, biographically, to detach the historical figure from the accretions of interpretation, and to point up the latent ideological purposes of texts which claim no such overt intention.

The authors' use of Elizabeth Siddal was of course equally

purposeful, with its own avowed intentions. This serves, too, to illustrate how all accounts are informed by their own concerns, specific to their age and origin. In common parlance, no narrative, whether in biography, art history or literary criticism, is 'value-free': each has its own specific relation to the events or objects it attempts to explain.

Thus my own account of Elizabeth Siddal in *Pre-Raphaelite Sisterhood* (1985), which was based on contemporary documentary sources and a strongly sceptical reading of the legend, had the aim of presenting a feminist revision or redefinition of her story, seeing her as one of a number of talented and ambitious women, who 'in real life tried to challenge the prescriptions of class and gender' and for whom modelling, drawing and marriage were a means to upward mobility and access to a wider cultural world. Lizzie's drug addiction and subsequent death were interpreted as the consequence of the broken 'engagement' and the unhappy social position of a rejected woman without income or occupation of her own.[9] Itself a narrative contribution to the ongoing 'story of Elizabeth Siddal', this account clearly owed much to current concern over women's roles, relationships, aspirations and economic opportunities in the 1980s.

I will not criticize that work harshly – it still represents in large measure what I believe to be an accurate account of Lizzie's life – except to say that by aiming at such a notion of unproblematic 'truth', it too shared in the posthumous reconstruction of biography shaped by contemporary perspectives. In this regard no biography is fully and absolutely differentiated from fiction or other forms of literary creation.

Also in 1985, Gillian Allnutt published her seven-part poem *Lizzie Siddall: Her Journal (1862)*, which presented the persona of a woman musing on her own representation in men's images of her:

> In bare grey light he slept
> like a saint.
> I crept
> into his empty room – and that paint

153

woman was grinning as if she had risen
from the grave –
as if she had removed the stone
of love

that laid her
tenderly in earth,
that stayed her
hand, her mouth –

. . .

She beckoned me to come
plain as I was in my nightdress,
and gave me her own name,
Beatrice.

Late this afternoon I stole
into the room
again – but she, subdued and sorrowful
looked only out from the little window of his dream.[10]

Subsequently, Gillian Allnutt and I devised *No Man Cares for My Soul: The Life and Legend of Elizabeth Siddall*, a programme of poetry, paintings, music and biography, presented at literature festivals and art galleries. This contained both the poetic sequence, and the biographical narrative, together with pictorial, prose and verse descriptions of Elizabeth Siddal, and a selection of her own poems and paintings.

The responses to these publications and performances from audiences and readers – my book has prompted what is to me an unexpected number of personal letters from strangers – has shown the powerful fascination still exerted by this quasi-historical, quasi-legendary figure. The desire to know 'what she was really like' is both combined with and countered by the desire to maintain the myth, in a paradigm of the tension inherent in the redefinitions of femininity in our time.

Thus Elizabeth Siddal has a historical significance beyond that of biography. Other, as yet unpublished or unperformed versions of her story have been produced, persuading me that writers seeking to express a female experience that has been dominantly refracted through a man-made prism have taken up her persona to explore their own emotional and social situation, and that of other women. In her image we find a reflection of our own, or perhaps a half-completed outline whose features wait to be filled in. In the voice of Lizzie from Gillian's poem:

> I said to him today, I'd love to draw –
> no, not another angel
> but the likeness of my own poor
> soul.
>
> . . .
>
> Beatrice may be
> the one
> who can undo her body
> like a button,
>
> who can let him
> in
> to his dream.
> Unknowing and unknown,
>
> I am beyond
> the pale
> and lovely land
> of lady. Wakeful
>
> now, I wait
> for morning light, the bright mane of her hair
> to burn out
> of the mirror.

In writing about Elizabeth Siddal, women are painting collective self-portraits.

13

Amiable Young Artist

As should by now be clear, although critical of writers who have used documentary sources in a careless or cavalier manner while claiming to construct objective biographies, I do not believe that any past, present or future texts relating to Elizabeth Siddal, however imperfect or imaginative, should be rejected as worthless: in showing how the past is perceived, they at least reveal the preoccupations of their own time. Nor do I believe, despite being naturally persuaded of the correctness of my own interpretations, in the possibility of a definitive biographical account, whether based on illuminating insights or on accumulated fact, or on both combined: biographers should be always aware of the provisional nature of our endeavours. There will always be new information and new perspectives, and I want therefore to conclude this study, at least for the time being, by considering in these final chapters some additional or alternative ways in which Elizabeth Siddal's story may currently be approached.

This latest approach is based in part on my discovery of further unpublished materials, in Sheffield and elsewhere, including what must be the earliest biographical record of Elizabeth Siddal, published in the month of her death as an obituary notice. As far as I am able to ascertain, this has not hitherto been reproduced. Since it antedates all other accounts of her life, it is not dependent upon any previous written or rumoured information and thus has the unique status of being unencumbered by the accretions of myth. And it calls into question all previous versions, including my own, in a manner that makes the biographer pause.

The obituary seems to derive substantially from information supplied by Elizabeth Siddal herself, and is thus the closest we have yet come to her autobiography. None the less, it does not represent gospel truth nor clarify all the mysteries of her life, for it contains a number of verifiable inaccuracies and omissions. This is not altogether surprising: autobiographies are often unreliable. Moreover, its author had evidently little first-hand knowledge of his subject's life in London or of the Pre-Raphaelite world. Indeed, his errors attest to the text's authenticity: it was written close to the events, before the PRB had entered the history books, and from a provincial distance. It was printed in the *Sheffield Telegraph* on 28 February 1862,[1] and is here given in full:

THE DEATH OF MRS D. G. ROSETTA [*sic*]
To the Editor: Mrs D. G. Rosetta, whose unfortunate death you mentioned in your Saturday's paper, was not a native of Sheffield, but her father was. Mr Charles Siddall, her father, was for many years a member of the Queen Street Church, and after the celebrated Samuel Frith resigned the office of leading singer at that place, Mr Siddall became the leader until he removed to London. He there became the leading singer at Mr Raisen's chapel. When his daughter was twenty years old, she was a dressmaker and as such was introduced into the family of an artist who held some office at the Royal Academy. This artist had a son, a most promising student, the friend of Rosetta, Maclise, Holman Hunt and others – the nucleus, the founders of the Pre-Raphaelite school. Miss Siddall showed some outlines, designs of her own leisure hours, to the elder artist Mr D— and he, much pleased with them, introduced them to Mr D— Jnr and the other young artists. She was encouraged to practise by them and did so at her leisure. But this was not all; similarity of mind is the true source of attachment and affection, and young D— formed a strong attachment to Miss Siddall and proposed a friendship to her that was to last for life. After consulting her friends, she accepted his offer. But alas in two and a half years from that time Mr D—, his wife and son died, and left the amiable young artist a disappointed lover. Mr Hunt, deeply sympathizing with Miss Siddall and believing her to be really clever, introduced her and her works to Mr Ruskin, who was much pleased with her efforts. He called at her father's residence and, finding she could not afford to give her trade up, made a most liberal offer of pecuniary assistance, upon three conditions – 1st that she devoted herself entirely to the fine arts; 2nd that she placed herself under the instruction of Hunt or Rosetta; and 3rd that he had her productions until he thought her progress warranted the supposition that she could maintain an independent position as an artist. She selected as her instructor Mr Rosetta, the father of the pre-Raphaelite school. Mr Ruskin wrote to her most kindly, advising her

not to apply herself too closely to her studies, for fear her injured health should not sustain her labours. It did fail and he sent her down to Oxford, to an eminent physician, under whose care she much improved. The following year she went for the same object to the continent, still pursuing her studies. He also introduced her to William and Mary Howitt, their daughter and many other literary friends. I am not aware that her pictures have appeared in any exhibition but one got up by the pre-Raphaelites at which Mr Ruskin arranged several of her sketches and one oil painting, which sold to an American gentleman for forty guineas.

The intimacy with Mr Rosetta led to an attachment between the two artists, and he proposed marriage to Miss Siddall. But a cloud passed over their friendship and she came down to Sheffield and visited Little Matlock, Wharncliffe, Endcliffe and other places; and liking the scenery of our delightful neighbourhood she took a house on Eccleshall road. But the intimacy between her and Mr Rosetta was renewed; they met at Matlock, she returned to London, and shortly they were united in marriage. But alas! the mental labour and anxiety to do credit to her most liberal and honourable patron had been too great for her feeble constitution; it induced a secret habit which has proved fatal to many, and her premature death has only added another proof of 'how frequently the fairest prospects fail'.[1]

[*signed*] W.I.

A marginal note in the scrapbook where this item is pasted in the Sheffield Local Studies Collection identifies 'W.I.' as William Ibbitt, the silverchaser and designer, artist and local councillor mentioned in the later Sheffield source materials as supposed cousin and friend of Elizabeth Siddal during her time in the city in 1857; he escorted her, for example, to visit the parents of 'Senex'.

Born in 1804, William Ibbitt was an admired and respected figure in Sheffield. Apprenticed to the silverplating trade, he was also a self-taught artist whose ambition to delineate the beauties of nature was realized in a well-known series of landscape views of Sheffield and its surrounding countryside. He was a Radical and member of Sheffield town council, with a special sympathy and concern for the welfare of the working classes and an 'intense hatred of every form of imposition and oppression and wrong', coupled with 'more than ordinary respect and deference to persons in the higher stations of life'. He supported the Mechanics Library, was a staunch Wesleyan and lay preacher, and died in March 1869.[2] Extensive genealogical research has so far found no relationship by blood or marriage, or religious denomination between the Siddall and Ibbitt families,[3] but it is possible that the precise nature of the connection may one day become known.

His account of Miss Siddall (for whose name the usual local spelling was given) is intriguing and deserves analysis, as the only life story not based on other versions. Firstly, it confirms the history of her origins that was pieced together over the years, showing her to be the London-born daughter of a Sheffield father. Charles Siddall is here identified not by trade – in Sheffield virtually everyone was connected with the cutlery business – but by his chapel. This confirms various later references to his choral singing, and confers a certain status: the lead singer was a person of some importance, and in the fluid social formation of the early nineteenth century an ambitious tradesman with religious connections could often attain a solid social standing. Mr Raisen's chapel in London has not yet been identified, but was clearly self-explanatory to Sheffield readers. And this confirms Elizabeth Siddall's connections with the Queen Street Congregational Church, from which her own religious beliefs may be inferred.

Alone among the early accounts, this obituary gives her correct age, stating that she was twenty when first introduced to the young artists. Mr Deverell senior is incorrectly assigned a position at the Royal Academy when he was secretary of the School of Design, but this is an understandable error, for the RA had previously occupied the same premises.

It was 'as a dressmaker', that Miss Siddall was introduced to the Deverell family. The wording suggests that, as was common practice, she called on the ladies of the house for instructions and fittings. This does not necessarily imply that she was not a milliner after all: at this date dressmaking and millinery were both aspects of the fashion trade and not regarded as different occupations. But it casts some doubt on Fred Stephens's colourful tale of how Miss Siddal was first glimpsed in the back room of a shop, and incidentally confirms William Rossetti's 1891 version of Lizzie as a dressmaker's assistant. It is indeed more likely that, in whatever capacity, she called upon Mrs Deverell at home – in 1850 middle-class women seldom bought ready-made clothes or bonnets – and that this was how she first met Walter, friend to the founders of

159

the Pre-Raphaelite school. Writing in 1862, William Ibbitt evidently had only a sketchy knowledge of this new movement, giving the name of Maclise (an older artist and Academician) in place of Millais, and misspelling Rossetti, who at the time was the least-known of the major members of the PRB, exhibiting only rarely.

More significant than her occupation, however, is the information that Miss Siddall showed the 'designs of her own leisure hours' to Mr Deverell and that he then showed her drawings ('designs' in this period meaning sketch or drawing rather than pattern) to his son and his friends. For this indicates that, before she ever met the PRB, she was producing pictures on her own account, and that it was as a result of her initiative in showing this work that aroused the artists' interest and encouragement. By this account, Rossetti was not the discoverer and begetter of her talent.

It is possible that she showed her work with the idea of joining classes at the School of Design, where Mr Deverell was administrative head from 1842. This was for the training of artisans and offered classes in drawing and ornamental design for those entering the decorative trades. The institution also embraced the Female School of Design, whose aims were 'to ensure young women of the middle class to obtain honourable and profitable employment' and to cultivate the taste of ornamental designers; it was open to girls over the age of thirteen who needed training 'in order to get their livelihood' and offered daily classes to about fifty pupils. Elizabeth Siddall was of the appropriate social class to enrol in the Female School; her work in the fashion trade was appropriate to the vocational bias of the school; her artistic aspirations were in keeping with those of the other students (the principal was rebuked for allowing her students to stray towards the fine arts); and her home in Southwark was within reach of the Strand. But there is no evidence that she did attend classes there and it is likely that the encouragement offered by Walter and his friends suggested another route to art training, via the studio.

The obituary, however, makes no mention of modelling for the young founders of the Pre-Raphaelite school. This is curious, for, together with the artists' own recollections, the pictorial evidence is unequivocal: from 1850 to 1852 Lizzie sat to a number of different artists for a variety of figures.

The first of these sittings were for Viola in Deverell's *Twelfth Night*. As well as the better known oil painting (exhibited in May 1850 at the British Institution) with Viola, disguised as the youth Cesario, listening to Duke Orsino and Feste, there was another subject showing a courting scene between Cesario and Olivia, which was published in the fourth issue of *The Germ*. In both images the model for Viola was Elizabeth Siddal.

Deverell was attracted by theatrical themes (he was a keen amateur actor) and by the dramatic motif of women in disguise: he also painted the forest scene from *As You Like It* with Rosalind in male attire. In *Twelfth Night*, Viola is an androgynous figure in short tunic over long hose, and the young critic William Rossetti, reviewing the painting, remarked that this was 'too flimsily theatrical' to be wholly convincing. He also took exception to Viola's costume on moral grounds, criticizing the artist for the 'immodesty of her very short dress'; even in disguise, Shakespeare's heroine embarrassed Victorian viewers by displaying so much leg. Finally he noted that the figure's face was 'not physically beautiful enough' to represent Viola.[4] Fifty years later, he had forgotten this judgement – made at a time when his brother was supposedly head over heels in love with Deverell's model – but he noted revealingly of the engraving in *The Germ* that 'this face does not give much idea of hers, and yet it is not unlike her in a way'[5]. The truth was that, in 1850, Miss Siddal was neither beautiful nor beloved, but a young woman who, through her work as a dressmaker, was used to travelling unescorted around London, and was now varying her occupation and following her artistic inclinations by working as a model, probably in defiance of her family.

She sat, too, for the figure of a young woman in Holman Hunt's picture of *A Converted British Family Sheltering a Christian Priest from Persecution by the Druids* (exhibited at the Royal Academy in May 1850). The figure is seen tending the priest with bowl and sponge, with her red hair looped loosely back and wearing a rough skirt and sleeveless hessian cape.

William Rossetti claimed that Elizabeth Siddal was also the model for *Rossovestita*, a small painting of a female figure executed

by Gabriel in 1850. If correct, this would mark her first appearance
in his work, but the features do not resemble those in Rossetti's
other drawings. The red-robed figure's round face and small pert
mouth are in fact similar to those in a drawing of the same date
for which the model was Miss Mead, also with red hair, who
seems a far more likely sitter for *Rossovestita*.[6]

For Holman Hunt's *Valentine Rescuing Sylvia from Proteus*, based
on the final scene from Shakespeare's *Two Gentlemen of Verona*,
(shown at the RA in 1851), where Valentine intervenes to prevent
Sylvia's ravishment, Elizabeth Siddal was the model for Sylvia.
According to Hunt's memoirs, she sat first in August – September
1850 for preparatory studies, and then in the spring of 1851 for
the final picture; in the interval Sylvia's kneeling pose was altered,
making it somewhat easier to hold. A letter from Rossetti to
his brother, first published in 1965, described how, during the
preliminary sittings, Holman Hunt and Fred Stephens hoaxed
another friend 'by passing Miss Siddal upon him as Hunt's wife'.
This was the sort of practical joke characteristic of the young
painters' high spirits, if lacking in tact. On hearing the story,
Rossetti urged them to apologize to their embarrassed victim, the
young man who had been tricked into treating an artist's model
as a married lady.[7] There is no evidence that Miss Siddal was
embarrassed by this incident: indeed, she was presumably party
to the hoax, which suggests a friendly relationship with Hunt,
and also with Stephens (both of whom naturally omitted this
incident from their account of Miss Siddal's discovery, since it
would have reflected badly on their own behaviour).

When *Valentine Rescuing Sylvia* was exhibited, Ruskin complained in print of the 'unfortunate types' chosen as models by
Holman Hunt, noting in particular the 'commonness' of Sylvia's
features. Hunt therefore repainted the face to give it a nobler
aspect. Together with other incidental evidence such as the artists'
use (among themselves) of the jocular titles 'Miss Sid' or 'the
Sid', it is therefore clear that Elizabeth Siddal was regarded as a
useful but not beautiful model, willing to wear costumes and hold
difficult poses, with a lively sense of humour and no false modesty. Hunt's tale of how she travelled to Chelsea to alert him to
a possible rival rendering of *The Light of the World* illustrates that
she also took a serious interest in the business of art.

In the closing weeks of 1851 she went, probably for the first time, to sit to Gabriel Rossetti, for the figure of Delia in a water-colour composition based on verses addressed by the Roman poet Tibullus to his beloved, showing her at the spinning wheel holding a distaff, her hair loose and feet bare. In one of the preliminary studies, the bodice of Delia's dress is discreetly open to the waist, indicative like her loose hair of intimate *déshabille*; it signifies, however, no more than that as a model Miss Siddal was willing to wear artistic costume for a poetic subject. There is no evidence that she ever posed naked or semi-draped.

It is also likely that she modelled for a second female figure in this picture, representing Delia's older companion, for in the compositional sketch a woman with two stringed instruments seated on the floor as Tibullus bursts into the chamber also has Elizabeth's aspect.

She sat to Rossetti again for three kneeling figures, one also with a stringed instrument, in studies for an unexecuted picture of St Elizabeth of Hungary praying with two companions, and possibly also for a standing figure in a pencil composition showing the Virgin being comforted after the Crucifixion, presented by Rossetti to a friend in May 1852.[8]

In this month, the floating figure of Millais's now famous *Ophelia* was hung at the Royal Academy. Contemporary correspondence shows that this was painted in the artist's studio during February and March 1852. It was the only occasion on which Millais used Miss Siddal as a model, perhaps owing to her unfortunate experience in the rapidly cooling water. Her father's anger and anxiety for her health, recorded by Arthur Hughes, are readily understood when it is remembered that only weeks previously her elder brother Charles had died after a long illness. Yet perhaps Mr Siddall's hostility had other causes, too, for modelling was scarcely a respectable occupation. Not many months later, Ruskin was told that Lizzie's family disapproved of her pursuit of art, and unchaperoned activities in young artists' studios may have had much to do with this.

She was evidently not deterred. Later in 1852 she was the model for Rossetti's Beatrice in a small watercolour entitled *Beatrice, Meeting Dante at a Marriage Feast, Denies Him Her Salutation*, and for Mary in Rossetti's second rendering of *The Annunciation*, unusually depicted as an outdoor scene with the Virgin washing clothes in a stream as the Archangel materializes amid the trees.

She also sat for another Mary bending to gather herbs in the unfinished *Preparation for the Passover in the Holy Family* and possibly also for *Mary Nazarene*, gardening with knapsack and spade. From 1853 onwards, indeed, she modelled exclusively for Rossetti's biblical and poetic women.

These were described by Ruskin as Rossetti's 'higher female faces', and the term indicates his consciousness that modelling was a questionable activity, only acceptable in this case because the subjects were moral figures such as the Virgin Mary. The Pre-Raphaelites' principle was to seek a spiritual as well as a physical correspondence in their models, preferring friends to professional models, who posed for groups of students in art schools or subscription classes. Nevertheless, the job remained dubious and even improper; however much artists insisted on the prosperity of the work, most models were regarded as little better than whores, and it is not surprising if Lizzie omitted to mention this aspect of her career to Mr Ibbitt in Sheffield, or if he omitted it from his obituary. To include it would probably have been regarded as deeply offensive to the deceased lady and her bereaved husband.

Indeed, modelling clearly impeded their marriage more than has previously been understood. In the spring of 1854, Barbara Leigh Smith wrote to her friend Bessie Parkes:

> Private. Now my dear I have got a strong interest in a young girl formerly model to Milais [*sic*] and Dante Rossetti, now Rossetti's love and pupil . . . Alas! her life has been hard and full of trials, her home unhappy and her whole fate hard. Dante Rossetti has been an honourable friend to her and I do not doubt if circumstances were favourable would marry her. She is of course under a ban having been a model (tho' only to 2 PRBs) ergo do not mention it to anyone.[9]

This shows why modelling should have been censored from William Ibbitt's account but raises the further question why, if it was such an unmentionable occupation, did Miss Siddal, from a respectable shopkeeper's family, undertake to pose for artists in the first place, and continue to do so for different painters for at least three years?

Money may have been one reason, although the modelling sessions were intermittent and it is likely that a steadier income would have been earned from dressmaking and millinery. My guess – it can be no more – is that modelling provided her above all with access to the studio and the world of art practice, which she had sought by displaying her work to Mr Deverell.

It was difficult for women in general to obtain professional art training in the 1840s and '50s and more so for those without means. However highly it was regarded as a ladylike accomplishment, art was not considered a suitable profession for women. The hints of Lizzie's situation contained in contemporary correspondence must be treated with caution, since they derive from Rossetti's presentation of her case to others, concealing his own motives, yet both Ruskin's account of the Siddall family's lack of sympathy and Barbara Smith's reference to a life 'full of trials' may well point to an unconventional female determination to be an artist, in opposition to parental wishes.

By the summer of 1852, Rossetti was promising to show Gug's drawings to Christina; by the beginning of 1853 he was referring to her as his pupil. In the summer of 1854, he told Allingham in melodramatic terms of her attempts to escape 'from degradation and corruption' and the danger that she would 'sink out again unprofitably in that dark house where she was born'. Quoting Psalm 42, she had complained that 'no man cared for her soul' and he was ashamed to admit that only recently had he paid any attention to her aspirations.[10]

Put together, these fragments suggest something of a strategy on Elizabeth Siddal's part in pursuit of artistic training. Having initially interested the young painters in her own talent and having been a willing model, she may have aroused Rossetti's sympathy for the difficulties she faced in obtaining instruction, especially if her father was unwilling to pay for classes. The simplest solution (which also partly disguised the developing romantic attachment) was for her to become Gabriel's pupil.

This was unconventional, but no means unknown. Being a private pupil, taught in the artist's studio, was one form of art training, especially for women, who were not admitted to the Royal Academy Schools. In most cases, however, female students were chaperoned, either by their own attendants or by the artist's wife. In this case the arrangement was somewhat irregular; as far as is known, Lizzie paid for her tuition by modelling and was therefore at the studio frequently, not at appointed weekly intervals. Gabriel's brother William was discouraged from calling on this account and sometimes instructed to keep others from calling, as in June 1853 when Lizzie was there painting on her own.[11]

What, however, is to be made of William Ibbitt's claim that Walter Deverell 'formed a strong attachment to Miss Siddall and proposed a friendship to her that was to last for life' – that is, marriage? And that his proposal was accepted, before the end of 1851? As Deverell was still alive in the summer of 1853, what was Lizzie doing in the Blackfriars studio at all?

This notion of a romance between Lizzie and Walter has been previously conjectured, notably by Paddy Kitchen but also by Brian and Judy Dobbs, authors of *Dante Gabriel Rossetti: An Alien Victorian* (1977) who resurrected a throwaway line by Violet Hunt, to the effect that Elizabeth Siddal's 'heart, such as it was, was buried with Deverell',[12] to put forward a new interpretation. This explained her sorrowful poetry as a response to Walter's untimely death:

> To be taken from a milliner's by a well-off young man, acknowledged universally to be handsome, and launched on a new career among his artist friends at the impressionable age of sixteen; when all this is considered it must have been very odd if Lizzie had *not* fallen for Walter Deverell . . .

and concluded 'There is no love like a first love, especially one with a tragic end.'[13] Until the discovery of the Sheffield obituary, the documentary evidence offered no corroboration of this. No Deverell family tradition recorded any such attachment; Walter's own diary did not mention Lizzie[14]; several other young women feature as models in the pictures he completed between 1850 and 1853. Walter's mother died in October 1850 and his father in June 1853, leaving the family in financial straits; he himself suffered from kidney disease for some years and was in no position to offer marriage. A proposal would have led to more formal relations, both with the Deverell family and with the other artists, who could hardly have passed Lizzie off as Hunt's wife if she was known to have accepted Walter's offer. All this evidence makes it hard to believe that she could have been engaged to Walter in, say, the summer of 1852, when surprised by Bell Scott's arrival at the Hermitage, or when Gabriel told Christina of the lock of hair shorn from her dear head, 'radiant as the tresses of Aurora', or indeed the following year when left alone in Rossetti's studio, with instructions to keep the doors locked.

Yet William Ibbitt evidently believed that Lizzie and Walter were engaged lovers, and is unlikely to have invented the story himself, since both their families were, as far as he knew, able to refute it. He repeated the story elsewhere, for it was recounted many years later by a Sheffield woman who remembered being told of a young artist who wished to marry Miss Siddal but died shortly afterwards from consumption, and through whom she was introduced to the PRB.[15] Moreover, Violet Hunt's notes record that Holman Hunt also apparently believed that Miss Siddal had 'been on the point of marrying someone else' when Rossetti paid court to her.[16]

In the absence of firmer evidence, however, it must be assumed that, if there was, at some early date, a romantic attachment to Walter Deverell, retrospectively confided to Lizzie's Sheffield friends, this largely represented wishful rather than literal truth. It may be, in the early days of her acquaintance with the Deverell family, that the 'amiable young artist' dreamt of romance with the handsome eldest son. It certainly seems unlikely that they were ever formally engaged.

Returning to the rest of the obituary, it was not Holman Hunt but Rossetti who introduced Miss Siddal and her work to John Ruskin. By this date, as we have seen, she was already under Rossetti's tuition, and the chronology presented by Ibbitt is contradicted by contemporary evidence. Yet perhaps, at one stage, Lizzie considered becoming Hunt's pupil, possibly while working as his model. But by 1853 Hunt was planning his trip to the Holy Land, and was not available as a teacher; in any case, he had found another protegée, the beautiful Annie Miller, who modelled for the fallen woman in *The Awakening Conscience*, and whom Hunt was planning to save from degradation by education and possibly marriage.

Ibbitt was correct, however, in stating that the intimacy of teacher and pupil led to an attachment between Lizzie and Gabriel, even if all the evidence shows that this was not a formal engagement. Barbara Smith described Miss Siddal as Gabriel's 'love and pupil' in the early summer of 1854, and the pictorial evidence for their attachment is compelling.

From the later part of 1853 and the early months of 1854 Rossetti's love is clearly visible in his drawings of Lizzie. They depict, amongst other things, the change in her position from that of model to friend and beloved. As has frequently been remarked, the drawings produced in Hastings are among the most perfect of his portraits, expressive of tender and delicate affection. Less often noted is the difference between these and the earlier drawings, which typically show a figure in careful or difficult poses – standing, kneeling, or sitting upright – such as a hired model might be expected to hold. She is also seen dressed either in costumes or her own outdoor clothes; in one early sketch she is on a hard chair, reading, with her bonnet on. In the Hastings drawings, by contrast, Lizzie is seen in relaxed poses, sitting in an armchair, reading, resting, leaning her head on her hand or a pillow, wearing a day dress. These images have often been invoked as evidence of Lizzie's inherent weakness, ill-health and lassitude, but are more simply interpreted as poses that were easier to hold, showing the artist's beloved rather than a paid model. They are indicative of greater intimacy; as Gabriel wrote to his mother from Hastings: 'No one thinks it at all odd my going into the Gug's room to sit there' – to sit and, on the visual evidence, to spend long hours drawing her.

Hitherto unpublished correspondence reveals that, at this date, Barbara Smith also told Bessie Parkes, who was already in Hastings, of Rossetti's secret interest in Miss Siddal because Bessie was to help, by providing tea on Lizzie's arrival in Hastings, and by finding lodgings. If the room by St Clement's church was not to let, Bessie was to ask Mrs Elphick to find a suitable room with sun and a good landlady, for seven or eight shillings a week, 'or less if possible.' The day before departure Barbara wrote to Bessie again: Dante Rossetti would be accompanying Miss Siddal, who 'is a genius and very beautiful, and although she is not a lady her mind is poetic'. While Rossetti did not much consider the class issue, nevertheless he wished her to meet 'ladies' such as Barbara and Bessie, in order to 'keep her self-esteem from shrinking'. She was weak and failing, and Barbara did not think of the future, for Lizzie was unlikely to recover. Romantically, she declared 'The present is all we have, do not let us or them cast it away.'[17]

A week or so later, Bessie had returned to London and Barbara was at Hastings with Anna Howitt. They had seen 'Mr R and Miss S sitting on the top of the East Cliff' and looking so cheerful that Barbara could hardly believe she was ill. Yet she still claimed that Lizzie was 'going fast' and that Gabriel was foolishly ignoring the danger. Neither would entertain the idea of Lizzie entering hospital, and they were planning to visit Barbara and Anna at Scalands on Saturday – 'now I know that is not prudent but she is doing every day as imprudent things therefore I shall not say: you must not go', Barbara concluded with her characteristic lack of punctuation.[18]

Mrs Elphick's lodging room, Barbara had specified, should be large enough for eating and sleeping and drawing. For Miss Siddal was an aspiring artist. And this is also the evidence in Rossetti's other portrait sketches and drawings from 1853 onwards, in which Lizzie is frequently seen with easel or drawing board – also informal poses rather than those of a model – and which are a testament to the seriousness with which she pursued her art. These also support Ibbitt's account, with its clear statements that Miss Siddal's aim was to 'maintain an independent position as an artist', and that her search for health went together with pursuit of her studies. The romantic attachment of tutor and pupil was also that between two artists, and assisted her own career.

Her participation in the exhibition 'got up by the Pre-Raphaelites at which Mr Ruskin arranged several of her sketches and one oil painting, which sold to an American gentleman for forty guineas' was proof of this professionalism, as also of Ibbitt's accurate knowledge of the details, evidently communicated to him by the artist himself. (He mistook only the medium – the picture of *Clerk Saunders and May Margaret*, purchased by Ruskin's Bostonian friend Charles Eliot Norton, was not in oils but watercolour; the single oil exhibited was a head study, thought to be her self-portrait.) It would seem therefore that Ibbitt's information was gained during Lizzie's visit to Sheffield in 1857, shortly after the exhibition at Russell Place, which represented the high point of her career.

The journey north, according to Ibbitt, was a more serious affair than has previously been supposed, for here his information is likely to be correct. Thus we learn that although Mr Rossetti had proposed marriage, 'a cloud passed over their friendship', and it was after this that she visited Sheffield, where, 'liking the scenery of our delightful neighbourhood, she took a house on Eccleshall Road'. This suggests a relatively long visit, which is supported by the recollections of her fellow students at the art school and the records of the Congregational church – both activities consistent with the intention of staying in Sheffield for some time. In fact, Lizzie can have been there for four months at the most, between the Russell Place exhibition in June 1857 and her summons to Gabriel from Matlock in November, as recorded by Crom Price in Oxford. The Manchester Art Treasures exhibition closed at the end of October, which is consistent with Lizzie's attendance at the art school and the rail excursion during the early autumn term that began in August.

The obituary corroborates this chronology, albeit in telescoped form, by stating that, the intimacy being renewed, the lovers 'met at Matlock, she returned to London, and shortly they were united in marriage.'

Tantalizingly, this is not only inaccurate – Rossetti returned alone to London in the spring of 1858 – but it fails to account for the subsequent two-year gap in Lizzie's history, between Gabriel's departure from Matlock and their marriage in May 1860. Contemporary records of Rossetti's activities in London during this period by Val Prinsep, Burne-Jones and others, show that neither friends nor family were aware of any continuing commitment to a prospective bride. She does not feature in any reminiscences, and there is in fact no information on Lizzie's whereabouts during these twenty-two months.

My deduction is that this period represented the real cloud or estrangement in their relationship, such as was hinted at by other informants, and that in Derbyshire the troubled 'engagement' was finally called off. Lizzie does not seem to have returned to Sheffield, since the local evidence relates only to 1857, and presumably went back to her family in Southwark. Unprompted, her great-niece noted that after having Gabriel's companionship for so long, 'one could hardly imagine that she would have married some perhaps ordinary working man', which suggests that this was, in the family, seen as a possible alternative now that Mr Rossetti had failed to honour his promises.[19] In this light, Gabriel's refusal to mention the engagement in front of Lizzie's mother during the quarrels of 1857 would suggest that his intentions had never been publicly declared, as a formal engagement would have given Lizzie grounds for an action for breach of promise.

In July 1859, Lizzie's father died, making marriage even more desirable, for the cutlery business at Kent Place was now reliant on the skills of her brother James, who had still to finish his apprenticeship; in addition the shop had to support the widow and her other unmarried children – three daughters and one slow-witted son. Soon, Lizzie's sister Lydia was to marry a young railway clerk ten years her junior, the marriage being hastened by Lydia's pregnancy. Lizzie's thirtieth birthday fell in the same month as her father's death, and she faced a bleak future.

There are hints, in the unpublished gossip recorded by Hall Caine and Violet Hunt, that she or her family made a last appeal to Rossetti, in the early months of 1860. Hall Caine remarked that Ruskin had done Rossetti 'an ill turn with a high intention when he persuaded him to go on with the marriage', while Holman Hunt reputedly told Violet that Lizzie asked to see Gabriel in order 'to bid him goodbye' when she was dangerously ill; he came, was touched by her condition, and professed love for her, saying 'if she would but get better, he would marry her'.[20] Bessie Parkes's daughter believed that her mother had also played a part in bringing about the marriage. Christina Rossetti, not knowing of this role as intermediary, met Bessie in the street soon afterwards, and greeted her with the announcement that 'Gabriel has married poor Lizzie at last'.[21] In July Christina told Pauline Trevelyan that Gabriel's marriage 'would be of more satisfaction to us if we had seen his bride', whom the family had not yet met. 'Some years ago I knew her slightly', Christina continued, 'I hope we shall be good friends some day'.[22]

It is clear that the marriage came as a surprise to the Rossetti family, as Bell Scott noted. And it must be assumed that, on learning that Lizzie was grievously ill, Gabriel's sense of honour roused him finally to fulfil his promise. From the brevity with which Ibbitt's obituary treats of his young friend's married life, it appears that nothing more than the formal announcement reached Sheffield and that he knew no more of her activities until receiving news of her death. As befitted the obituary form, Ibbitt aimed only to present a coherent account without including (if indeed he was privy to the exact nature of Miss Siddall's relationship with her wayward lover) too much candid detail. He was franker than might have been expected in his acknowledgement of Lizzie's addiction, however, and his phrasing – 'a secret habit which has proved fatal to many' – suggests personal disapproval of opiates, which perhaps tempered his sorrowful response to the sad news of the amiable young artist's untimely death.

14

Life's Work

The most notable feature of William Ibbitt's obituary is its view of Elizabeth Siddal as an artist in her own right, not simply as Rossetti's model and muse. This redefinition, which accords with the interests of the late twentieth century in rediscovering women who have been 'hidden from history', also indicates another area of original source material relating to her life which has hitherto seldom been explored. This is, of course, her pictorial art, which has so commonly been dismissed as derivative and worthless that its biographical role has been ignored. Yet it offers first-hand evidence of her activity and deserves closer attention. This chapter therefore looks at the story which Elizabeth Siddal's work tells of her life.

The production of art by a woman aiming at professional achievement rather than amateur accomplishment was sufficiently unusual in the mid-nineteenth century to make this aspect of Elizabeth Siddal's life at least of equal importance as her emotional affairs. Indeed, in many ways her art is of more interest than the history of her troubled courtship and marriage, since it was generally assumed in the 1850s that all women sought marriage, while only a few aspired to an artistic career. Of those who did, moreover, only a very few shared Elizabeth Siddal's social position, which makes her even more exceptional. The majority of women artists in the nineteenth century came from the families of professional artists and thus followed, so to speak, in their fathers' or brothers' footsteps. Others came from upper- or middle-class families with enlightened views, like Elizabeth Siddal's friends and near-contemporaries Anna Mary Howitt (born 1824) or Joanna Mary Boyce (born 1831), both of whom enjoyed sufficient parental support to enable them to study in Britain and on the Continent. Both women exhibited and sold their work, and were known to the men of the PRB, and their example may well have encouraged Elizabeth Siddal to seek her own career.[1] In this context, her display of drawings to the Deverells, her work as a model, her acceptance of Ruskin's allowance, her endeavours in illustration, participation in the Russell Place exhibition and her attendance at Sheffield Art School, can all be interpreted as evidence of artistic enterprise and ambition. As befits an artist with a recognizable if shortlived career, she may, too, be referred to by her surname, as well as the more familiar Lizzie.

Siddal was less fortunate than Howitt or Boyce in her training, for Rossetti's tuition appears to have consisted largely of encouraging his pupil to follow her own devices. He himself had been impatient of instruction and study, which at this date involved painstaking and graduated practice in drawing outlines, forms, shading, draperies, casts and still life, before moving on to figure studies from live models, draped and nude. The prospectus of the Sheffield classes – regarded as progressive in their time – indicates the parameters of conventional training:

> Drawing in Outline – Ornament and Figure from the Flat, the Round and from Models, with Blackboard Illustrations.
> Shading – from the Flat and the Round.
> Drawing – Flowers, Foliage etc from Nature.
> Painting – in Oil and Watercolour, from Copies and Still Life, Fruits and Flowers from Nature.
> Modelling – from Fruits, Flowers and the Cast.
> Anatomical Studies, and Studies from the Human Figure (Male Students only)[2]

Rossetti preferred to work from imagination, and encouraged his pupil to do the same. The results were idiosyncratic, in terms of conventional Victorian art. Thus William Rossetti claimed in 1903 that Siddal's works 'resembled those of Dante Rossetti at the same date . . . he had his defects and she had the deficiencies of those defects'.[3] To Evelyn Waugh in 1928, her drawings had 'so little real artistic merit and so much of what one's governess called "feeling" . . . they were tentative, imitative, flickering'.[4] As time went on, she was denied even the credit for their defects: to Graham Robertson in 1931, the works consisted of 'small paintings purporting to be by Elizabeth Siddal and indeed drawn and tinted by a faltering and unskilful hand, but quite obviously, in all save execution, fresh from the brain of her magician husband'.[5] Doughty in 1949 saw 'Gabriel always looking over her shoulder and sometimes taking pencil and brush from her hand to complete the thing she had begun'.[6] More recently, John Nicoll remarked that although Lizzie's paintings were 'technically even less satisfactory than Rossetti's, they have exactly the same direct and personal appeal and, probably because of the extensive help which he gave her, are closely related to them'.[7] Timothy Hilton, as we have seen, imagined Lizzie and Gabriel loving, living and painting together.

The pictures themselves hardly support such negative judgements. Since Siddal's art has been so overshadowed by her husband, it is difficult to gain a clear picture of its development, but a combination of documentary and pictorial evidence – thanks in part to Rossetti's care in collecting and photographing her drawings and sketches – makes it possible to reconstruct a modest *oeuvre* of between twenty-five and thirty subjects, not all completed, from a short working life of about a decade between the early 1850s and the artist's death in 1862. The evidence is of assiduity, imagination and originality. Technical accomplishment along the lines of Academic art was not achieved, but in the Pre-Raphaelite world of the 1850s this was not the main aim.

The subjects of the first 'designs of her own leisure hours' cannot now be guessed, although since they impressed the Deverells they were perhaps already poetic images rather than, say, the sketches of fashionable dress that might be expected from a young milliner. Arthur Hughes's anecdote about Siddal finding Tennyson poems wrapped round a pat of butter indicates that she was aware of contemporary literature before she met the PRB, whatever the limits of her education.

The earliest extant reference to her pursuit of art comes in the letter written by Rossetti in the summer of 1852, warning his sister 'not to rival the Sid' in drawing; but this does not mention any specific subject. At the end of the same year, she declined a request from Charles Collins for her services as a model, as she had 'other occupation'.[8] From this it may be inferred that her studies were in progress. By the beginning of 1853 Rossetti was referring to her as his pupil, and he told Madox Brown that her composition from Wordsworth was 'very advanced and nearly done'.[9] This was the watercolour of *We are Seven*, showing a grieving child in a churchyard among mountains, which was later presented to Henry Acland. In the summer of 1853, as we have seen, while Gabriel was visiting friends in the north of England, Lizzie had the freedom of his studio so that she could get on with her work; at this time she was engaged on her self-portrait, in oils. On his return, Gabriel told Madox Brown that this was nearly finished, and would probably be sent to the Winter Exhibition. It was not sent, however, and the artist evidently encountered problems that her tutor could not solve, for the following year the picture was 'improved greatly' by means of practical advice from Brown. In August 1853, Rossetti reported that Lizzie was 'going to begin a picture at once' for the following year's Royal Academy show, based on a Tennyson subject.[10]

Tennyson, appointed Poet Laureate in 1850 on the death of Wordsworth, and author of the acclaimed *In Memoriam*, was a newly fashionable source among the artistic avant garde. After a slow start, his early works, published in *Poems* (1832), *English Idylls* (1842) and *The Princess* (1847) were gaining popularity; eventually they became the most familiar texts of the century and, as subjects and titles for paintings, an almost inexhaustible pictorial resource, especially favoured by Pre-Raphaelite artists and their followers. In the early 1850s, however, Siddal's *Lady of Shalott* was among the earliest representations of his verse.

It is her first dated work. The finished drawing is inscribed 'E. E. Siddal Dec 15 1853', and both signature and distinctive spelling of the surname suggest a new self-conscious identity as an artist. The scene depicted is the critical moment in the poem, when the imprisoned Lady, 'sick of shadows', sees Sir Lancelot in the mirror and turns from her loom to look directly, causing the glass to crack and provoking the curse that leads swiftly to her death. In Siddal's picture, the Lady is presented as 'pure, chaste and calm', occupying a cool, airy and spacious workroom which holds evidence of past labours in the tapestry hanging on the far wall and a crucifix for devotional use; she thus accords with prevailing Victorian prescriptions of womanhood, being quiet, modest, devout and usefully occupied with a specifically feminine skill.[11]

Artistically, the drawing recalls the early work of the PRB, in terms both of its presentation of a single female figure and of its awkward, *faux-naïf* manner. Through her acquaintance with Holman Hunt, Siddal may already have known of his own *Lady of Shalott* drawing, done in 1850 and offering a different image of the same moment, while the religious references in her picture, absent from the poem, echo comparable elements in Millais's *Mariana*, first exhibited at the Royal Academy in 1851. In this context, Siddal's drawing is less naïve than has been assumed. Moreover, the extreme awkwardness of the Lady's pose and the stiffness of her anatomy, normally interpreted as evidence of the artist's lack of skill, relate even more strongly to a specific source much favoured in early Pre-Raphaelitism – that of medieval art. A strikingly similar image, showing a fifteenth-century woman seated on a stool, working at a tall tapestry loom in a bare room with a window behind her, is contained in an illuminated manuscript of Christine de Pisan's *Cité des Dames*, now in the British Museum. It cannot be proved that Elizabeth Siddal knew this picture, for the manuscript was only acquired by the museum in 1855, but the similarities are remarkable, and Pre-Raphaelite interest in medieval illumination is well documented: Charles Collins, for example, used an Italian book of hours in the Soane Museum for his *Convent Thoughts* in 1850. Siddal's reference to a similar source was thus probably due to conscious study, not ineptitude. A few years later, Rossetti himself used similar medieval illuminations of women carding and weaving for the background in *Before the Battle* (1858).

In both subject and treatment, therefore, *Lady of Shalott* displays the Pre-Raphaelite style in its first phase, when drawings of archaic and literary subjects characteristically contained flat, stiff figures, small spaces and odd, irregular compositions. Taken together, however, Siddal's early works also display unexpected variety. *We are Seven* is a relatively amateurish piece, although it is, as Henry Acland noted, ambitious in its landscape scope for an artist working entirely within the studio. By contrast, the bold, unglamorized presentation of the contemporaneous self-portrait – strongly contrasting with Rossetti's saccharine images of her at the same period – indicates a firm, Ruskinian honesty or truth to nature.

As has already been noted, this period of Siddal's apprenticeship in 1852–4 was reflected in Rossetti's own works, as already noted. For example, his drawing *A Parable of Love* (sometimes known as *Love's Mirror*) depicts a young man in archaic costume teaching a woman to paint, by guiding her hand as she attempts a self-portrait. A caricature sketch dated September 1853 shows Gabriel sitting to Lizzie as she works intently on a portrait study. A virtual companion piece of the same period shows a male artist and female model over the title *Giorgione Painting*. Taken together, these three images convey the various aspects of the reciprocal partnership of teacher-pupil and artist-model. Other studies of Lizzie at her easel or drawing board, together with a caricature of her hiding a picture among stacked canvases in the studio, also attest to her pursuit of art. Not surprisingly, these images are less well known than those showing Lizzie reading or resting, because they have, up till now, been less popular with biographers: the passive rather than active poses have been selected as representations of the romantic artist and his muse.

Her own works contain fewer images that can be directly related to personal circumstances, since virtually all are subject pictures and illustrations. But within these are contained several motifs that are indirectly personal, and some which can be described as self-images similar to that of Rossetti's *Giorgione*. The most important of these is the pen-and-ink drawing *Lovers Listening to Music*, which was given to William Allingham around the end of 1854. The title is not that chosen by the artist, being derived from Gabriel's description of the subject the following year as 'the two nigger girls playing to the lovers'.[12] (When reproduced in 1897, they were more politely called 'Egyptian Girls'.) This appears to have been an original subject and was in my view inspired by the weeks Lizzie and Gabriel spent at Hastings in the early summer of 1854. This was when they were most in love, and when Barbara Smith was convinced they would marry 'if circumstances were favourable' – and it was where, as Gabriel told his mother, the pair rambled along the cliffs carving their initials on the rock, in the time-honoured tradition of young lovers.[13]

The background in *Lovers Listening to Music* is similar to that of a popular cliff walk between Hastings and Fairlight (itself a landscape view popular with several Pre-Raphaelite painters) passing a spot locally known as 'Lover's Seat'. In the picture, the Indian-looking girls playing to the seated lovers are symbolic of love's 'song of joy', and the small figure by the gate is probably intended to personify Love, as a sort of non-classical cupid who featured frequently in Pre-Raphaelite art. The lovers themselves are idealized images of the artist and her beloved. Clearly not a literal scene – the oriental musicians are not inhabitants of rural England – this is an imaginative representation of the lovers' relationship. Its companion piece is Rossetti's *Writing on the Sand*, where two figures in modern dress, not dissimilar to those listening to music, are walking on the beach; with his stick the man draws the woman's profile in the sand. Again, this is a gesture of love akin to carving initials, and almost certainly the picture drew its original inspiration from the time at Hastings. It should be stressed that neither *Writing on the Sand* nor *Lovers Listening to Music* was intended as a love token, yet a strong element of personal meaning is present in both works, especially when seen together.

Companionship in love went with partnership in art. Another source of inspiration for Siddal was Rossetti's own poetry. When they met, he had written very little verse, but among the published pieces was *Sister Helen*, a ballad tale in which a young woman melts the waxen image of her faithless lover while her young brother watches the man's death from the battlements. The critical moment when Helen realizes that she has forfeited her soul was selected by Siddal for her sketch with the same title. As the choice suggests, she shared with Rossetti a liking for macabre and supernatural subjects. Her later watercolour known as *The Haunted Tree* (sometimes *The Haunted Wood*), in which a woman shrinks from a ghost in a woodland setting is based on an as yet unidentified source, but shares its spooky atmosphere with Edgar Allan Poe's *Ulalume*, and the 'ghoul-haunted woodland of Weir' – a poem and a poet from whom Rossetti had taken several picture subjects in the late 1840s.

Both artists were also attracted to border ballads. 'I think I told you that she and I are going to illustrate the Old Scottish Ballads which Allingham is editing for Routledge,' Gabriel told Madox Brown from Hastings. 'She has just done her first block (from *Clerk Saunders*) and it is lovely,'[14] This ballad had long been a favourite of his and it is likely that he introduced his pupil to the text. In the event, no such illustrated book was issued by Routledge, but Lizzie began several ballad subjects taken from Walter Scott's *Border Minstrelsy*. Two volumes of this collection, inscribed with the artist's name – 'Eliz⁄th. E. Siddal' – show that at one time she considered a total of seventeen texts.[15] Four are known in pictorial form: preparatory sketches for *The Gay Goshawk* and *The Lass o' Lochryan*, and finished watercolours of *Clerk Saunders* and *The Ladies' Lament* from *Sir Patrick Spens*.

Clerk Saunders began as a woodblock engraving, with stiff figures and a stark setting appropriate to the subject, where the Clerk appears as a ghost, wrapped in his shroud, in the bedchamber of his lover May Margaret, having been slain by her brothers. Rossetti praised his pupil's originality. 'Her power of designing increases greatly,' he told Brown from Hastings; 'and her fecundity of invention and facility are quite wonderful, much greater than mine.'[16] Again, despite the lack of anatomical understanding, the work is remarkable for the stiff spikiness characteristic of early Pre-Raphaelite drawing and for its emotional expressiveness. But the composition and subject were less purely original than Rossetti believed, for both display close links to his own works at the same period. Similar two-figure compositions were a feature of Rossetti's pictures around 1853–4, and the principal figures in his *Salutation of Beatrice in Eden* (finished in the spring of 1854) are echoed in *Clerk Saunders*. This does not mean that Siddal's work was simply imitative: the themes of the revenant and of the lovers reunited after death were recurrent motifs in both artists' work, and compositional similarity is indicative of a collaborative artistic relationship. Rossetti was certainly right to regard Siddal's work as original in the sense of being uncontaminated by conventional academicism, and himself strove to produce the same archaic effect in his own pictures.

Later, after the ballad-book idea had been dropped, Siddal reworked *Clerk Saunders* as a watercolour, losing in the process some of the attractive naïveté but gaining in fluency and depth as well as colour. It proved one of her most successful designs, and was exhibited in London and North America in 1857, where it was described as a study for a larger oil painting, suggesting still further potential development. Retrieving the watercolour from its purchaser some years later, Rossetti was 'truly pleased to see its face again. It even surprised me by its great merit of feeling and execution and now takes its place among its fellows on my drawing-room walls.' He also arranged for the original silver surround to be gilded.[17]

By the spring of 1855, Siddal had completed sufficient drawings and watercolours for Rossetti to show her work to Ruskin with a view to obtaining his patronage. The previous year Ruskin had lost his favoured protegé Millais when Millais had rescued Effie Ruskin from an unconsummated and unhappy marriage, and for a time Rossetti became the chief beneficiary of Ruskin's patronage. He was thus eager to bring his pupil to Ruskin's attention and the ground was carefully prepared. On seeing Siddal's works Ruskin offered to purchase them all for a total of £30. 'He is going to have them splendidly mounted and bound together in gold, and no doubt this will be a real opening for her, as it is already a great assistance,' Gabriel told Allingham with excitement.[18] Lizzie's first purchase with the money, with Brown's aid, were her own brushes and paints from the artist's supplier Robersons.

This sale, and Ruskin's subsequent offer of an allowance of £150 a year (which Lizzie was, if necessary, to be 'coerced' into taking, as Gabriel wrote) have sometimes been interpreted as evidence of Ruskin's desire to secure Rossetti's allegiance, rather than a demonstration of genuine faith in her talent. It is true that Ruskin was, at this date, much influenced by Rossetti – he commissioned a number of pictures and wove Rossetti's praises into the third volume of *Modern Painters* – but he was also patronizing other, more grateful disciples such as John Brett and Anna Blunden, with financial assistance, and his response to Siddal is in keeping with his self-assumed role as Pre-Raphaelite mentor. He undertook to instruct Blunden in Pre-Raphaelite principles, for example, and attempted to do the same to Siddal.

Ruskin's ideal was the fusion of heightened realism from detailed observation of nature with the expressive power of Gothic 'grotesque'. And he evidently felt Siddal's work was over-weighted in favour of the latter. Apparently referring to her 'spectral subjects' like *The Haunted Tree* and *Clerk Saunders*, he advised her to desist from 'those disagreeable ghostly connections',[19] and concentrate on sketching from nature, in colour.

Later he told her to stop designing 'fancies' or imaginative scenes, saying that she should be 'made to draw in a dull way sometimes from dull things'.[20] At this, Rossetti intervened to insist that he alone would act as Miss Siddal's instructor.

Ruskin also offered to show Lizzie his collection of illuminated manuscripts, as if in recognition of the archaic references in her work. And he played an active role in managing her health, inviting her to meet his parents (when his mother presented Lizzie with the ivory dust with which to make a restorative jelly) and sending her to consult Henry Acland, who, as we have seen, was given a slightly garbled account of her origins that included the information that Miss Siddal's father was a watchmaker. Acland's diagnosis was that she was over-excited, and his advice was that she stop painting and rest. When Lizzie proved less than grateful for Mrs Acland's hospitality, Ruskin confessed that all his so-called 'geniuses' were wrong-headed. Then, after ascertaining from Rossetti that it was not lack of money that prevented his marriage with Miss Siddal, Ruskin insisted that she take a cottage in the country, preferably in Devonshire. Lizzie went to the sea-side resort of Clevedon in Somerset where she met the donkey boy, and was later prevailed upon to go to France for the winter. With Mrs Kincaid she left for Paris and finally reached Nice, from where she wrote to Ruskin about the landscape. 'I am rejoiced at your entirely agreeing with me about the vapid colour of that southern scenery,' he replied in January 1856. 'I hate it myself. The whole coast of Genoa, with its blue sea, hills, and white houses, looks to me like a bunch of blue ribands dipped in mud and then splashed all over with lime.' He commended the 'fine green and purple' of Menton, and advised her to go to the Italian Alps where, he concluded, 'if with red campaniles, green and white torrents, purple-grey and russet rocks, deep green pines, white snows and blue valley distance, you can't make up a sauce to your satisfaction. I shan't pity you'.[23]

But Siddal's art was not the vivid landscape of John Brett, whom Ruskin dispatched in the same direction. Indeed, she seldom used outdoor settings for her imaginative scenes. One of her few landscapes with figures, however, is the ballad scene from *Sir Patrick Spens*, known as *The Ladies' Lament*. Signed and dated 'E.E.S. 1856', this is a gentle composition in greens and blues and yellows, showing a group of young mothers gazing out to sea from the low cliffs around a grassy cove. The landscape may have been taken from the Somerset coast near Clevedon, where Rossetti joined her for a short holiday, and the tones and mood are echoed in his watercolour version of *Writing on the Sand*, for which he borrowed a north Devonshire background. *The Ladies' Lament* exhibits all Siddal's facility of invention, or visual imagination, for the grouping of the figures is unlike anything seen in contemporary work. There is no clear centre of attention, and indeed the action, such as it is, takes place off canvas, as the women watch vainly for their shipwrecked menfolk.

Another sequence of subjects selected by Siddal, perhaps with Ruskin in mind, was wholly conventional, for her series of religious subjects from the life of the Virgin were standard themes from Christian art and iconography. During 1855 Ruskin attempted to persuade Rossetti to complete his pictures of the Nativity and the Holy Family at the Passover, for sale to an ecclesiastical friend. At the same time, he was advising a fellow patron in Leeds that some day a commission might be an encouragement, to Rossetti's pupil, 'a poor girl – dying I am afraid – of ineffable genius'.[24] Many patrons preferred obviously moral and uplifting pictures and it is possible that Siddal turned to religious subjects hoping that Ruskin could sell them for her.

Three were variations on the same theme: a watercolour *Nativity* showing Mary with an angel in the stable; a series of sketches depicting the Virgin laying the child in the manger, watched by ox and ass; and a watercolour *Madonna and Child*, where Christ is a red-haired infant standing sturdily on his mother's lap. Scenes for a *Deposition from the Cross* and *The Empty Tomb* were also sketched out.

These subjects do not prove that Elizabeth Siddal was a believer, but they show she was responsive to and ready to use the same Christian themes that were among the main subjects of Pre-Raphaelite religious art. Rossetti himself had painted the *Girlhood of Mary Virgin* and *The Annunciation*, Holman Hunt selected *Christ in the Temple* and *The Light of the World*, as well as an earlier, unfinished image of Christ and Mary Magdalene. Millais's *Christ in the Carpenter's Shop* had of course been the subject of Charles Dickens's notorious attack on the religious and artistic principles of Pre-Raphaelitism in 1850. With what is now known of Elizabeth Siddal's Congregational affiliations, her choice of religious subjects is surprising only in so far as it suggests the conscious adoption of a mode frequently criticized – by Ruskin among others – of papistical tendencies or 'Mariolatry'. In fact, however, pictures of sacred subjects such as the Nativity and Empty Tomb were also typical of 'low church' or Sunday School teaching, and Siddal's choice of subjects need not imply any abrogation of Protestant belief.

Having begun her professional career with a subject from Tennyson, she was an obvious contender, as Rossetti thought, for the list of artists commissioned by Edward Moxon to produce engravings for an illustrated edition of Tennyson's early poems. Millais, Hunt and Rossetti were invited to represent the younger generation, and in January 1855 Rossetti protested to Allingham that Brown, Hughes and Miss Siddal ought also to have been included. He urged his pupil's merits on both publisher and poet, and in March reported triumphantly that 'Mrs T[ennyson] wrote immediately to Moxon about it, declaring that she would rather pay for Miss S's designs herself than not have them in the book.'[25] This did not happen, but it is probable that several of Siddal's designs were prepared in expectation.

She began another Lady of Shalott composition, showing the Lady lying in the boat that bears her downriver to Camelot, and six other subjects: *Lady Clare, Morte d'Arthur, Sir Galahad, St Agnes' Eve, Jephtha's Daughter* (from *A Dream of Fair Women*) and *Saint Cecilia* (from *The Palace of Art*). The last is a careful composition showing the patron saint of music, from the following verse:

> Or in a clear-walled city on the sea,
>   Near gilded organ pipes, her hair
> Wound with white roses, slept St Cecily;
>   An angel looked at her.

In an interior setting, the saint's head is thrown back, her eyes closed in a trance or transport of ecstasy rather than sleep, while an angel with folded wings kneels beside the organ. This image, as Marillier and William Rossetti established, was adapted by Gabriel for his own later illustration to *The Palace of Art*, in which the saint, high up on the city wall, is kissed by a large enfolding angel.[26] As is frequent in their work, where Siddal placed her figures apart, Rossetti brought them together in an embrace.

The embrace, however, featured in Siddal's composition for *Jephthah's Daughter*, who was the Hebrew martyr who gave her life for her people and became a popular figure in Victorian art. In Siddal's study, Jephtha's kiss is not romantic but ominous, representing the critical moment when the woman's sacrifice is sealed. The figures are strongly drawn and evidently studied from life.

Another Tennyson subject was *St Agnes' Eve*, a small painting in gouache, based on the short poem about a novice contemplating her vows. Images of nuns were popular, if controversial, subjects in the paintings of the 1840s and '50s, when the issue of Anglican sisterhoods was much debated, and Siddal's image falls within the Pre-Raphaelite mode, where the religious woman devoting her life to Christ was an admired representation of femininity. The saintly figure is positioned to the right of a high window, with a snowy landscape beyond; below, a door opens into a chapel, with altar and crucifix.[27]

Lady Clare deals with more complex issues of gender and class relations. In the short ballad-style poem, Nurse Alice reveals that Lady Clare is her own daughter and not of aristocratic birth. Once more, Siddal's composition depicts the moment of moral dilemma, when Alice implores Lady Clare not to disclose the truth.

> 'Nay, now, my child,' said Alice the nurse,
> 'But keep the secret for your life,
> And all you have will be Lord Ronald's
> When you are man and wife.'

Nobly, Lady Clare rejects this deceit:

> 'If I'm a beggar born,' she said,
> 'I will speak out, for I dare not lie,
> Pull off, pull off the brooch of gold,
> And fling the diamond necklace by.'

The Legend of Elizabeth Siddal

This watercolour, begun around 1854 and finished in 1857, when it was signed and dated 'EES/57' in an elaborate new monogram of her initials characteristic of Pre-Raphaelite practice, is an awkward representation of an awkward moment, set like several of Siddal's other works within an enclosed space, with small openings into daylight. Lady Clare covers Alice's face with her hand and turns stiffly away from her supplication. 'The drawing of the figures and the organisation of the architectural space oppose renaissance notions of anatomy and perspective which were enshrined in academic traditions . . . as calculated strategies in the production of "medievalness",' noted Deborah Cherry,[28] just as the mid-Victorian poem takes the self-consciously archaic form of a traditional ballad. In the happy ending, Lady Clare reveals her humble origin and Lord Ronald marries her none the less, recognizing her nobility of nature. Problems of class and sex – the staple of Victorian literature – are thus resolved.

Into Lady Clare's story, Siddal's painting also inserts a pictorial reference to another tale of maternal affection, in the form of a stained-glass window showing the Judgement of Solomon, in which the true mother's identity is revealed by her willingness to forgo her claim to the child to save it from death. This was a parable of maternal self-sacrifice frequently cited in Victorian sermons and scripture lessons, and such typological insertion was characteristic of Pre-Raphaelite art. Here it is indicative of an intellectual approach that is seldom attributed to this artist, and also of a somewhat unexpected focus on the figure of the mother rather than the young marriageable woman. Again, the device echoes a similar use of stained glass in Millais's *Mariana*, while the figures are locked in an embrace that recalls those of other couples – as in Millais's *Huguenot* of 1852, Hunt's *Claudio and Isabella* of 1853, and Arthur Hughes's *April Love* of 1856 – similarly full of tension and conflict.

If Elizabeth Siddal's work was wholly derivative, as has so frequently been claimed, her borrowings prove to have been carefully selected from a range of sources, rather than being unconsciously absorbed from her tutor, as the 'deficiencies of his defects' as William Rossetti unkindly put it. A simpler explanation is that, with her entry into the Pre-Raphaelite circle as model and aspiring artist, she noted and adopted the currency of the school, as did other painters. And in some areas, she was at the forefront of new ideas.

The last Tennyson subject she selected was *Sir Galahad*, from *English Idylls*, a subject that is in fact one of the earliest representations of Arthurian themes in Pre-Raphaelite art, indicating that Siddal was among the first to develop the medieval motifs that now became a hallmark of the school, although later images drew more frequently on Malory than Tennyson. It also demonstrates the close collaborative artistic partnership between herself and Rossetti. Whatever the vicissitudes of their emotional relationship, their artistic practice was reciprocal.

A number of sketches for *Sir Galahad and the Holy Grail* show the development of the idea from a conventional composition of the virgin knight with angels in a chapel consecrating himself to the quest for the Grail, to the much stranger final scene which places him in a skiff, drifting through a ruined and flooded church, as in a dream landscape. The image is a conflation of the lines spoken by Galahad:

> Sometimes on lonely mountain meres
> I find a magic bark;
> I leap on board: no helmsman steers:
> I float till all is dark,
>
> . . .
>
> A gentle sound, an awful light!
> Three angels bear the holy grail:
> With folded feet, in stoles of white,
> On sleeping wings they sail.

The sketches were all executed by Siddal (and included as such in the photographic portfolio of her drawings compiled by Rossetti) indicating that the idea and design was her work, but the finished watercolour was a joint production: its inscription reads: 'EES inv. EES & DGR del.', showing that both artists were involved in its execution. It was presented to Ruskin, presumably under the terms of his allowance during 1855–6.

If the standard view of duality between Rossetti and Siddal in terms of male/female, strong/weak, innovative/imitative is abandoned in favour of one that sees their artistic relationship as a matter of mutual exchange and collaboration, much of the debate over his role in her work will dissolve. Although manifestly the junior partner in the artistic enterprise, Siddal supplied Rossetti with several ideas – for example *St Cecilia* and the *Morte d'Arthur* (where her three weeping queens were multiplied into seven) – while in his role as instructor he assisted some of her work. The joint inscription on *Sir Galahad* should be taken at face value: in this instance both artists worked on the picture together.

The notion that the works 'purporting' to be by Siddal were in fact by Rossetti derives largely from Charles Fairfax Murray, Rossetti's former studio assistant and, subsequently, collector. On a label stuck to the back of *Clerk Saunders* (which he purchased from William Rossetti in 1884 and sold to the Fitzwilliam Museum thirty years later) Murray claimed that: 'There is no doubt that Gabriel Rossetti himself worked on this picture as was customary with him.' Citing Burne-Jones as his authority, he went on to assert that 'much of the merit' possessed by Siddal's works properly belonged to Rossetti, and 'his aid is frequently visible in the preliminary drawings'.[29] But Murray had not known Siddal and was above all interested in the promotion of Rossetti as an 'uniquely gifted artist', and in his own role as expert and arbiter when works came on to the market. A picture that could be said to have had Rossetti's hand in its execution was self-evidently worth more money than one by Siddal. Burne-Jones's role in this debate, incidentally, suggests that he recalled seeing Gabriel and Lizzie working together presumably after marriage.

There is, as it happens, no evidence of Rossetti's hand in the sketches for *Sir Galahad*. But a degree of influence in exactly the opposite direction is visible in Rossetti's works of the mid–1850s, for deliberate imitation of Siddal's stylistic lack of sophistication, in homage to Ruskin's praise of Gothic grotesque, is the only plausible explanation for Rossetti's 'inept' pictures of this period, such as the cramped *Arthur's Tomb* of 1855. This, Ruskin confessed, he dared not show any 'anti-Pre-Raphaelites', who would jeer at its amateurish composition.[30] On similar grounds he refused to buy the unsatisfactory *St Catherine* two years later, justifiably complaining of its poor execution. Rossetti could indeed draw and paint in a much more accomplished manner, and the grotesquerie of these works is explicable only by reference to the genuine naïveté he admired and fostered in the work of his 'love and pupil'.

From this survey of her pictures, it can be seen that from the start of Lizzie's relationship with Gabriel she was tackling Pre-Raphaelite subjects in her own distinctive style, which made up for its lack of technical accomplishment (she seems never to have learnt how to draw, in the sense in which it was understood in the nineteenth century) by its freshness and direct, expressive manner. She might almost, in today's terms, be characterized as a naïve or primitive painter.

But she was not ignorant or unaware of prevailing artistic thought. Indeed, her subjects reflected the standard motifs of the age – religious, poetic and legendary themes drawn from sources in the English bible and English literature, at a time when the establishment of an English visual culture was being promoted to challenge the high ground of French artistic superiority. They also addressed closer concerns, both social and personal, and specifically in regard to issues of class and gender, from which it is possible to deduce some of the private responses behind the artist's selection of subjects.

Devout and moral figures are strongly featured in her work, as we have seen, from the Virgin Mary through *Jephtha's Daughter* and the novice nun of *St Agnes' Eve* to the spiritual male hero Sir Galahad and the flower of Victorian chivalry, Tennyson's King Arthur. These were the approved models of nineteenth-century masculinity and femininity, to which as artist Siddal paid more than lip service, for her renderings of the subjects are thoughtfully chosen and deeply felt. She also celebrated family affection and grief, in her pictures of the mourning women in the *Ladies' Lament* and the bereaved child in *We are Seven*. The choice of Wordsworth's text may, indeed, indicate a directly personal subject, for Siddal herself had seven siblings, and the watercolour – her first finished painting – followed hard on the death of her eldest brother Charles in 1850.

Lady Clare is also a type of Victorian virtue, in her uncompromising insistence on truth. This was a period when honesty and frankness in personal relations as well as business affairs were the twin ethical pillars of the emerging middle class, and Siddal's own sense of honourable truth-telling is visible in her *Self-Portrait*, with its utter absence of vanity or glamorization. *Lady Clare*, however, is also an example of the superiority of moral integrity over aristocratic birth, and it is no coincidence that Siddal's painting was completed in the same year that the hugely popular novel *John Halifax, Gentleman* was published, with its paradigmatic story of the social triumph of innate nobility of soul over the accident of birth.

In class terms, Siddal herself was upwardly mobile. Her father, born into the skilled working class in Sheffield, had risen to become a prosperous retail shopkeeper in London, with social aspirations (and also, if family tradition is correct, a fixed belief in his family's ancestral gentility). His daughters were not born ladies – they lived over the shop, with no resident servants, and were trained to earn their own livings in the dressmaking trades – but their mother had pretensions, and in the fluid social formation of mid-Victorian London, it was enjoined on them to marry as well as they were able: romantic love was well-tempered by hopes of social advancement. Despite her unorthodox entry into the artists' world, Lizzie's upward path was indeed checked only by Gabriel's failure to make good his promises of marriage. In this context, the triumph over class divisions in *Lady Clare* takes on an additional meaning.

So, too, does the story of *Clerk Saunders*, although here the class position is reversed, for it is Saunders who is low-born and slain by Margaret's brothers for his presumption. And Siddal's other choices from Scots balladry echo the theme of ill-fated and obstructed love. *The Lass o' Lochryan* is prevented from reaching Lord Gregory by his mother's enchantments, while *The Gay Goshawk* tells of a woman who by feigning death outwits her father in order to marry her beloved.

As an artist, Siddal was evidently also attracted to tales of magic and the supernatural, with their strong element of fantasy. Her illustrations of contemporary verse included not only the mysteriously accursed Lady of Shalott and Sister Helen's sorcery, but also a sketch for Keats's cold enchantress La Belle Dame sans Merci. As other women artists found, in the poetic sphere femininity was not disadvantaged, for there were no strict standards of heroic naturalism to meet, and the pictorial world of fantasy and imagination was perceived as an appropriate artistic arena for women. The male Pre-Raphaelites, indeed, had more to worry about, for their choice of poetic subjects laid them open to the criticism that their work lacked 'virility' and the 'broader masculine life and temper' that produced great and noble art.[31]

The majority of Siddal's works also show women as chief subject or protagonist. Of these, perhaps the most intriguing are two pictures which, while drawing on the work of Shakespeare and Browning – two popular Pre-Raphaelite sources – articulate unexpected issues around the question of womanhood, reflecting contemporary debates over definitions of gender.

Her careful ink drawing of *Pippa Passing the Loose Women* from Browning's poetic drama *Pippa Passes* dates from 1854, the same period as *Lovers Listening to Music*. Removed from the poetic setting, its subject is prostitution: the virginal Pippa passes three 'poor girls' sitting on the steps gossiping about their clients. In the 1850s, prostitution was an urgent social issue. The increase in the visible numbers of 'circulating harlotry' in the streets of London formed the background to a cultural discussion of the problem that included Dickens's portrayal of Little Em'ly in *David Copperfield*, and Tennyson's oblique account of a seduced girl in *The Woodman's Daughter* (painted by Millais in 1851). In 1853 Holman Hunt's *Awakening Conscience* was the talking point of the Royal Academy show, prompting Rossetti to lay claim to the subject with his never-finished *Found* on the same modern-life topic. Richard Redgrave and Augustus Egg were among the other artists who offered variations on the theme, and in 1854 Anna Howitt caused a stir with her picture of the seduced Margaret from Goethe's *Faust*, a picture that was sought by the philanthropist Angela Burdett Coutts, then engaged in the reclamation and retraining of fallen women. The following year Howitt exhibited *The Castaway*, which Rossetti said contained a 'dejected female' with lilies lying in mud, all 'symbolical of something improper'.[32] *Pippa and the Loose Women* was thus Siddal's treatment of a popular if controversial subject, generally regarded as rather 'strongminded' for a female artist. Her image juxtaposed the pure and corrupted types of womanhood, showing Pippa as a demure and modest self-image, and the Loose Women as large, blowsy and vulgar. These opposing types are visually separated by an unmistakable barrier of strong vertical lines.

The Shakespearean subject is equally interesting, for the PRB were famous for their renderings of Shakespeare, and Siddal herself had modelled for Viola, Ophelia and Sylvia. Yet her own choice of subject was no such virtuous heroine but the evil and tragic Macbeths. Her pen-and-wash drawing for this depicts the moment after the murder of Duncan when, with the words 'Give me the daggers', Lady Macbeth seizes the weapons from her husband to smear the grooms' faces with blood. In concept this is the most violent and melodramatic of Siddal's subjects, and shares the same fascination with evil intent as *Sister Helen*. For a young woman artist it was a distinctly unexpected choice of subject and, if entirely her own invention, this image of a murderess would be a somewhat startling addition to Siddal's artistic *oeuvre*, in stark contrast to her other heroines such as the self-sacrificial Jephtha's Daughter.

Indeed, her brother-in-law evidently thought so, for in his account of Siddal's career, he described the subject as 'Macbeth taking the Daggers from his Wife who meditates Suicide'.[33] But no such scene is found in the play, and in any case in the picture Lady Macbeth is clearly seen grasping the knife from her irresolute husband, who twists his body ineffectually as she grits her teeth for the task. The dramatic implications are obvious. However, it seems likely that the image was not invented by the artist but adapted by her from a similar engraving in a contemporary edition of Charles and Mary Lamb's *Tales from Shakespeare*, one of the nineteenth century's favourite texts. It was indeed responsible for introducing many people to Shakespeare's work at a time when the theatre was generally considered too vulgar for respectable persons, especially women, to attend. The Lambs' text, with its detailed account of the witches's spells, Banquo's ghost and other apparitions, was calculated to appeal to Siddal's taste for the macabre, while their characterization of Lady Macbeth as a 'bad, ambitious woman' and the chief villain of the piece established her as an 'unsexed' antitype of femininity.

When Lizzie returned to Britain in the spring of 1856, she took rooms of her own in Weymouth Street. She found that Gabriel's attention had wandered, and that he had been chasing Annie Miller, among others. 'Miss Sid complains enough of his goings on,' commented Madox Brown, who believed the best solution to be marriage.[34] Yet her painting flourished. She at once set to work to turn the *Clerk Saunders* woodblock into a watercolour, and by the end of the year was planning an oil version too. She completed the *Ladies' Lament*, and also *The Haunted Tree*. In September, Gabriel promised to set a wedding date when he received money for a painting, but the cash came and went and no date was fixed. Lizzie left for Bath, telling the Browns she wanted no more to do with her wayward lover. On her return to London in February, came the great quarrel over the artists' colony, followed by another promise of marriage, and another failure to act. Gabriel had his new friends from Oxford, Morris and Burne-Jones (to whom Miss Siddal was not introduced) and a painting commission in Wales, at Llandaff Cathedral.

Her career continued. In 1857, she completed her picture of *Lady Clare* and was invited to participate in the exhibition of Pre-Raphaelite art organized by Madox Brown and held in Russell Place, in June. This was the first public showing of her work, in the illustrious company of Millais, Hunt, Brown, Rossetti and other much better established artists than herself. She was the only woman included, and Rossetti and Ruskin helped mount her pictures, which included *We are Seven, The Haunted Tree*, and *Clerk Saunders*, together with drawings from Tennyson and Browning, and a study of a head which was presumably her self-portrait. The show was not warmly reviewed – Pre-Raphaelite painting was still something of a minority interest – but Siddal's work received relatively favourable private and public attention. Holman Hunt, who had not previously seen her work, compared it with that of Walter Deverell, which he admired, and Rossetti sprang to his pupil's defence by asserting it was far better.

In the *Saturday Review*, the poet Coventry Patmore was complimentary, commending the archaism of style and the elevated sensibility. 'There was one lady contributor, Miss E. E. Siddal whose name was new to us,' he wrote.

Her drawings display an admiring adoption of all the most startling peculiarities of Mr Rossetti's style, but they have nevertheless qualities which entitle them to high praise. Her 'Study of a Head' is a very promising attempt, showing great care, considerable technical power and a high, pure and independent feeling for that much misunderstood object, the human face divine. . . . 'Clerk Saunders', although we have heard it highly praised by high authorities [i.e. Ruskin], did not please us so much.

He added that *We are Seven* and *Pippa Passes* deserved more attention than he was able to give.[35]

William Rossetti, in a *Spectator* review, praised Miss Siddal's designs as being quite unlike the general run of lady artists' work. She did not, it may be noted, choose to exhibit with the newly-founded Society of Female Artists, organized by friends of Anna Howitt and Barbara Leigh Smith as a specific saleroom for women's work. But she was honoured when *Clerk Saunders* was included in the show of British art seen in New York at the end of the year – even if this came about partly because the painting had to cross the Atlantic anyway, having been purchased by Ruskin's friend Professor Norton of Harvard. This sale helped compensate for the fact that Ruskin's allowance had been permitted to lapse, apparently by default. He wished his protegée well on the open market.

In July Gabriel went to Oxford to lead the 'jovial campaign' in the university debating chamber, and Lizzie, perhaps angry at being excluded (several of those recruited had less painting experience than herself but were of course all men), went to Sheffield, where she was welcomed for both her local and metropolitan connexions by William Ibbitt – a self-taught artist himself – and Young Mitchell, head of the art school. From Sheffield she travelled to the Art Treasures Exhibition in Manchester, where several of her friends and acquaintances, including Millais, Hunt and Howitt, had works on display.

It is tempting to see her enrolment at the art school as evidence of a belated desire for a solid grounding in drawing, but the truth is probably that it afford the most congenial working space and companionship. If the other women students laughed at her artistic dress, as 'A.S.' recalled, they were probably motivated partly by envy of this visitor from London, who knew the great critic Ruskin and moved in such avant-garde circles. As A.S. noted, with Miss Siddal Young Mitchell was able to discuss the new trends in art of which the other students had not heard.

194

In November Lizzie moved to Matlock (medical advice commended leaving the urban areas in winter owing to soot- and sulphur-laden fogs) and summoned Gabriel north. At this point a curtain falls on their relationship, in terms of documentary information. Artistically, however, they resumed their partnership, both being engaged on similar subjects during the succeeding months. These were directly derived from the interest in medieval chivalry and jousting that had been stirred by the Oxford enterprise, and by William Morris's proselytizing enthusiasm for armour, tourneys and Froissart's chronicle of the French wars. By 1857–8, virtually all the Pre-Raphaelite circle were busy with pictures of knights and ladies.

The most popular of these subjects showed a medieval damsel tying her favour to the lance or helm of a knight riding out to joust or battle in her honour. Millais, Rossetti, Burne-Jones and Siddal all produced variations on this theme in the late 1850s. Siddal's image, *Before the Battle* (also known as *Lady Affixing Pennon to a Knight's Lance*) is one of shared activity as the lady assists her knight to nail her favour – a scarf in love's own colour of red – to his long lance. Through the door, his squire waits, holding the horse, while through the window is seen a moorland landscape, perhaps taken from the Derbyshire hills. If, as the Sheffield historians stated, the artist visited Haddon Hall, the fortified medieval house in the Peak District, famed for its association with Walter Scott, the setting would have provided apt inspiration for the scene in the picture. The mood is companionate, although the subject is structured in terms of gender difference, and the almost-conjugal embrace of the figures is cut across diagonally by the length of the lance. In Rossetti's companion piece, also entitled *Before the Battle*, the lady is centred and foregrounded, standing. As she ties the embroidered banner to his lance, the young knight gazes out beyond the spectator. In the background coifed ladies are carding and weaving while knights muster with their spears and banners.

From the spring of 1858 the documentary trail of Elizabeth Siddal's life goes cold, and there is no further record of her artistic activity until her wedding in 1860. After this date there are several references to her painting – including her mural contribution to the decoration of the Morrises' Red House – but only one specific subject is mentioned. This is her last unfinished work *The Woeful*

Victory, first shown to Georgie Burne-Jones after the visit to the zoo in the summer of 1860. This again is a tournament scene, with a tragic theme: 'Two Knights fight for a Princess – the one she loves is vanquished,' explained William Rossetti, adding that: 'This fine subject was I believe wholly her own invention.'[36] The further tragedy is that the Princess must now marry the victor, who has slain her lover, according to summary of the plot given by Gabriel when he took the story as the projected ending for his long, unfinished ballad *The Bride's Prelude*. Although the poem was composed in various stages between 1849 and 1878, this ending was proposed long after Lizzie's death, and it is virtually certain that *The Woeful Victory* was independently conceived, to be later borrowed by her husband. Its melodramatic motif is in keeping with her liking for such archaic themes. The complex picture, as it survives in unfinished drawings, includes another squire with horse, and demonstrates the artist's growing confidence and skill in dense, detailed composition and ambitious figure poses.

These chivalric scenes in Siddal's late works share in the Pre-Raphaelite group's interest in medieval art, which was at its height in the late 1850s and early 1860s, and was reflected in the Medieval Court at the 1862 International Exhibition in London, where a large range of ecclesiastical and decorative art was on display. Siddal died shortly before the exhibition was opened, but in her social circle the medievalist enthusiasm is also seen in the furnishings and furniture created for Red House during preceding months, with which she was actively involved. Her own participation in this process is seen in the decoration of a wooden Gothic Revival jewel box she began to paint in the last months of her life. On this, one of the small panel pictures was taken directly from an early fifteenth-century illuminated manuscript in the Harley collection of the British Museum (incidentally another Christine de Pisan text) showing a lady and her lover in a battlemented terrace garden.[37]

The jewel box was unfinished: only seven of the fourteen tiny panels are painted and of these some scenes remain half-completed. One resembles a slight sketch in Siddal's portfolio showing two figures in a shallow boat. The painted panels are now worn, for the box later belonged to Jane Morris, probably having been given to her by Gabriel after Lizzie's death in remembrance of her. May Morris believed it to have been painted by Lizzie and Gabriel together; it would thus form another joint artistic enterprise, so characteristic of their working partnership.

A number of other sketches and drawings are included in the surviving portfolios of Siddal's work, showing that over the years she began other subjects and practised drawing from life. Besides the figures rowing in a shallow skiff, there is a rough compositional sketch which Rossetti or his brother called *Wreck of a Fishing Boat*, and an unidentified *Landscape with Castle*. A figure study of a girl holding an infant may have been drawn from a girl in charge of a young brother whom the artist met on the cliffs at Hastings and took back to her lodgings to draw; alternatively, her elder sister Annie MacCarter had children of the appropriate age. There is also a pencil study of a young woman reading, reminiscent of Rossetti's own images of Elizabeth in similar poses, which may have been done from her sister Lydia, her frequent companion; it is more softly and skilfully executed than the majority of her sketches. In addition, there is a head study of a girl which in its conventional non-Pre-Raphaelite rendering of soft features and round 'chocolate-box' eyes is utterly unlike any other work from her hand. In the photographic portfolio it looks frankly like a cuckoo in the wrong nest, yet is must be supposed that in compiling the portfolio Rossetti knew his wife's work. In total, sixty-seven items – drawings, sketches and scraps of sketch – were photographed and recorded, some of which are extremely faint and exiguous, suggesting that nothing done by Elizabeth Siddal had been discarded or excluded. Together with the eleven known works in oil or watercolour, which were not reproduced owing to the poor results expected in monochrome, this compilation stands as a full record of her work.

Viewed overall, her artistic career is both more varied and more independent than has previously been assumed. At the same time, her evident partnership with Rossetti and links with other painters in the group show her to have been not so much an 'original' as a junior member of the Pre-Raphaelite band, sharing their preoccupations and concerns. The personal element in her work is subdued but detectable. Above all, the story of her work over the years places the story of her love life in a new and firmer perspective. We are beginning to be able to reconstruct her biography in detail.

15

Poetic Endings

Painting was only part of Elizabeth Siddal's artistic output. Just as her work as a visual artist has been ignored in the histories in favour of her role as model, so her verse writings have been dismissed, or invoked as examples of simple self-expression in support of biographical interpretations of weakness and self-pity.

But her poetry – fifteen more or less complete poems, plus some fragments – is also an important part of her 'own story'. In the absence of autobiography, letters, diaries, notebooks or the like – whatever such materials existed at her death were destroyed by her husband on leaving Chatham Place – they represent the only surviving texts produced by herself, as opposed to the many tales about her created by other people. Like the drawings and paintings they are self-conscious works of art, not raw autobiographical writings. They are not exclusively concerned with direct personal feeling and meanings; indeed, several are composed in dramatic voices, as in the ballad form, where the 'I' is not the poet's subjective self. Yet all, of course, tell us something about the poet. In this they belong to the same class of verse as many of Christina Rossetti's poems: simple-seeming lyrics dramatizing a mood or emotion, or telling a tale. Most are in ballad form, with four- or six-line stanzas; some employ simple couplets. The style is unsophisticated, the content often unexpectedly layered and complex. And, while they are not as deftly wrought or densely allusive as verse by Emily Brontë or Christina Rossetti, they nevertheless inhabit the same poetic world.

Elizabeth Siddal does not seem to have accorded the same status to her poetry as to her painting. Her visual art was undoubtedly practised in a professional manner – studied, displayed, exhibited and sold – and continued even after marriage and despite the impediments of pregnancy, depression and drug addiction. By

198

contrast, verse writing seems to have been a private activity. No
documentary references exist from her lifetime and it is difficult
to judge the dates of most of the poems. The established view is
that Lizzie began writing poetry before 1854,[1] but this merely
represents William Rossetti's best guess and seems founded on no
evidence, internal or external. If she was indeed writing during
the early 1850s, when Gabriel was full of enthusiasm for her
wondrous talent, he would surely have included it in his praise
of her genius to Ruskin, for example, and would have also told
Madox Brown. But neither Ruskin's letters nor Brown's diaries
contain any reference to 'Ida' or 'Guggum' as a budding poet.
Bessie Parkes was also an aspiring poet in her youth, but left
no mention of this as a shared interest in her friendship with
Lizzie.

The first extant mention of Elizabeth Siddal's poetry was indeed
not until some years after her death, when Rossetti fair copied
six poems for possible inclusion in Christina's volume *The Prince's
Progress* (1866). The six poems selected but not then published
were those now titled 'True Love', 'A Year and a Day', 'Dead
Love', 'Shepherd Turned Sailor', 'Gone' and 'At Last'. Apart
from the first, the titles were apparently supplied at this date,
rather than by the poet. Between 1895 and 1906 all fifteen poems
were published by William Rossetti, and thereafter were quoted
from time to time in biographies and other accounts of the Pre-
Raphaelite circle, until the publication of the Wombat Press limited edition of 1978, and the inclusion of 'Silent Wood' and 'Dead
Love' in the *New Oxford Book of Victorian Verse* in 1987. Elizabeth
Siddal is still not widely known as a poet, however; at the literary
festivals where Gillian Allnutt and I have included six of the
poems in our presentation of poetry and paintings audiences have
expressed surprise at learning that she also wrote verse.

The corrupt and fragmentary texts of the poems – in holograph,
fair copy and print – present some difficulties of interpretation,
especially with regard to authorial intentions, which were only
partly resolved in the Wombat edition where 'author's manuscript' was claimed as copy text, although several of the holograph
versions are incomplete or almost impossible to decipher. Only
'True Love' exists as an author's fair copy, signed with the initials
'E.E.R'; according to a note by William Rossetti, this was 'written
before her marriage but the copy is made afterwards',[2] although

the logic of this deduction is not apparent; the whole piece may well date from after the marriage. Two previously unpublished fragments complete the Wombat edition, one taken from an author's manuscript and the other from Violet Hunt's *Wife of Rossetti*, where no authority for its authorship is cited; further unpublished fragments exist in the Bryson collection of manuscripts in the Ashmolean Museum.

These technical details mean that, with the exception of 'True Love', it is impossible to regard the texts as representing the author's finished work; in many ways they are drafts of poems variously amended by subsequent editors. However, little is gained by scholarly examination of variant readings; the verses now current must simply be regarded as uncertain and not necessarily the texts the author would have published had she lived to do so. Similarly, it is virtually impossible to establish any chronology or dating for the poems. Some drafts are on notepaper bearing the author's married monogram 'EER'; some are on eighth- and quarter-inch mourning stationery, which may signify that they were written after her father's death in July 1859. On the back of one manuscript sheet is an unfinished draft of a letter to Emma Madox Brown in 1855, with a reference to Lizzie's imminent departure abroad. The handwriting of the various copies varies from a small, thin-lined cursive script to a broad, straggling and illegible hand which seems accurately identified by William Rossetti as 'done under the influence of laudanum . . . and probably not long before her death'.[3]

In terms of content, the poems can be divided into two broad groups – those dealing in one way or another with sorrow and death, and those dealing with 'the passing of love' – the actual title of one piece. Some contain both themes, but overall the 'death' verses are marked by melancholy and the 'love' verses by anger. At this point, I want initially to consider the texts as literary productions, not as autobiographical outpourings, and discuss their poetic content and meanings. Because the verses are not easily available, this entails fairly extensive quotation, although none of the poems is long in itself. The critical discussion, however, is integral to an understanding of what part the poems played in Elizabeth Siddal's life story. With circumspection, they can be used as biographical materials.

In *Early Death*, the dying lover addresses the beloved with words of sorrowful consolation:

> Oh grieve not with thy bitter tears
> The life that passes fast;
> The gates of heaven are open wide
> And take me in at last.

The speaker foresees reunion in heaven:

> But, true love, seek me in the throng
> Of spirits floating past
> And I will take thee by the hands
> And know thee mine at last.

He and She and Angels Three treats the same theme in the third person, as the beloved awaits her lover in heaven:

> Ruthless hands have torn her
> From one that loved her well;
> Angels have upborn her,
> Christ her grief to tell.

> She shall stand to listen,
> She shall stand and sing,
> Till three winged angels
> Her lover's soul shall bring.

Both these pieces are slight and unsophisticated, deriving their feeling and imagery from the standard consolations of mid-Victorian religious verse with its emphasis on heavenly meetings with lost loved ones, in a world of unseen idealities. This, of course, was also the world of Gabriel Rossetti's poem *The Blessed Damozel*, where the beloved leans from heaven seeking her lover on earth, and with erotic religosity imagines being married to him by God in paradise. Elizabeth Siddal's verse is plainer and more truly pathetic; its *vrai naïf* qualities carry genuine feeling, within a long tradition of poetic lamentation and farewell. In this mode, too, Christina Rossetti wrote several first-person poems about approaching death, and the imagined consolation of heavenly reunion, also viewing the afterlife with desire. And Siddal's images are active; the lover is envisioned as searching for his beloved in a 'throng' of souls moving past like an urban crowd, and seizing her from its midst. The lost one has been ruthlessly torn from life and carried to heaven, to await – the repetition of 'she shall stand and listen, she shall stand and sing' is fully expressive of anxious expectation – the arrival of her lover by the same angelic transport.

Lord, May I Come is longer and more complex. The speaker contemplates death with a paradox linking death with light rather than darkness:

> Life and night are falling from me
> Death and day are opening on me.

Life is perceived as a 'stony way of woe':

> Hollow hearts are ever near me,
> Soulless eyes have ceased to cheer me,
> Lord, may I come?

Although following the contours of devotional verse, this piece is impelled not by piety but by sorrow and despair:

> My outward life feels sad and still
> Like lilies in a frozen rill;
> I am gazing upward to the sun,
> Lord, Lord, remembering my lost one
> O Lord, remember me!

Approaching death raises queries about heaven:

> How is it in the unknown land?
> Do the dead wander hand in hand?
> . . .
> Do we clasp dead hands and quiver
> With an endless joy for ever?

Again, here are echoes of the *Blessed Damozel*, although the dead hands clasped and quivering in an endless unconsummated embrace is an original and vivid image of ghostly lovers. It was, incidentally, a motif picked up and used by Swinburne in *The Triumph of Time* not many years later, where spirit lovers 'feel the dust quiver and quicken, and seem Alive as of old to the lips', and while it is possible – and would be intriguing to know – that Swinburne read Siddal's lines, it must be said that the motif was so common in Victorian verse for no such direct cross-fertilization to be necessary. Equally striking is the fusion of religious and romantic language, the blend of erotic and devotional desire, that brings sacred and secular together. This too was a contemporary habit, clearly displayed in the work of Christina Rossetti and others, but strongly felt and expressed by Siddal. Loss and lamentation in this world go hand in hand with faith and hope in the hereafter.

Biographically, it is tempting to interpret these poems as expressions of the author's sorrow when her estrangement from Gabriel seemed permanent, but they fall into a familiar mode much practised in mid-century, and to place them within their cultural context serves to counter the critical view that all are simply morbid and self-indulgent, expressive only of personal distress.

Frequently, the work borrows from archaic sources. *Shepherd Turned Sailor* begins like a medieval carol:

> Now Christ ye save yon bonny shepherd,
> Sailing on the sea,

and modulates into a lament:

> If he is lost then all is lost
> And all is dead to me.

> My love should have a grey head-stone
> And green moss at his feet,
> And clinging grass above his breast
> Whereon his lambs should bleat,
> And I should know the span of earth
> Where some day I might sleep.

The conjunction of unresolved elements creates an atmosphere of awkward innocence that is characteristically Pre-Raphaelite in

203

feeling, and also owes much to the ballad tradition, with its fragmentary, contradictory texts.

True Love invokes the ballad form in its opening lines, addressed to 'Earl Richard' (the title of an actual ballad in *Border Minstrelsy*). Siddal's Earl is dead, 'lying alone' under his marble effigy, 'with hands pleading earnestly, All in white stone'. The image is taken from observation of Gothic tombs infused with dramatic feeling; it evokes the ruined chapel of the watercolour of *Sir Galahad and the Holy Grail* and also the story of *The Woeful Victory*, to whose subject the poem may well be connected, but is in no sense a ballad pastiche. Kneeling to kiss the dust from his grave, the speaker is Earl Richard's beloved saying farewell:

> Soon I must leave thee
> This sweet summer tide;
> That other is waiting
> To claim his pale bride.

The ambiguity – is 'that other' another husband or death itself? – is maintained through to the final verse, foreseeing the 'dead leaves' of autumn:

> Then shall they find me
> Close at thy head
> Watching or fainting,
> Sleeping or dead.

The short, lilting lines are deceptively simple, deploying nursery rhythms with ambivalent assurance.

At Last begins like a ballad – 'O mother, open the window wide' – and moves to another death-bed valediction:

> The hills grow darker to my sight
> And thoughts begin to swim.

The dying narrator entrusts her son to his grandmother and gives instructions for her laying-out:

> And mother, wash my pale pale hands
> And then bind up my feet;

My body may no longer rest
Out of its winding sheet.

And mother dear, take a sapling twig
And green grass newly mown
And lay them on my empty bed
That my sorrow be not known.

And mother, find three berries red
And pluck them from the stalk
And burn them at the first cock-crow
That my spirit may not walk.

And mother, dear, break a willow wand
And if the sap be even,
Then save it for sweet Robert's sake
And he'll know my soul's in heaven.

Together, the repetition, incantation, hints of archaic magic and the unexplained storyline – is the speaker dying of a broken heart? – carry an authentic sense of the old texts to which the verses pay tribute, such as *Lord Randal* or *The Demon Lover*, while making a new tale with its oblique, elusive narrative. In succeeding stanzas the speaker moves steadily towards death with both sorrow and joy:

And mother, when the big tears fall
(And fall, God knows, they may)
Tell him I died of my great love,
And my dying heart was gay.

With its unresolved story and delicate tone balanced between regret and desire, *At Last* is among the finest of Elizabeth Siddal's poems.

A Year and a Day combines the welcome approach of death with the loss of love. Again, it begins simply, with the repetition characteristic of traditional verse, yet quickly modulates into something different, with the dragging rhythm expressive of the mood:

The Legend of Elizabeth Siddal

Slow days have passed that make a year,
Slow hours that make a day
Since I could take my first dear love
And kiss him the old way;
Yet the green leaves touch me on the cheek
Dear Christ, this month of May.

I lie among the tall green grass
That bends above my head
And covers up my wasted face
And folds me in its bed,
Tenderly and lovingly
Like grass above the dead.

The subject has altered, from conventional lover's lament to a haunting death-in-life image of burial and embrace, in the vocabulary of love and desire.

This is one of the longer poems, with seven six-line stanzas, a form chosen several times by Elizabeth Siddal and similar to that used by Christina Rossetti in *Seeking Rest*, which also deals with the loss of joy. The verses progress irregularly, and the imagery is sustained. 'Dim phantoms of an unknown ill' as 'unformed visions' of life 'pass in ghostly train' indicating imminent death. In turn the spectral figures suggest kindly, grieving spirits:

Some pause to touch me on the cheek,
Some scatter tears like rain.

Another passage develops the grave-as-bed motif, where

A new face lies between my hands –
Dear Christ, if I could weep
Tears to shut out the summer leaves
When this new face I greet.

Firmer control over the verse here might have resulted in a loss of suggestive uncertainty; the broken rhythm and double hiatus of 'if I could weep Tears' reaches out towards the unconscious, the vision being 'but the memory Of something I have seen . . . so strange and far it seems'. Here again the poem turns on ambiguity: the new face is the shadow of the lost love so that 'old' and 'new' may be the same as 'then' and 'now'.

206

The present is lapped in obsessional natural imagery. Grass and leaves are repeatedly invoked: the 'river ever running down' hints at passing time; the voices of 'a thousand birds' do not sing but 'clang' overhead; and the final stanza employs a striking image of fruitful death:

> A silence falls upon my heart
>   And hushes all its pain.
> I stretch my hands in the long grass
>   And fall to sleep again,
> There to lie empty of all love,
>   Like beaten corn of grain.

This image of a woman who has lost her lover (specifically referred to as him, from which we may infer that the speaker is female) being as a threshed or beaten ear of wheat, for whom death or silence 'hushes' all pain, combines both comforting and disturbing associations.

Gone by contrast adopts the voice of a male lover – a deliberate device which indicates how the verses are not to be interpreted as simple, subjective expressions of unmediated personal feeling – recalling a now-shadowy happiness through simple synecdoche:

> To touch the glove upon her tender hand,
>   To watch the jewel sparkle in her ring,
> Lifted my heart into a sudden song
>   As when the wild birds sing.
>
> To touch her shadow on the sunny grass,
>   To break her pathway through the darkened wood,
> Filled all my life with trembling and tears
>   And silence where I stood.

The beloved is 'gone for ever', likened to 'the tender dove That left the Ark alone', a simile that recalls not only Rossetti's 'dear dove' symbol but also numerous Pre-Raphaelite paintings of girls and doves, notably Millais's *Return of the Dove to the Ark*.

The darkened wood is visited again in *Silent Wood*. This offers the most poignant of all Elizabeth Siddal's poems on love's passing, beginning as an evocation of deep, atmospheric melancholy:

The Legend of Elizabeth Siddal

> O silent wood, I enter thee
> With a heart so full of misery
> For all the voices from the trees,
> And the ferns that cling about my knees.
>
> In thy darkest shadows let me sit
> When the grey owls about thee flit . . .

In this profound gloom of place and mood, the speaker is 'frozen like a thing of stone', sitting in shadow yet 'not alone'. Leaving this unexplained, the verse breaks abruptly into a final anguished and unanswered long-lined couplet of regret:

> Can God bring back the day when we two stood
> Beneath the clinging trees in that dark wood?

According to tradition Elizabeth and Gabriel first pledged their hearts in the woods of the Leigh Smith estate at Scalands in 1854, and personal meaning may well give the verse its emotional edge here, but such an interpretation does not modify the power of its sudden emotional swoop, and the desolation of the ending.

The Passing of Love opens with a howl of pain:

> O God, forgive me that I ranged
> My life into a dream of love!
> Will tears of anguish never wash
> The passion from my blood?

Then the emotional tone is reversed, continuing with an evocation of happiness:

> Love kept my heart in a song of joy,
> My pulses quivered to the tune;
> The coldest blasts of winter blew
> Upon it like sweet airs in June.
>
> Love held me joyful through the day,
> And dreaming ever through the night;

> No evil thing could come to me
> My spirit was so light.

The loss of this bliss is especially bitter, in the last stanza's violent image:

> O heaven help my foolish heart
> Which heeded not the passing time,
> That dragged my idol from its place
> And shattered all its shrine!

This fierce, angry ending explains, contains and underscores the pain and distress of the opening, as the contrast between happiness and misery is laid bare, in an exceptionally unsentimental piece.

Passionate anger is again the emotion of *Love and Hate*, in which the faithless lover is dismissed with scorn:

> Ope not thy lips, thou foolish one
> Nor turn to me thy face
> The blasts of heaven shall strike thee down
> Ere I will give thee grace.

The rage is for betrayal:

> Turn thou away thy false dark eyes
> Nor gaze upon my face.
> Great love I bore thee; now great hate
> Sits grimly in its place.

And betrayal is corrosive: the false lover is a 'poisonous tree That stole my life away'.

These verses attempt no narrative explanation or justification; their feeling is rendered stronger by the lyrical simplicity and the blend of literary language with fierce and unexpected imagery:

> Take thou thy shadow from my path
> Nor turn to me and pray;
> The wild wild winds thy dirge may sing
> Ere I will bid thee stay.

Elizabeth Siddal's verse contains many similar elements to

The Legend of Elizabeth Siddal

Christina Rossetti's, in addition to the use of deceptively simple forms. Throughout both poets' work, cold and frozen imagery for the experience of lost or unrequited love alternates with that of fire and burning for passion and anger. It is not surprising that Christina found much in Lizzie's verses to admire, while recognizing that they were too sombre for public taste. Her own work was criticized as excessively melancholy; how much more so the handful of poems by her sister-in-law?

Dead Love she thought 'piquant . . . with cool bitter sarcasm', and as such no doubt inappropriate, as she judged, for publication by the author's husband in memorial form. It has indeed a fierce, unforgiving wit:

> O never weep for love that's dead,
>   Since love is seldom true
> But changes his fashion from blue to red,
>   From brightest red to blue,
> And love was born to an early death
>   And is so seldom true.

This is altogether the bitterest tone Elizabeth Siddal's verse employs, but it too modifies into complexity, for the second stanza contains an implicit dialogue over the romantic illusions of love:

> Then harbour no smile on your bonny face
>   To win the deepest sigh.
> The fairest words on truest lips
>   Pass on and surely die,
> And you will stand alone, my dear,
>   When wintry winds draw nigh.

The poem's resolution is bitterly but ambiguously sad:

> Sweet, never weep for what cannot be,
>   For this God has not given.
> If the merest dream of love were true
>   Then, sweet, we should be in heaven,
> And this is only earth, my dear,
>   Where true love is not given.

Who is being addressed, the false lover or grieving self? The slight break in rhythm accentuates the tragic quality of disillusion, as the bleak sense forces itself across the poetic form.

The opening of *The Lust of the Eyes* has exceptional piquancy in its implicit comment on the Pre-Raphaelite artists' aesthetic adoration of female beauty:

> I care not for my Lady's soul
>   Though I worship before her smile;
> I care not where be my Lady's goal
>   When her beauty shall lose its wile.
>
> Low sit I down at my Lady's feet
>   Gazing through her wild eyes
> Smiling to think how my love will fleet
>   When their starlike beauty dies.

Finally, there are two poems of terminal melancholy. One is in couplets and was given the title 'Speechless' by William Rossetti.[4] It opens:

> Many a mile over land and sea
> Unsummoned my love returned to me;
> I remember not the words he said
> But only the trees moaning overhead.

The speaker is almost beyond speech as well as hearing; her 'frozen lips' are 'still shut and dumb'. Nor does she know how her 'still and slow' words sound to her lover, who comes to rescue her from 'pain and wrong'. But this prince has come too late: he cannot revive his princess. Indeed, his arrival is a strange sort of comfort:

> I felt the wind strike chill and cold
> And vapours rise from the red-brown mould;
> I felt the spell that held my breath
> Bending me down to a living death.

Is the rescuer 'with his love so strong' a human figure, or perhaps Christ the Saviour, 'ready to take and bear The cross I had carried', or rather Death itself, with his fatal yet welcome embrace?

The Legend of Elizabeth Siddal

Worn Out reworks a similar theme, with what seems a more sentimental approach, yet retains a cool, almost ironic distance:

> Thy strong arms are around me, love,
>   My head is on thy breast;
> Low words of comfort come from thee
>   Yet my soul has no rest.
>
> For I am but a startled thing
>   Nor can I ever be
> Aught save a bird whose broken wing
>   Must fly away from thee.
>
> I cannot give to thee the love
>   I gave so long ago,
> The love that turned and struck me down
>   Amid the blinding snow.
>
>   . . .
>
> Yet keep thine arms around me, love,
>   Until I fall to sleep;
> Then leave me, saying no goodbye
>   Lest I might wake, and weep.

The poignancy of this ending, with its plaintive echoes of Christina Rossetti's *Song* beginning 'When I am dead, my dearest', is overshadowed only by Elizabeth Siddal's own death so soon after writing these lines.

Since the poems were not intended for publication, they may be regarded as more personal in conception than the paintings, which were undoubtedly produced within the framework of professional purpose, for exhibition and sale. And the dominant poetic themes of lost love and anger, tempered only by a faint hope of heavenly reunion, cannot easily be related biographically to any period of Elizabeth Siddal's life except that of the estrangement in 1858–60. The echoes of Border balladry, with which the author was familiar in her pictorial work from 1854 onwards, and the mourning edge to her notepaper offer circumstantial but not conclusive

212

support for this dating. The sad scraps of manuscript that survive can hardly be seen as evidence of sustained or self-confident literary art, and the absence of any contemporary references to verse suggests it was a very private activity. So, although it cannot be proved, it is very likely that Elizabeth Siddal's poetry was written during the period when she was out of touch with the artists' world, lacking support or encouragement to paint, possibly without painting materials, and that it represents both a substitute for her pictorial art and a means of expressing and assuaging her broken heart. In that experience, however, anger was at least as powerfully felt as sorrow.

Postscript

The analysis of Elizabeth Siddal's verse and visual art may seem dry and distant, a poor alternative to the flesh and bones or at least the living voice which is the proper subject of biography. And indeed, the discussion of works of art should not be confused with that of the author's life: analysis of poetry and pictures lies in the realms of literary criticism and art history, and is not a substitute for biographical explanation.

But it is an inadequate account of Elizabeth Siddal's life that does not discuss her art, and I have chosen to conclude with my account of her poems in order to introduce other ways of reading Elizabeth Siddal's story, and hence her life. What survives of the woman buried in Highgate Cemetery today is both an accumulation of more or less persuasive anecdotes, and a small but substantive body of work, which no one but myself as yet takes very seriously. Both pictures and poems possess an imaginative scope and unique flavour which convey an always individual vision, drawing inspiration from unusual sources and journeys of self-discovery, expressive of original imagination and emotion, within the true Pre-Raphaelite style. And both are major elements in her life story.

To place the emphasis here is not to claim that this account is 'better' or more correct than the biographies that have preceded it, nor to assert that critical analyses are above or outside history, untainted by the assumptions and prejudices of their times and authors. Clearly, each such narrative is itself a product of its own age, with its own details of meaning. The quest for the 'real Elizabeth Siddal' thus reveals more about the changing ideological context, and the uses to which the legend is put in the redefinitions and negotiations in the realms of gender and art.

If it is not possible, finally, to resurrect Elizabeth Siddal living and breathing as a 'real person', this is partly because the documentary materials have been destroyed, but more importantly because biography is not reincarnation but a form of exhumation. From the contents of her coffin, so to speak, each age remakes the image of Elizabeth Siddal to its own specification. And the image is only ever a shadow or ghost of the actuality.

Nowadays, Highgate Cemetery is much tidier, and there is a well-worn path through the tombs and massed headstones to the Rossetti grave where, frequently, one finds a bunch of flowers wilting in a jamjar. I have placed some there myself, in tribute to the woman about whom I am writing.

There are many aspects of her life that are still unknown, obscure or puzzling, and many fanciful tales are still repeated. All contribute to her legend, and have purpose and meaning in themselves. But a real change has occurred even as this book has been in preparation. Not only, as we have seen, is her poetry now represented, in its own right, in the current Oxford anthology of Victorian verse, but her painting has also been on show, in a touring exhibition. Moreover, her two pictures in the Tate Gallery, normally kept unseen in the basement archive, viewable only by appointment, have recently been on display, alongside other works of the same period and style, accompanied by Max Beerbohm's cartoons. Furthermore, in the month that I finished the first draft of this text, an article appeared in the Sunday press on the treatment of artists' remains by their family and friends. The passing reference was, of course, to the exhumation and retrieval of Rossetti's poems from his wife's coffin, 'under cover of darkness . . . thereby furthering both his career and his guilt'. To my delight, however, the victim of this 'cadaverous caper' was described plainly, without apology, as 'Elizabeth Siddal, the writer and artist'.[1]

Perhaps she is, therefore, now being allowed to relinquish her posthumous domain as a fantasy figure for generations of readers (and some ballerinas), and encouraged to enter a new incarnation. At one level, I wish she could now be left to rest in peace; at another, I trust there will, in time, be many further disinterments and re-creations of the legendary Elizabeth Siddal. She still has many more lives to be told, for we look into the past as into a mirror, to see ourselves.

Bibliography

Owing to the nature of this book, the bibliography of published sources is arranged in chronological order, with the works cited in the text listed by author or source according to date of publication. For easy cross-reference, works are then cited in the notes by author and date, followed by volume and page number where appropriate; full details may be found in the bibliography's chronological sequence. The aim of this chronological ordering is to give further demonstration of the 'biographical history' of Elizabeth Siddal as regards published works.

All students of the Pre-Raphaelite world and its inhabitants are indebted to William Fredeman's *Pre-Raphaelitism: A Bibliocritical Study* (1965), which lists every work on the subject up to that date and without which much subsequent research would have been much more laborious. For our further benefit, a welcome supplement to this valuable work is currently in preparation. Other important volumes, editions of letters and the like are also being prepared for publication so that the bibliography given here will continue to require updating.

Unpublished sources are listed alphabetically at the head of the bibliography.

Manuscript and Special Collections

Ashmolean Dept of Prints and Drawings, Ashmolean Museum, Oxford, GB.
BL Dept of Manuscripts, British Library, London, GB.
Cornell Dept of Rare Books and Manuscripts, Cornell University Library, Ithaca, NY, USA.
Fitzwilliam Dept of Manuscripts, Fitzwilliam Museum, Cambridge, GB.
Girton Library and Archive Collection, Girton College, Cambridge, GB.

Huntingdon   Henry E. Huntingdon Library, San Marino, California, USA.
Sheffield LS   Local Studies Collection, Sheffield City Libraries, Sheffield, GB.
Yale   Beinecke Rare Book and Manuscript Library, Yale University, New Haven, Connecticut. USA.

Publications

Place of publication: London, unless otherwise stated.

Daily News, 1862 'Death of a Lady from an Overdose of Laudanum', *Daily News*, 14.2.1862
Sheffield Telegraph, 1862 'The Death of Mrs D. G. Rossetta', *Sheffield Telegraph*, 28.2.1862, Sheffield, Yorkshire.
C. G. Rossetti, 1866 Christina Rossetti, *The Prince's Progress and Other Poems*.
Athenaeum, 1882 'Dante Gabriel Rossetti', obituary by Theodore Watts Dunton and F. G. Stephens, *Athenaeum*, 15.4.1882. Reprinted in Theodore Watts-Dunton, *Old Familiar Faces*, 1916.
Tirebuck, 1882 William Tirebuck, *Dante Gabriel Rossetti: His Work and Influence*.
Sharp, 1882 William Sharp, *Dante Gabriel Rossetti: A Record and a Study*.
Caine, 1882 Thomas Hall Caine, *Recollections of Dante Gabriel Rossetti*.
Royal Academy, 1883 Royal Academy, *Winter Exhibition of Works by the Old Masters . . . including a special selection from the works of John Linnell and Dante Gabriel Rossetti*.
Burlington Fine Arts, 1883 Burlington Fine Arts Club, *Pictures, Drawings, Designs and Studies by the Late Dante Gabriel Rossetti*.
W. M. Rossetti, 1886 William Michael Rossetti (ed) with preface and notes, *Collected Works of Dante Gabriel Rossetti in Poetry and Prose*.
Knight, 1887 Joseph Knight, *The Life of Dante Gabriel Rossetti*.
W. M. Rossetti, 1889 William Michael Rossetti, *Dante Gabriel Rossetti as Designer and Writer*.
Howitt, 1889 *Mary Howitt: An Autobiography*, edited by Margaret Howitt.
W. M. Rossetti, 1891 William M. Rossetti: (ed) *The Poetical Works of Dante Gabriel Rossetti*. New edition in one volume.
Scott, 1892 *Autobiographical Notes of the Life of William Bell Scott, and Notices of His Artistic and Poetic Circle of Friends 1830 to 1882*, edited by W. Minto, 2 vols.
Layard, 1894 G. S. Layard, *Tennyson and his Pre-Raphaelite Illustrators*.

Stephens, 1894   F. G. Stephens, *Dante Gabriel Rossetti.*

W. M. Rossetti, 1895   William Michael Rossetti (ed), *Dante Gabriel Rossetti: His Family Letters with a Memoir*, 2 vols.

C. G. Rossetti, 1896   Christina Rossetti, *New Poems.*

New Gallery, 1897   New Gallery, Regent Street, *Exhibition of Pictures Ancient and Modern by Artists of the British and Continental School, including a selection from the works of Dante Gabriel Rossetti.*

Hill, 1897   G. B. Hill (ed) *Letters of Dante Gabriel Rossetti to William Allingham*, New York.

Belloc, 1897   Bessie Parkes Belloc, *A Passing World.*

W. M. Rossetti, 1898–1900   W. M. Rossetti (ed), *The Poems of Dante Gabriel Rossetti*, 7 vols. 'Siddal Edition'.

Spielmann, 1898   M. H. Spielmann, *Millais and His Works*, Edinburgh.

Bell, 1898   Mackenzie Bell, *Christina Rossetti: A Biographical and Critical Study.*

Millais, 1899   J. G. Millais (ed), *Life and Letters of Sir John Everett Millais*, 2 vols.

Mackail, 1899   J. W. Mackail, *The Life of William Morris*, 2 vols.

Marillier, 1899   H. C. Marillier, *Dante Gabriel Rossetti: An Illustrated Memorial of His Art and Life.*

W. M. Rossetti, 1899   William Michael Rossetti (ed), *Ruskin: Rossetti: Preraphaelitism. Papers 1854 to 1862.*

Symons, 1899   Arthur Symons, *Images of Good and Evil.*

W. M. Rossetti, 1900   William Michael Rossetti (ed), *Pre-Raphaelite Diaries and Letters.*

W. M. Rossetti, 1901   William Michael Rossetti (ed), *The Germ: a reprint of the literary organ of the Pre-Raphaelite Brotherhood published in 1850*, with introduction.

Hueffer, 1902   Ford Madox Hueffer, *Rossetti: A Critical Essay on His Art.*

Atlay, 1903   J. B. Atlay, *Sir Henry Wentworth Acland: A Memoir.*

W. M. Rossetti, 1903 (1)   William Michael Rossetti (ed), *Rossetti Papers 1862–1870.*

W. M. Rossetti, 1903 (2)   William Michael Rossetti, 'Dante Rossetti and Elizabeth Siddal', *Burlington Magazine*, June.

Burne-Jones, 1904   Georgiana Burne-Jones, *Memorials of Sir Edward Burne-Jones*, 2 vols.

Benson, 1904   A. C. Benson, *Rossetti.*

C. G. Rossetti, 1904   *The Poetical Works of Christina Georgina Rossetti*, edited with a memoir and notes by William Michael Rossetti.

W. H. Hunt, 1905   William Holman Hunt, *Pre-Raphaelitism and the Pre-Raphaelite Brotherhood*, 2 vols, revised and reissued 1913.

W. M. Rossetti, 1906   William Michael Rossetti, *Some Reminiscences*, 2 vols.

Williamson, 1906   G. C. Williamson, *Catalogue of the Collection of Miniatures the Property of Mr J. Pierpont Morgan*, privately printed.

Allingham, 1907   William Allingham, *A Diary*, edited by H. Allingham and D. Radford.

Caine, 1908   T. Hall Caine, *My Story*

Hueffer, 1911   Ford Madox Hueffer, *Ancient Lights and Certain New Reflections*.

Le Gallienne, 1911   Richard le Gallienne, *Loves of the Poets*, New York. Reissued in Britain as *Old Love Stories Retold*, 1924.

Ruskin, 1912   *Collected Works of John Ruskin, Letters I and II*, edited by A. J. Cook and A. O. Wedderburn.

Beerbohm, 1922   Max Beerbohm, *Rossetti and His Circle*.

Williamson, 1925   G. C. Williamson, *Stories of an Art Expert*.

Waugh, 1928   Evelyn Waugh, *Rossetti: His Life and Works*.

Megroz, 1928   R. L. Megroz, *Dante Gabriel Rossetti: Painter Poet of Heaven in Earth*.

Caine, 1928   T. Hall Caine, *Recollections of Rossetti* (new edn).

Symons, 1929   Arthur Symons, *Studies in Strange Souls*.

Robertson, 1931   W. Graham Robertson, *Time Was*.

V. Hunt, 1932   Violet Hunt, *The Wife of Rossetti: Her Life and Death*.

Bickley, 1932   Francis L. Bickley, *The Pre-Raphaelite Comedy*.

Larg, 1933   David Larg, *Trial by Virgins: Fragment of a Biography*.

Winwar, 1933   Frances Winwar, *Poor Splendid Wings: the Rossettis and Their Circle*, New York; issued in Britain as *The Rossettis and Their Circle*, 1934.

Sitwell, 1936   Sacheverell Sitwell, *The Dance of the Quick and the Dead*.

Troxell, 1937   Janet Camp Troxell (ed), *Three Rossettis: Unpublished Letters to and from Dante Gabriel, Christina, William*, Cambridge Mass.

Ricketts, 1939   Charles Ricketts, *Self Portrait*, edited by Cecil Lewis.

Baum, 1940   P. F. Baum (ed), *The Letters of Dante Gabriel Rossetti to Fanny Cornforth*, Baltimore.

Lowndes, 1941   Marie Belloc Lowndes, *'I, Too, Have Lived in Arcadia': a Record of Love and Childhood*.

Gaunt, 1942   William Gaunt, *The Pre-Raphaelite Dream*, alternative title *The Pre-Raphaelite Tragedy*.

Birmingham, 1947   Birmingham City Museum and Art Gallery, *The Pre-Raphaelite Brotherhood*, exhibition 7 June to 27 July 1947.

Gray, 1947   Nicolette Gray, *Rossetti, Dante and Ourselves*.

Ironside and Gere, 1948   Robin Ironside and John Gere, *Pre-Raphaelite Painters*.

Whitechapel, 1948 Whitechapel Art Gallery, *The Pre-Raphaelites*, exhibition.

Doughty, 1949 Oswald Doughty, *A Victorian Romantic: Dante Gabriel Rossetti*, Oxford; second edition 1960.

Angeli, 1949 Helen Rossetti Angeli, *Dante Gabriel Rossetti: His Friends and Enemies*.

Hough, 1949 Graham Hough, *The Last Romantics*.

Procter, 1950 Ida Procter, 'Elizabeth Siddal: The Ghost of an Idea', *Cornhill Magazine*, no. 990.

Preston, 1953 Kerrison Preston (ed) *Letters from W. Graham Robertson*.

Shute, 1954 Nerina Shute, *Victorian Love Story: A Study of the Victorian Romantics Based on the Life of Dante Gabriel Rossetti*.

Angeli, 1954 Helen Rossetti Angeli, *Pre-Raphaelite Twilight: the Story of Charles A. Howell*.

Lang, 1959 C. Y. Lang (ed), *The Letters of Algernon Charles Swinburne*, 5 vols.

Packer, 1963 Lona Mosk Packer, *Christina Rossetti*, Cambridge.

Grylls, 1964 Rosalie Glynn Grylls, *Portrait of Rossetti*.

Doughty and Wahl, 1965–7 O. Doughty and J.-R. Wahl, *The Letters of Dante Gabriel Rossetti*, Oxford, 4 vols.

Fleming, 1967 G. H. Fleming, *That Ne'er Shall Meet Again*.

J. D. Hunt, 1968 John Dixon Hunt, *The Pre-Raphaelite Imagination 1848–1900*.

Russell, 1969 Ken Russell, *Dante's Inferno: The Private Life of Rossetti*, BBC TV.

Grieve, 1969 Alastair Grieve, 'A Notice on illustrations to Charles Kingsley's "The Saint's Tragedy" ', *Burlington Magazine*, vol 61.

D. H. Hunt, 1969 Diana Holman Hunt, *My Grandfather, his Wives and Loves*.

Hilton, 1970 Timothy Hilton, *The Pre-Raphaelites*.

Sonstroem, 1970 David Sonstroem, *Rossetti and the Fair Lady*, Middletown, Conn.

Nicoll, 1970 John Nicoll, *The Pre-Raphaelites*.

Surtees, 1971 Virginia Surtees, *Dante Gabriel Rossetti: The Paintings and Drawings, A Catalogue Raisonné*, Oxford, 2 vols.

Royal Academy, 1973 *Dante Gabriel Rossetti: Painter and Poet*, exhibition catalogue by Virginia Surtees.

Gere, 1973 John Gere, *Dante Gabriel Rossetti: Painter and Poet*.

Fredeman, 1975 William E. Fredeman (ed) *The P.R.B. Journal: William Michael Rossetti's Diary of the Pre-Raphaelite Brotherhood 1849–1853*, Oxford.

Nicoll, 1975 John Nicoll, *Dante Gabriel Rossetti*.

Bibliography

Delaware, 1976   *The Pre-Raphaelite Era 1848–1914*, exhibition curated by Rowland and Betty Elzea, 12 April to 6 June 1976.

Nochlin and Harris, 1976   Linda Nochlin and A. Sutherland Harris, *Women Artists 1550–1950*, Los Angeles.

Dobbs, 1977   Brian and Judy Dobbs, *Dante Gabriel Rossetti: An Alien Victorian*.

Edwards, 1977   Marion R. Edwards, 'Elizabeth Siddall – the age problem', *Burlington Magazine*, February.

Siddal, 1978   Roger C. Lewis and Mark S. Lasner (eds), *The Poems and Drawings of Elizabeth Siddal*, Wolfville Canada.

Grieve, 1978   A. I. Grieve, *The Art of Dante Gabriel Rossetti: Part III the Watercolours and Drawings of 1850 to 1855*, Norwich.

Weintraub, 1978   Stanley Weintraub, *Four Rossettis: A Victorian Biography*.

Edwards, 1979   Marion R. Edwards, 'This Modestly Educated Girl from Southwark: The Family & Background of Elizabeth Siddall', *Family History*, vol. 10, April.

BBC, 1979   BBC Television, *The Love School*, drama series.

Boyce, 1980   *The Diaries of George Price Boyce*, edited by Virginia Surtees, Norwich.

Delaware, 1980   Delaware Art Museum, *The Correspondence between Samuel Bancroft Jr and Charles Fairfax Murray 1892–1916*, edited by Rowland Elzea.

Kitchen, 1981   Paddy Kitchen, *The Golden Veil: A novel based on the life of Elizabeth Siddall*.

Battiscombe, 1981   Georgina Battiscombe, *Christina Rossetti: A Divided Life*.

Rose, 1981   Andrea Rose, *Pre-Raphaelite Portraits*, Oxford.

Brown, 1981   *The Diary of Ford Madox Brown*, edited by Virginia Surtees.

Wood, 1981   Christopher Wood, *The Pre-Raphaelites*.

Tate Gallery, 1984   Tate Gallery, *The Pre-Raphaelites*, exhibition 7 March to 28 May 1984.

Parris, 1984   Leslie Parris (ed), *Pre-Raphaelite Papers*.

Cherry and Pollock, 1984   D. Cherry and G. Pollock, 'Woman as Sign in Pre-Raphaelite Literature: A Study of the Representation of Elizabeth Siddall', *Art History* vol. 7, June.

Manchester, 1984   Joanna Banham and Jennifer Harris (eds), *William Morris and the Middle Ages: a Collection of Essays with Catalogue*, exhibition at Whitworth Art Gallery, Manchester, 28 September to 8 December 1984.

Marsh, 1985   Jan Marsh, *Pre-Raphaelite Sisterhood*.

Allnutt, 1985   Gillian Allnutt, *Lizzie Siddall: Her Journal (1862)*, Warwick.

Hilton, 1985   *Timothy Hilton, John Ruskin: the Early Years.*

Shefer, 1985   Elaine Shefer, 'Deverell, Rossetti, Siddal, and "The Bird in the Cage", *Art Bulletin*, New York, September.

Rochdale, 1987   Rochdale Art Gallery, *Painting Women: Victorian Women Artists*, exhibition 4 April to 30 May 1987.

Ricks, 1987   Christopher Ricks (ed), *New Oxford Book of Victorian Verse*, Oxford.

Nunn, 1987   Pamela Gerrish Nunn, *Victorian Women Artists.*

Marsh, 1987   Jan Marsh, *Pre-Raphaelite Women: Images of Femininity.*

Shonfield, 1987   Zuzanna Shonfield, *The Precariously Privileged: A Professional Family in Victorian London*, Oxford.

Marsh, 1988   Jan Marsh, 'Imagining Elizabeth Siddal', *History Workshop Journal*, no. 25.

Marsh and Nunn, 1989   Jan Marsh and Pamela Gerrish Nunn, *Women Artists and the Pre-Raphaelite Movement.*

Pollock, 1989   Griselda Pollock, *Vision and Difference: Femininity, feminism and histories of art*

Daly, 1989   Gay Daly, *Pre-Raphaelites in Love*

Marsh, 1990   Jan Marsh, 'The Woeful Muse', *Antique Collector*, April 1990

Surtees, 1991   Virginia Surtees, *Rossetti's Portraits of Elizabeth Siddal*

Marsh, 1991 (a)   *Elizabeth Siddal: Pre-Raphaelite Artist*, exhibition and illustrated catalogue, Ruskin Gallery, Sheffield

Marsh, 1991 (b)   'Looking for Lizzie', *Kaleidoscope Special, BBC Radio Four*, March 1991

Sulter, 1991   Maud Sulter, *Echo: Works by Women Artists 1850–1940*, exhibition and illustrated catalogue, Tate Gallery, Liverpool

Mancoff, 1992   Debra N. Mancoff, 'Is there Substance behind the Shadows?' *Journal of Pre-Raphaelite Studies*, Arizona, Spring 1992

Notes and References

Key to Abbreviations

ACS	A.C. Swinburne
BLS	B. Leigh Smith
BRP	Bessie R. Parkes
CEN	C.E. Norton
CGR	C.G. Rossetti
DGR	D.G. Rossetti
DM	Desmond MacCarthy
EES	Elizabeth Siddal
EG	Edmund Gosse
FLR	Frances L. Rossetti
FMB	F. Madox Brown
GBJ	Georgiana Burne-Jones
GBS	George Bernard Shaw
HRA	Helen R. Angeli
JEM	J.E. Millais
JR	John Ruskin
MBL	M.B. Lowndes
PRB	Pre-Raphaelite Brotherhood
SCC	Sydney Cockerell
THC	T. Hall Caine
TJW	T.J. Wise
WA	William Allingham
WBS	W. Bell Scott
WHD	Walter Deverell
WHH	W. Holman Hunt
WMR	W.M. Rossetti

Notes and References

For full details of works cited, see Bibliography on pp. 216–221 under name and date as given here. For key to abbreviations, see opposite page.

1 The Overgrown Grave (pp. 1–6)

1   *Observer*, 8.12.1985.

2 Dimmed in Death (pp. 9–23)

1   *Daily News*, 14.2.1862, 6.
2   Shonfield, 1987, 112.
3   Weintraub, 1978, 150–2.
4   C. G. Rossetti, 1904, 461.
5   Surtees, 1971, 93–4.
6   CGR to DGR Jan–Feb 1865 in W. M. Rossetti 1903, 76–8.
7   EES Portfolios are preserved in the Fitzwilliam and Ashmolean Museums; the glass negatives are in the Ashmolean. DGR's plans to photograph EES's watercolour works were not accomplished owing to the poor results expected of balck-and-white photography at this date.
8   DGR to GBJ 17.10.1864 in Burne-Jones Papers, Fitzwilliam.
9   Allingham, 1907, 144.
10 see Surtees, 1971, no. 168.
11 Robert Buchanan, *The Fleshly School*, 1872.
12 *Athenaeum*, 1882.
13 ibid.
14 Tirebuck, 1882, 32, 19.
15 David Hannay, 'The Paintings of Rossetti', *National Review*, March 1883, 126–32.

16 Sharp, 1882, 22.
17 Sharp, 1882, 22–3.
18 Sharp, 1882, 26.
19 DGR to ACS 26.10.1869, first printed in *The Times Literary Supplement*, 16.10.1919, 565; also Doughty & Wahl, 1965–7, 761.
20 'A Cheap Edition of a Great Man', *Pall Mall Gazette*, 18.4.1887.
21 Caine, 1882, 226.
22 Caine, 1882, 43–5.
23 Caine, 1882, 57.
24 Caine, 1882, 58.

3 Icon of Decadence (pp. 24–32).

1 Royal Academy 1883, cat. nos A. B, C and D.
2 Burlington Fine Arts, 1883, no. 329. There was, in addition, a third, unofficial show organized by DGR's former model Fanny Cornforth and her second husband, held in the 'Rossetti Gallery' at 1a Old Bond St, where the works displayed were for sale.
3 BL Ashley MS 3840, f. 4. The connection with the notebook is doubtful.
4 ACS to WMR 4.12.1895, BL Ashley 1427.
5 see above: Ch. 2 n. 20.
6 Ricketts, 1939, 294.
7 *Observer* 14.10.1928, 6.
8 Symons, 1929, 25.
9 J. Comÿns Carr, *Some Eminent Victorians*, 1908, 65.
10 *Pall Mall Gazette* 18.4.1887.
11 This picture of EES is now in the collection of the Walters Art Gallery, Baltimore, USA. Its history is given, with minor variations, in Williamson, 1906, 114 and Williamson, 1925, 36.

4 Dear Dove Divine (pp. 33–49)

1 Waugh, 1928, 85.
2 W. M. Rossetti, 1886, xvii.
3 Knight, 1887, 69–70.
4 Knight, 1887, 71.
5 see Troxell, 1937, 40.
6 Knight, 1887, 71.
7 Knight 1887, 78.
8 Knight 1887, 75.

9   Knight 1887, 76–8.
10   Howitt, 1889, 340.
11   W. M. Rossetti, 1889, 22.
12   W. M. Rossetti, 1891, xvii.
13   Scott, 1892, i, 316.
14   Scott, 1892, i, 316–17.
15   Scott, 1892, ii, 58–64.
16   ACS to WMR 4.12.1892, BL Ashley 1427.
17   Correspondence in *Academy* 10/17/24.12.1892.
18   Stephens, 1894, 35–6.
19   W. M. Rossetti, 1895, i, xii.
20   W. M. Rossetti, 1895, i, 172. This statement was circumstantially supported by one of WMR's convoluted footnotes to the effect that, on her death, DGR believed EES to be aged twenty-nine, but that her sister told him, in WMR's hearing, that the correct age was twenty-eight. Neither was accurate.
21   W. M. Rossetti, 1895, i, 173.
22   W. M. Rossetti, 1895, i, 172.
23   W. M. Rossetti, 1906, i, 200 n.1.
24   W. M. Rossetti, 1895, i, 173.
25   W. M. Rossetti, 1895, i, 173–4.
26   W. M. Rossetti, 1895, i, 177.
27   C. G. Rossetti, 1904, 284.
28   CGR to WMR 10.11.1893, quoted Battiscombe, 1981, 204.
29   Diary entry for 23.10.1855, in Brown, 1981, 155.
30   DGR to CGR 4.8.1852, W. M. Rossetti, 1895, ii, 95–6.
31   DGR to WMR 20.6.1853, W. M. Rossetti, 1895, ii, 98.
32   DGR to FLR 7.5.1854, W. M. Rossetti, 1895, ii, 127.
33   W. M. Rossetti, 1895, ii, frontispiece.
34   W. M. Rossetti, 1895, i, 209.
35   W. M. Rossetti, 1895, i, 225

5   Pre-Raphaelite Mascot (pp. 50–68)

1   W. M. Rossetti, 1895, i, 173.
2   Belloc, 1897, 24.
3   Le Gallienne, 1911, Chapter xii.
4   Hill, 1897, 3.
5   Hill, 1897, 5.
6   Hill, 1897, 225–6.
7   ibid. The child was later identified as Catherine Madox Brown.
8   Spielmann, 1898, 76. This work also mentioned a portrait by Millais

dated 1854 currently on the market for which the sitter was erroneously identified as EES; this 'mistake' indicates how EES's name was believed to raise the value of any work of art.

9   Millais, 1899, i, 144.
10   'The PRB and Walter Deverell', 1899, Huntingdon.
11   New Gallery 1897, with list of works on show and available in reproduction: 'for prices please apply to the Secretary'.
12   C. G. Rossetti, 1896, 114.
13   Marillier, 1899, 38, 48.
14   Marillier, 1899, 58.
15   Delaware, 1980, no. 112.
16   W. M. Rossetti, 1901, 5.
17   W. M. Rossetti, 1903(2), 273.
18   ibid.
19   see Marsh, 1985, for discussion of this issue.
20   W. M. Rossetti, 1903(2), 278.
21   W. M. Rossetti, 1899, 19.
22   W. M. Rossetti, 1899, 63. The full texts of this and subsequent letters by Ruskin were also reprinted in Ruskin, 1912, i, 200–220.
23   W. M. Rossetti, 1899, 76.
24   W. M. Rossetti, 1899, 80–1.
25   see Ruskin, 1912, i, 204–7.
26   W. M. Rossetti, 1899, 110–13.
27   W. M. Rossetti, 1899, no. 17, where the Valentine verses were misdated 1855.
28   W. M. Rossetti, 1906, i, 196.
29   W. M. Rossetti, 1903(2), 295.
30   DGR to WMR 17.4.1860, in W. M. Rossetti, 1903(2), 284–5.
31   W.M. Rossetti, 1903(2), 285.
32   Burne-Jones, 1904, i, 219.
33   W. M. Rossetti, 1895, i, 220.
34   Burne-Jones, 1904, i, 218–19.
35   Burne-Jones, 1904, i, 219.
36   Burne-Jones, 1904, i, 228.
37   Burne-Jones, 1904, i, 216.
38   ACS to WMR 4.12.1895 in W. M. Rossetti, 1906, i, 194–5.
39   Burne-Jones, 1904, i, 237.
40   W. H. Hunt, 1905, i, 198–9.
41   W. H. Hunt, 1905, i, 199.
42   W. H. Hunt, 1905, ii, 97–8.

6 Sheffield Siddalites (pp. 69–76)

1 Hueffer, 1911, 26.
2 July 1911, 942. 74. SQ f. 33, Sheffield LS.
3 3.8.1911, 942. 74. SF. ff. 99–100, Sheffield LS.
4 August 1911, 942. 74. S. f. 95, Sheffield LS.
5 18.8.1911, 942. 74. SQ f. 89, Sheffield LS.
6 Abstract of paper read 5.3.1912 on 'Elizabeth Eleanor Siddal', Sheffield Literary and Philosophical Society Annual Report 1912, 9–11.
7 11.2.1913, 942. 74. S. ff. 141–3, Sheffield LS.
8 ibid.
9 J. W. Ibbotson, 1928, 942. 74. S. f. 93, Sheffield LS.
10 This and subsequent extracts from the correspondence are taken from various scrapbooks dated 1928–35 in Sheffield LS.

7 Suicide and the Sex War (pp. 79–95)

1 Clive Bell, *Nation and Athenaeum*, December 1924, quoted Quentin Bell, Parris, 1984, 11.
2 W. M. Rossetti, 1895, i, 202–3.
3 Allingham, 1907, 100.
4 Shonfield, 1987, 112.
5 Delaware, 1980, nos. 5 and 7.
6 Delaware, 1980, 55.
7 Benson, 1904, 44–6.
8 Benson, 1904, 56.
9 Benson, 1904, 218.
10 Caine, 1908, 81–2.
11 W. M. Rossetti, 1903(2), 284.
12 Caine, 1908, 83.
13 Caine, 1908, 83–4.
14 Caine, 1908, 183.
15 Caine, 1908, 218.
16 Caine, 1908, 201–2.
17 GBS to THC 21.9.1928, BL Add 50531.
18 ibid.
19 Delaware, 1980, nos. 112 and 132.
20 EG to TJW 2.10.1923, BL Ashley 3854.
21 Beerbohm, 1922, pl. 7.
22 Waugh, 1928, 55–6.
23 Waugh, 1928, 55–8.

24 DGR to FMB 26.2.1857, W. M. Rossetti, 1899, 162, quoted Waugh, 1928, 87–8.
25 Waugh, 1928, 110.
26 ACS to Lady Swinburne, 13.3.1862, *The Boyhood of Algernon Charles Swinburne: Personal recollections by his cousin Mrs Disney Leith, with extracts from some of his private letters*, 1917, 102–3; see Lang 1959, i, 50.
27 Shonfield, 1987, 112.
28 Note in MS of WBS *Autobiographical Notes*, ii, 65, Princeton University Library.
29 see Martin Stannard, *Evelyn Waugh: The Early Years 1903–1939*, 1986, 152.
30 Caine, 1928, 40.
31 Caine, 1928, 198.
32 *Observer*, 14.10.1928.
33 Megroz, 1928, 59.
34 Megroz, 1928, 67.
35 Megroz, 1928, 76.
36 For a complete bibliography and analysis of sex-reform manuals in the 1920s and '30s, see Sheila Jeffreys, *The Spinster and her Enemies*, 1985.
37 Waugh, 1928, 107.

8   Violet's Elizabeth (pp. 96–106).

1 see Martin Green, *The von Richthofen Sisters*, 1974.
2 D. H. Lawrence, *The Rainbow*, 1926 edition, Chapter xv.
3 'Holman Hunt and the PRB', Cornell.
4 ibid.
5 This and subsequent information is collated from items in Cornell and Sheffield; owing to the fragmentary nature of this material it is not possible to construct a complete narrative.
6 Notes dictated 16.3.1930 by Mrs E. E. Higgins, Cornell.
7 V. Hunt, 1932, 113.
8 V. Hunt, 1932, 96.
9 V. Hunt, 1932, 278.
10 V. Hunt, 1932, 303–5.
11 MBL to DM, 21.4.1942, BRP A, 21, Girton.
12 *Letters from W. Graham Robertson*, ed. Kerrison Preston, 1953, 274–5.
13 *What is Fascism and Why?*, ed. Tomaso Sillani, London, 1931, trans-

lated by H. R. Angeli from *Lo Stato Mussoliniano e le realizzazioni del Fascismo nella Nazione*, Roma, 1930.
14 HRA to CC 9.19.1932, BL Add MSS 527501.
15 Book review and letter to the editor, *The Times Literary Supplement*, 22.9.1932, 655 and 27.10.1932, 789.

9 Costume Cinema (pp. 107–119).

1   Winwar, 1933, 61.
2   Winwar, 1933, 107.
3   Winwar, 1933, 213–4.
4   Baum, 1940, 12.
5   Larg, 1933, 241.
6   Larg, 1933, 278–9.
7   26.5.1935, Preston, 1953, 331.
8   8.6.1935, Preston, 1953, 332–3.
9   Sitwell, 1936, 223.
10 Sitwell, 1936, 225.
11 Sitwell, 1936, 240.
12 Robertson, 1931, 208.
13 Robertson, 1931, 89.
14 Troxell, 1937, 8.
15 Troxell, 1937, 8–9.
16 Baum, 1940, 10.
17 Baum, 1940, 3–8.
18 BRP A, 21, Girton.
19 Lowndes, 1941, 207.
20 BRP B, 159, Girton.
21 Gaunt, 1942, 11 Gaunt's book was long considered the best on its subject: see Bevis Hillier, *Connoisseur*, October 1975, quoted Jeremy Maas, Parris, 1984, 226.
22 Gaunt, 1942, 28–30.
23 Gaunt, 1942, 45–7.
24 Gaunt, 1942, 102–3.

10 Hysterics on the Hearthrug (pp. 120–130)

1   Birmingham, 1947, 53.
2   Ironside and Gere, 1948, 17.
3   Doughty, 1949, 120–4.
4   Doughty, 1949, 130.

5   Doughty, 1949, 176–89.
6   Doughty, 1949, 195.
7   Edward Clodd, *Memories*, 1916, 200.
8   W. M. Rossetti, 1895, i, 201.
9   Brown, 1981, 178.
10 Doughty, 1949, 265.
11 Ford Madox Ford, *Mightier than the Sword*, 1938, 248–51.
12 Doughty, 1949, 291–301.
13 Doughty, 1949, 297. Wilde's predilection for sensational stories conveying symbolic rather than literal truth perhaps might have alerted Doughty to the questionable nature of this anecdote.
14 Doughty, 1949, 299.
15 Angeli, 1949, xv.
16 Angeli, 1949, 190 n.2.
17 Angeli, 1949, 197.
18 Angeli, 1949, 203.
19 Angeli, 1956, 79.
20 see J. A. C. Brown, *Freud and the Post-Freudians*, 1961, Harmondsworth, 63.
21 Hough, 1949, 77–81.

11   Sixties Swinger (pp. 131–144)

1   Grylls, 1964, 78.
2   Virginia Surtees (ed), *Sublime and Instructive*, 1972, 158.
3   Virginia Surtees (ed), *Reflections on a Friendship*, 1979, 99.
4   *Apollo*, February 1973.
5   Gray 1947, 51–2.
6   Procter, 1950, 369.
7   Procter, 1950, 375.
8   Procter, 1950, 385–6.
9   see Yale MSS. for this unpublished work by HD (Hilda Doolittle).
10 Shute, 1954, 158–9.
11 Russell, 1969.
12 Robert Melville, *New Statesman*, 20.11.1970, quoted Jeremy Maas, Parris, 1984, 233–4.
13 Hilton, 1970, 101.
14 Hilton, 1970, 179.
15 Kitchen, 1981, 286.
16 Doughty and Wahl, 1965, i, 261.
17 Brown, 1981, 126, 148.
18 Brown, 1981, 149–50.

19 ibid.
20 Brown, 1981, 154–5.
21 Brown, 1981, 156–60.
22 Brown, 1981, 174, 180–7.
23 Brown, 1981, 191–6.

12   Emergent Feminist (pp. 147–155)

1   Shefer, 1985, 437–48.
2   Edwards, 1977, 112 and Edwards, 1979, 189–98.
3   Information from Mrs Elizabeth Oliver, descendant of Robert Evans, cousin to EES.
4   see Edwards, 1979; also letters from Clara Siddall at the University of British Columbia.
5   Siddal, 1978.
6   Tate Gallery, 1984, no. 217.
7   Tate Gallery, 1984, nos. 198 and 222.
8   Cherry and Pollock, 1984, 206–27. Reprinted in Griselda Pollock, *Vision and Difference: Femininity, Feminism and Histories of Art*, 1988.
9   Marsh, 1985, Chs 1–11.
10 Allnutt, 1985; reprinted in Gillian Allnutt, *Beginning the Avocado*, 1987.

13   Amiable Young Artist (pp. 156–172)

1   *Sheffield Telegraph*, 28.2.1862.
2   *Sheffield and Rotherham Independent*, 3.4.1869. My thanks to Sheffield Local Studies Library for biographical information on William Ibbitt.
3   My thanks to Marion Edwards of the PRO for sharing her extensive researches into Siddall family history.
4   *The Critic*, 1.7.1850.
5   W. M. Rossetti, 1901, 25.
6   Surtees, 1971, nos. 47, 48, 48a; Boyce, 1980, 24.2.1860.
7   DGR to WMR 3.9.1850, Doughty & Wahl, i, 92.
8   for details of the dating of these subjects, see Surtees, 1971, no. 62; Grieve, 1969, 290ff; and Grieve, 1978, 39–40.
9   BLS to BRP, May 1854, BRP V / 172, Girton.
10 DGR to WA, 23.7.1854, Doughty & Wahl, 1965, i, 209. Thanks to Gillian Allnutt for identifying the Biblical quotation.
11 DGR to WMR 20.6.1853, Doughty & Wahl, 1965, i, 146.

12 V. Hunt, 1932, 109; see also Fleming, 1967, 174. Kitchen, 1981 also imaginatively reconstructed a romantic relation between EES and WHD, following Dobbs, 1977.
13 Dobbs, 1977, 95.
14 see Mary Lutyens, Parris, 1984, 76–96, n.4.
15 Isabella M. Gilchrist, 18.5.1928, Sheffield LS. This communication derives from William Ibbitt via Ms Gilchrist's mother; the relevant parts of it read as follows: 'I wonder whether you will come to hear of [my mother's] remembrances of Miss Elizabeth Eleanor Siddal. My mother never met her – to her regret – but heard often of her great beauty from Councillor Wm Ibbitt, with whom she had the privilege of a long friendship. Mr William Ibbitt senior was an artist and silver chaser who painted among other works, a charming series of six views of Sheffield, of which replicas are in the Mappin Art Gallery. Miss Siddal was a cousin of his.

'Miss Siddal's people might be poor, but they were eminently respectable. "Tizzie" was so beautiful that she was never allowed to walk out unless accompanied either by her father or mother, or her younger brother. She was first engaged as a saleswoman in a milliner's shop in London, where a young artist, I forget his name – fell in love with her when he escorted his sister to choose a bonnet. He wished to marry her, but died shortly after from consumption. It was through him that she was introduced to the Pre-Raphaelite Brotherhood. Her engagement with Dante Gabriel Rossetti lasted about ten years; they had not at one time enough money to marry. She was once threatened with consumption, and John Ruskin, to set her mind at ease financially, gave her a chance to recover, and made her a money allowance for a year or two, for which she was to give him all her pictures and sketches in return. Rossetti was occasionally very violent in temper, and on the occasion of her visit to Sheffield, and to Mr Ibbitt's house, they quarrelled, and she had left London to get out of his way. Her relations were very averse indeed from her marriage with him on account of these brain storms. However, the quarrel was made up, and Rossetti wrote to ask her to meet him at Harrogate, Sheffield being altogether "too squalid and smoky" for a meeting of lovers. She did, and they were married soon afterwards. They were not unhappy together, but Mrs. Rossetti's health had failed after the birth of a dead baby, and she was deeply depressed and unable to sleep, which accounted for her taking chloral.'

In essence, this is not an inaccurate version of EES's story; but it is impossible to tell how much derived from oral tradition, how much from the author's own interpretation and how much from her reading of contemporary biographies such as Waugh's. She also claimed that her mother had met EES's 'elder sister' at William Ibbitt's house, whom she said was a forewoman in a leading London mantle warehouse and had 'kept house' for DGR after EES's death. EES's younger sister Clara was listed as mantlemaker in the 1861 Census, but there is no record of her housekeeping for her bereaved brother-in-law, although it is possible that she was asked to clear her sister's personal belongings when DGR left Chatham Place in 1862 on his removal to Chelsea.

16 VH Notes, Cornell.
17 BLS to BRP May 1854, BRP v, 172, Girton.
18 BLS to BRP May 1854, BRP v, 174, Girton.
19 Miss E. E. Higgins, Cornell.
20 Marsh, 1985, 178–9.
21 BRP A, 21, Girton.
22 Quoted Raleigh Trevelyan, *A Pre-Raphaelite Circle*, 1978, 161.

14 Life's Work (pp. 173–197)

1   see Marsh and Nunn, 1989.
2   Sheffield School of Art Annual Report 1857. My thanks to Dr. E. Mackerness for this information.
3   W. M. Rossetti, 1903 (2), 273.
4   Waugh, 1928, 55.
5   Robertson, 1931, 89.
6   Doughty, 1949, 268.
7   Nicoll, 1970, 65.
8   JEM to WHH 4.11.1852, first quoted D. H. Hunt, 1969, 92.
9   DGR to FMB 29.1.1853, Doughty & Wahl, 1965, i, 127.
10 DGR to FMB 25.8.1853, Doughty & Wahl, 1965, i, 153.
11 Tate Gallery, 1984, no. 198.
12 DGR to WA 17.3.1855, Doughty & Wahl, 1965, i, 245.
13 DGR to FLR 1.7.1855, Doughty & Wahl, 1965, i, 259.
14 DGR to FMB 23.5.1854, Doughty & Wahl, 1965, i, 200; see also DGR to *Athenaeum* 21.8.1852, Doughty & Wahl, 1965, i, 110–11.
15 now in Fitzwilliam Museum, Cambridge.
16 DGR to FMB, 23.5.1854, Doughty & Wahl, 1965, i, 200.
17 DGR to CEN, 22.1.1870 Doughty & Wahl, 1965, ii, 783.
18 DGR to WA 17.3.1855, Doughty & Wahl, 1965, i, 245.
19 JR to EES, 1855, Ruskin, 1912, i, 207.
20 JR to DGR 1855, Ruskin, 1912, i, 201.
23 JR to EES, 27.1.1856, Ruskin, 1912, i, 231–2.

24 JR to Ellen Heaton, c. 1855 in *Sublime and Instructive*, ed. V. Surtees, 1972, 157.

25 DGR to WA 17.3.1855, Doughty & Wahl, 1965, i, 245.

26 Marillier, 1899, 57 and 78; and W. M. Rossetti, 1903(2) 295; the attribution of the composition to EES may have been provoked not by a sense of justice but rather in order to transfer some of the blame, DGR's illustration of Saint Cecilia having been vigorously criticized for showing 'a shaggy-haired angel' apparently 'munching the face of the fair martyr', in Layard, 1894, 56.

There is also, in the Victoria and Albert Museum, another drawing of Saint Cecilia now attributed to EES, which is not reproduced in the photographic portfolio of her work prepared by DGR and does not appear to be by her hand. As a tentative explanation, I suggest that the attribution may have arisen in the absence of a signature following an incorrect attribution to DGR, whose early work it resembles, and was reassigned to EES when this was queried, through a misinterpretation of WMR's words. Compositionally, this third version has little similarity to the 'Moxon' versions and may possibly be an early work by the sculptor Alexander Munro.

27 This image bears a curious coincidental resemblance to JEM's *St Agnes' Eve* of 1854.

28 Tate Gallery, 1984, no. 222.

29 in Fitzwilliam Museum, Cambridge.

30 JR to Ellen Heaton, 11.11.1855, Ruskin, 1912, i, 229. Although this work is inscribed '1854', 'all the documentary evidence indicates that this watercolour was painted in the late summer of 1855' (Alastair Grieve, in Tate Gallery, 1984, 276); the deliberate falsification of the date may have been DGR's attempt to suggest that the work antedated EES's Arthurian subjects such as *Sir Galahad*. Although DGR praised EES' talent, like other PRB painters he was acutely conscious of the importance of artistic innovation.

31 *Magazine of Art*, 1880, 474.

32 DGR to WA, August, 1854, Doughty & Wahl, 1965, i, 214; *The Castaway* was exhibited at the Royal Academy in 1855 and may have inspired EES; its present location is unknown.

33 W. M. Rossetti, 1903 (2), 295.

34 Brown, 1981, 183.

35 *Saturday Review*, June 1857. The North American reception was less friendly, the *Evening Post* (14.11.1857) criticizing the 'childish vagaries' of *Clerk Saunders*, and the *New York Times* (7.11.1857) remarking that the work of EES and Arthur Hughes represented 'Pre-Raphaelitism run mad' – see Susan P. Casteras 'The 1857–58

Exhibition of Art in America' in *The New Path: Ruskin and the American Pre-Raphaelites* ed. Linda Ferber and William Gerdts, New York, 1985.
36 Elizabeth Siddal portfolio, f. 5, Ashmolean.
37 BL Harley 4431, f. 376; see Manchester, 1984, no. 57.

15 Poetic Endings (pp. 198–213)

1 see Siddal, 1978.
2 Bryson MSS 2599c, Ashmolean.
3 W. M. Rossetti, 1906, i, 199.
4 'Fragment of a Ballad' in Siddal, 1978.

Postscript (pp. 214–215)

1 Robert Liebman, *Sunday Times*, 29.5.1988.

Index